Disaster and Fiction

Disaster
and Fiction

Modern Greek Fiction
and the
Asia Minor Disaster
of 1922

Thomas Doulis

University of California Press
Berkeley   Los Angeles   London

University of California Press
Berkeley and Los Angeles, California

University of California Press, Ltd.
London, England

ISBN 0-520-03112-1
Library of Congress Catalog Card Number: 75-22654
Printed in the United States of America

Contents

To
Nikos and Ismene Avyeris
and
Philocles and Maria Anthopoulos

Acknowledgements

I do not think I would have begun to do research for this book if Basil Laourdas, then Director of the Institute for Macedonian Studies, had not mentioned to me his belief that Greek critics had completely ignored the impact of the Asia Minor Disaster on their culture. Although I am a novelist, and was one at the time, I, like most Neohellenists (so pervasive is the hold of verse in Greek letters) immediately considered the Disaster's effect on poetry. Yet, the more I pursued the issue, the more I realized that a major landmark in modern Greek culture had been reached as a result of the events of 1922 and that prose held the key to its interpretation.

In the almost ten years that intervened between the chance comment of Laourdas and the publication of this book, I have encountered and been compelled to entertain ideas that I would never have considered if I had "remained" a novelist only. The relative importance of poetry and prose in a national culture, the novel as a social document, the ideological underpinnings of art, all of these issues would never have occurred to me as problems that had to be assessed and confronted. The book has, therefore, been a profound educational experience for me. I would have preferred not to learn some of the things that I did learn in the course of writing this book, but few of the bargains one makes with the Devil, or any one of his numerous cohorts, can be negotiated after the fact.

I came to the study for which this book is the culmination with a commitment to fiction, both as a novelist and as a long-time student of Greek literature. Besides this, I have always had an interest in matters pertaining to Asia Minor, for as a child I listened to my mother's stories of life in Smyrna and of the last memory she had of the Ionian city, her terrorized flight from the Fire and her escape on the last ship leaving Asia Minor.

It would be impossible for me to thank all of the people who helped me on this book. First and foremost, my wife, Nancy, for being at my side throughout the hectic years of its writing. Then, my parents, John and Argiro Doulis, and my sister and brother-in-law, Stella and Phaedon Kozyris, who supported me whenever I faltered.

Almost every conversation with Greeks in the arts about the subject tended to confirm the thesis implicit and explicit in this book. I am indebted to many, though none should be held responsible for any errors of omission or commission in the book. At this point, I would like to thank those whose advice and suggestions, even though they may not have been aware that they were advising and suggesting, helped me considerably in gaining some awareness of the problems I would need to face. They are, in alphabetical order: Elli Alexiou, Markos Avyeris, Peter Bien, John Cavarnos, Constantine Dimaras, Stratis Doukas, Athina Kallianesi, Andreas Karandonis, George Katsimbalis, Basil Laourdas, John Petropulos, Kosmas Politis, Nikos Psyroukis, Apostolos Sachinis, Tatiana Stavrou, Stratis Tsirkas, George Valetas, Ilias Venezis, Eva Vlami, and Speros Vryonis. For Basil Laourdas, Kosmas Politis, Ilias Venezis, and Eva Vlami these thanks, alas, are posthumous: may their memory be eternal.

A Note on
the Transcription of Greek

With heavy heart I admit that I have not been as lucid or as consistent as I should have been in transcribing Greek names, but like most other Neohellenists I plead extenuating circumstances. I beg the reader to be indulgent with contradictory listings such as Andreas (rather than Andrew) Karkavitsas and George (rather than Yorgos) Seferis or Theotokas. Andrew Karkavitsas somehow sounds absurd, while George Seferis and George Theotokas somehow do not. No one seems to have trouble any longer with Nikos Kazantzakis (though at first his surname was being written as Cazantzakis), but, with the exception of Kimon Friar, we all continue to write Cavafy rather than the more consistent Kavafis, or Kavaphis, because we have accustomed ourselves to the appearance of the name. The most consistent system seems to be that devised by Kimon Friar and perhaps the rest of us Neohellenists should adopt it, although I don't think I will ever get to the point where I won't hesitate briefly before writing Pinelópi instead of the less consistent Penelope. By and large, I have tried to respect the sound of words and the look they have when spelled. I have, moreover, tried to retain the spellings of names that have appeared in English previously — for example, Yianis Kordatos, instead of the more usual Yiannis, as in Yiannis Psycharis. But I chose to write Ilias Venezis rather than Elias Venezis because the sound of the former is more accurately written with the "I." Maria Katchis Boyer has brought her considerable linguistic knowledge to bear on this problem, for which I thank her very much. Any inconsistencies the careful reader may notice are due probably to a last-minute irrationality on my part or to my obdurate character rather than to any error or inattention of hers.

Introduction

The interplay of literature with history is a vast subject, because no creative artist, however hermetic his art, can divorce himself from the political and social tensions of the world he inhabits. In many cases, his very hermeticism can be interpreted as a comment upon the world by which he finds himself surrounded. From this point of view, the work he produces is as important a document of his era as that of his less retiring brother-artist. Historical events are invaluable watersheds for the study of art, therefore, and they may range from those of worldwide importance – the French and Russian Revolutions, for example, or the two World Wars – to those of purely national significance.

To trace the impact of a specific historical event on the cultural life of a people requires a careful assessment of the previous cultural milieu, a brief but objective recapitulation of the causal chain of political, social, and economic developments that coalesced to create the historical "fact" and, finally, the new cultural reality that emerged as a result of the "fact."

All this must be accomplished without imputing a greater importance to the matter in question than it could legitimately claim, or by trimming the complexity of reality to fit the Procrustean bed of theory or prejudice. Both falsifications are ever-present dangers for the scholar: the first because his work is the product of many years' labor, and the second because he has all the weaknesses and liabilities of the human being. He is limited, moreover, by his intelligence and by his ability to endure the presence of inexplicable facts. Though he wants to rest, the bed he chooses, Procrustean or not, must nevertheless be suited to him and to the project upon which he has spent so much time and labor.

Conscious of the risk of overstating my case, therefore, I must assess the "fact" of the Asia Minor Disaster and compare it, briefly, to other historical events. Since neither Greece nor Turkey can be considered a major power, the interactions between them (though they may have been triggered by developments whose origins are to be found deep in the national past of both nations, as well as in the general European developments of the early twentieth century) affected only themselves. Because their levels of cultural development were — by European standards — fairly modest, we must not expect the consequences of the war they waged to have had the impact that that other bi-national event, the Franco-Prussian War of 1870, had on the plastic arts, the literature, and the political thought of Europe. The Greco-Turkish War of 1920-1922 was important only for Turkey and Greece. Though it may have changed somewhat the power structures of the Balkans, the Near East, and the Eastern Mediterranean, this effect had little more than local significance. For the two nations in question, however, the war was of decisive importance.

There are, I think, few parallels in modern history for what occurred as a result of the war, whose end for Greece was catastrophic. In fact, "disaster" — used as the English equivalent of the Greek "catastrophe" — has provided the present writer with a great many problems throughout his research and writing.

The "Asia Minor Disaster" can be interpreted to mean two vastly different things. In its most narrow sense it can mean the events that occurred during the months of August and September in various regions of Asia Minor. In fact, the events of 1922 have entered the English language as "The Asia Minor *Disaster*," a phrase initially used interchangeably with "The Smyrna Disaster," which was the phrase Western journalists used to describe the looting, rapine, and massacre that occurred when Turkish troops entered the Ionian city, as well as the fire that was started four days later to destroy all traces of the pillage and murder in the Greek and Armenian quarters. In its broadest and most comprehensive sense, however, the phrase embraces the whole process of the catastrophic eradication of the age-old Hellenism of Asia Minor.

For the purposes of this study, the reader must bear in mind that my theme is not limited to an analysis of the events, as reflected in prose fiction, of a week or two of officially sanctioned barbarism in Smyrna or elsewhere; it is also concerned with the ideological and psychological trauma that resulted from the uprooting of a million and a half Greeks from an Anatolia whose Hellenism was an undisputed fact for three millennia, and with the effect that this trauma has had on the fiction of modern Greece.

Let us try to place the Asia Minor Disaster in historical perspective. One event differs from another because each is the result of hundreds of thousands of intangibles and unassessables intricately developed and evolved in historical time. The most one can do is compare the magnitude of the event objectively, study it in relation to its immediate effect, and assess its long-range impact on the cultural life of the nation in question. The Asia Minor Disaster left approximately one million dead and one and a half million permanently uprooted, and would therefore rank, in

European terms, as one of the major upheavals of our time. When we compare it to Asiatic upheavals, it may at first seem much less significant, but this first impression is misleading. The crucial factor is that a million and a half Anatolians were absorbed *permanently* by five million free Greeks, who lived in a country much poorer than that which the refugees had left. In proportion, therefore, the Greek experience is much greater than most of the Asiatic upheavals that have periodically stunned the Western mind with their vast population figures. Three out of every ten people living in Greece in the autumn of 1923 were Anatolians who had arrived only a few weeks before. Very few Asiatic upheavals have resulted in the migration and permanent absorption of 30 percent of a population and the death of another 15 percent.

In terms of population and property, as well as in moral and ideological terms, the destruction of European Jewry in Hitler's death camps is a much greater event. In lives, of course, the difference is obvious. Whereas the destruction of Hellenism in Asia Minor only proved what most European, and Christian, peoples believed about the "barbarity" of the Turk, however, the horror of the concentration camps and the gas ovens compelled all civilized men – not only Europeans – to question themselves and their achievements in science, upon which they had founded their faith in the post-Christian era.

Attempts to equate the Asia Minor Disaster with the loss of empire experienced by Great Britain, or the loss of colonies as experienced by Spain, Germany, France, or Italy, are ultimately invalid. They rest on the assumption that the Disaster meant a "loss of empire" for the Hellenes. Anatolia was not an "empire" but a reminder of the empire they lost centuries ago and a perpetual promise that their national greatness would once again be restored. It was not, therefore, an unmitigated "imperial adventure," as Marxist critics after 1922 tend to view it and as Monarchists (such as Gounaris) claimed it was; it was instead an irredentist struggle. After the Disaster, however, and with the arrival of the refugees from Asia Minor, the Greek nation lost forever its chances of becoming an important force in European politics. Greece became a minor nation, perpetually dependent on the disposition of the major powers, a pawn in their struggles, unable to chart its own progress in history.

But Greece also gained much from the Asia Minor Disaster. It attained, for the first time, territorial integrity, since the one and a half million refugees were settled either in sparsely populated provinces like Macedonia and Thrace that had previously been disputed territory in the Balkans, or in cities that were little more than large towns. In gaining territorial integrity, Greece gained ethnic integrity, for the population exchanges had moved out the non-Greek and non-Christian elements. In gaining both, Greece began to develop an alert and large urban class, previously scattered throughout the unredeemed lands, and thus began to develop a unified national culture.

I do not mean to imply that Greek culture did not exist, or existed only in a rudimentary form, before the Disaster. Though great figures such as Adamantios Korais, Dionysios Solomos, General Makriyannis, Nicholaos Politis, Kostis Palamas, Alexandros Papadiamandis, and Yiannis Psycharis flourished before 1922, Hellenism as such — as I hope to establish in this study — was not limited to or identical with Helladic Greece. In fact, alternative centers of Hellenism, such as Constantinople, Alexandria, and Smyrna were, if not culturally, then certainly commercially richer than Athens. But the events of 1922 virtually destroyed non-Helladic Hellenism. Today, in the wake of the Greek emigration from Egypt and excluding the Greek communities which, for economic or political reasons, are scattered throughout the world (in most cases being gradually assimilated by the host countries), the majority of the Greek people live within the boundaries of the Greek state. For the first time Helladic Greece and Hellenism are almost identical.

But what effect did all of this have on the nation's fiction, a genre viewed by most critics as the mirror of its society? Many Greek critics have claimed that the impact of the Disaster on Greek fiction has been minor, and to support this statement they have mentioned the relatively few works that have dealt with the theme. This, however, would seem to be no better than claiming that the effect of the First World War on European or American fiction should be sought only in works that describe the actual events of the war. By and large, these critics seem to expect a concentration on the subject-matter of Asia Minor (the war, the imprisonment, the massacres, the refugees), ignoring the fact that the major impact of the Disaster would come as fiction began to reflect its aftermath in a changed view of man, of Greek society, and of the role and destiny of Greece.

I propose to study modern Greek fiction and the impact of the Asia Minor Disaster of 1922 in the following way. In Chapter One I hope to do two things: discuss the ideological and historical background of the Asia Minor Disaster and provide a brief retrospective view of Greek fiction as it existed before 1922. In this segment I claim that the development from ethography to social fiction would not have been achieved as quickly as it had been if the military defeat, the subsequent ideological repercussions, and the arrival of the refugees, with the social problems this caused, had not occurred: it is only after 1922 that fiction becomes a forum where important issues are raised and discussed. Chapter Two will contain a careful analysis of the direct impact of the Disaster and its consequences as mirrored in fiction. Chapter Three will document the ideological reactions of Greek intellectuals to news of the Disaster, focusing particularly on the reorientation and disorientation in the lives and art of two men ordinarily never considered in terms of the Disaster, Kostas Varnalis and Nikos Kazantzakis. Chapter Four will treat the Generation of the 1930s, a group of writers who broke from the ethography that had been the near-exclusive concern of Greek fiction and established the novel as the comprehensive genre of creative literature that speaks directly of man within society. Chapter Five will study the latest manifestation of interest in the theme of the Asia Minor Disaster, an interest that has benefited from the perspective of time and distance. Chapter Six will offer a discussion of Greek literary criticism on the subject, beside clarifying and emphasizing the result of the study.

1 Ideological, Historical, and Cultural Background

The Birth and Death of the Megale Idea

The Greek Revolution of 1821 against the Ottoman Empire had an electrifying effect throughout
the Greek world. For four centuries the Greek Christians had
lived as subjects in lands they considered historically theirs,
nurtured since the Fall of Byzantium in 1453 by the hope that
eventually the Eastern Roman Empire, *Tó Roméiko*, would again
be led by a Christian Emperor in Constantinople and a reconse-
crated Saint Sophia would again be the spiritual heart of Byzantine Christendom.

There is evidence to suggest that this hope of recapturing past
Byzantine glories — much later and with a somewhat different
meaning called the Megale Idea[1] — precedes the Fall of Byzantium to the Turks. It may have begun with the efforts of the
Byzantine Greeks to retake the Imperial City from the Franks
who had conquered and sacked it during the Fourth Crusade.

1. This phrase is often translated as Grand or Great Idea. The phrase
Megale Idea itself, according to Constantine Dimaras in a series of articles
in *Vima,* January 1970, was first used by Ioannis Kolettis in the National
Assembly on January 15, 1844. Alexandros Soutsos, using Kolettis's state-
ment that Greece is a bridge between Europe and Asia, says: "With
[Byzantium's] fall she had shed light on the West, with her standing erect
again [she] will enlighten the East." (Μέ τήν πτώσιν της τά φῶτα εἰς τήν
Δύσιν εἶχε χύσει — μέ τήν ὄρθωσίν της θέλει τήν ᾿Ανατολή φωτίσει.)

Michael VIII Paleologos, exclaiming at Nymphaion — 28 kilometers east of Smyrna — that his general, Alexander Stratigopoulos, had recaptured Constantinople from the Franks in 1261, forcefully expresses for the first time the desire to reconstitute the glories of Byzantium. Whether or not we accept this clarification, the Megale Idea nevertheless emerges as the ideal, nurtured by the Greeks, that Constantinople would once again become — and perpetually remain — the capital city of a reconstituted Christian Greek Empire, to whose jurisdiction all lands historically considered integral parts of the Greek world would adhere.[2]

That this was not merely the "idea" of an elite but was supported in great measure by the aspirations of the folk can be seen in the wealth of demotic songs, in folk expressions, and in the tales of the Greek tradition. If the folk expression is enriched by narratives and songs relating the Fall of the City and the profanation of Saint Sophia, it is equally rich in works prophesying the eventual defeat of the Turk, his retreat back to the "Red Apple Tree" (*Kókkini Miliá*), and the restoration of the City and Saint Sophia, the major architectural monument of Christian Hellenism, to the Virgin-Protectress and the Greek people.

The permeation of religious themes with racial freedom and integrity is the first and abiding impression one receives in studying the folk mind during the centuries of *tourkokratía*, the period under Turkish rule. The bondage to the Turk was considered an interval, a fitful slumber between moments of wakefulness, a nightmare that would end with the reimposition of sane consciousness. This can be seen in several of the folk tales Nicholaos Politis has gathered in his *Traditions of the Greek People.*

2. J. C. Voyatzidis, "La Grande Idée," *L'Hellénisme Contemporain, Le Cinq-Centième Anniversaire de la Prise de Constantinople, 1453-1953* (Athens, May 29, 1953), pp. 279-287. The precise statement from Michael Paleologos can be found in George Pachymeris, *De Michaele Paliologo,* ed. Bekker, I. (Corpus Scriptorum Historiae Byzantinae), Bonn, 1835, p. 153.

In "The Seven Half-Fried Fish," a monk, ready to turn his fish dinner over in the pan, is stopped by the news that Constantinople has fallen to the Moslem. "The Turk will never set foot in the City," he says. "I'll believe it when these fried fish come to life again." The fish, at that point, "leaped alive from his frying pan and fell into a nearby pool. Those fish are alive to this day in Baloukli and will remain there half-fried but living until the time comes when we retake the City. Then, it is said, another monk will come to finish frying them."[3]

Besides the certitude that Constantinople's reconquest will be fulfilled, there is the unmistakable psychological demand that the human agent present at the City's Fall will — though with another identity, perhaps — be present at its recapture. The folk mind seems to demand the satisfaction of a termination that neatly ties up all the loose threads of the break with the past. There is no doubt, moreover, that the City will be reconquered and that the Christian traditions will be reconstituted so that the break with the past would appear no more than an unfortunate interval in a chain of events reaching to perpetuity.

But this is not enough, for what the folk mind longs for, besides certitude and the restoration of severed continuity, is the feeling that the Fall of the City occurred because of the mysterious dictates of God. We see this in "The Priest of Saint Sophia."

> When the Turks had entered Saint Sophia, the Holy Liturgy had not finished. The celebrant priest immediately took the holy chalice, climbed to the upper storeys, and entered a door that shut behind him. The Turks, who had chased him, saw him disappear and found themselves before a wall. They tried to break it down with their weapons but to no avail. . . . For it is the will of God that the door will open of its own accord when the time comes and that the priest will emerge from it to

3. Nicholaos Politis, *Meletai peri tou Viou kai tis Glossis tou Ellinikou Laou: Paradoseis* (Athens, 1904), vol. 1, No. 31, p. 21.

complete the liturgy in Saint Sophia, when we retake the City.[4]

The implication in this vividly expressed "traditional story" is unavoidable that, as far as the folk mind is concerned, time — at the mythic level — has stopped since the conquest of Constantinople, at least in the City itself, and that it will begin again only when the City is reconquered by the Greeks. The historical present is frozen during the long period of Greek servitude; everything is in a state of suspension, awaiting the day when the city is retaken so that time can advance again.

But tradition did not allow the agent of the City's recapture to remain unspecified. The expression, "Constantine gave, Constantine will take back" (Κωνσταντῖνος ἔδωκε, Κωνσταντῖνος θα λάβει) is clear in its certitude that the name Constantine and Constantinople will be fused for all time, for it was Constantine the Great who founded the New Rome and Constantine XI Paleologos who died fighting on the walls. The implication is that another Constantine will retake "his" City in the name of its Virgin-Protectress and of the Greek people.[5]

---

4. *Ibid.*, vol. 1 No. 35; vol. 2 p. 678. Gaspard Fossati was supposed to have discovered a secret door leading to a chapel near the *gynaeceum* when he restored Saint Sophia in 1847 under Sultan Abdul Medjid. The triforium, "the upper storey," was called *catechumena* until the fall of the City in 1453. Porphyrogenitos (*De Ceremoniis,* I, 125, 157, 635) mentions a "wooden stairway" that led from a passage constructed by Justinian to connect the church with the palace. See W. R. Lethaby and Harold Swainson, *The Church of Sancta Sophia, Constantinople* (London, 1894), pp. 154-155; and Emerson Howland Swift, *Hagia Sophia* (New York: Columbia University Press, 1940), pp. 120-123.

5. This can be seen in a number of incidents whose resonance can only be felt at the mythic level. On the first night after the Greek army's landing in Smyrna, May 2, 1919, Colonel Zaphiriou selected "Paleologos" as the password his soldiers would use. "Konstantinoupolis" was the answer. See Yiannis Kapsis, *Hamenes Patrides* (Athens, 1962), p. 13. King Constantine arrived in Smyrna at 4:20 P.M. on May 30, 1921, hours after the "date" when Constantinople fell, 468 years before. There should be no doubt that everything possible would have been done to fulfill the mythical requirement if the city had been Constantinople, but even Smyrna would have

11

Constantine's refusal to come to terms with the Turks, and his heroic death, exalted this last Emperor of Byzantium in the consciousness of the nation. He left behind him a great lesson that survived the Fall and emphasized in the minds of those who came after him "the certitude that duty had been fulfilled to the utmost."[6] Only this certitude was able to imbue the Greek nation with the hope that Constantinople would once again be a Greek Christian capital, despite the fact that for many years before the Fall many horrible predictions of its conquest had circulated. Immediately after the Fall, the hope in the eventual reconquest by the Greeks sprang up at once, as seen in "The King Turned to Marble."

When the time came for the City to become Moslem and the Turks entered it, our King galloped on his horse to stop them. The Turks were a vast multitude, thousands encircled him, and he slashed and cut them down without pause. Then his horse was killed and he fell down. When a black had raised his sword to strike the King, an angel of the Lord came, took him up and carried him to a cave deep in the earth, near the Golden Door. There the King remains, turned to marble, and awaits the hour

seen him one day earlier if the political issues had been less complex. See Christos Angelomatis, *Chronikon Megalis Tragodias* (Athens, 1963), pp. 111-115. Besides, even Muhammed II did not enter the city and give his thanks to Allah in Saint Sophia until May 30, 1453. See Charles Diehl, "An Outline," *Byzantium,* ed. N. H. Baynes and H. St. L. B. Moss (Oxford University Press, 1969), p. 49. A number of prominent citizens of Proussa had the good fortune to meet King Constantine on his trip to Asia Minor on August 21, 1921. They felt "deeply that those were historic moments . . . before our king, the king of all the Greeks, before him who bore the name that for centuries nurtured the imaginations of all of us and which was joined with all the legends of the race. Wasn't that the name we imagined would be borne by him who would have realized the vision of all the previous generations?" See Ad. N. Adamantiadis, "Ta Teleftaia Chronia Tis Ellinikis Koinonias Tis Proussis," *Mikrasiatika Chronika,* vol. 4, 1948, pp. 96-125.

6. G. A. Megas, "La Prise de Constantinople dans la poésie et la tradition populaires Grecques," *L'Hellénisme Contemporain,* pp. 125-133.

when the angel will come to raise him up. The Turks know this but cannot find the cave where the King is. That is why they sealed the door from which they know the King will enter to take the City back from them. When it is the will of God, though, the angel will go down into the cave, free him from the marble, and place the sword he carried in battle in his right hand. The King will rise and enter the City through the Golden Door and, pursuing the Turks with his armies, he will chase them to the Red Apple Tree. There will be such great slaughter, that the calf will swim in blood.[7]

Some historians, in fact, feel that the legend of "The King Turned to Marble" and the Megale Idea are intricately meshed. Because the end of Constantine Paleologos (like that of Arthur, or Siegfried, or Holger) was not clear, doubts about his death immediately emerged. Citing the "traditions" of Politis, George Megas maintains that the legend of "The King Turned to Marble" is important as a promise and a hope of eventual reconquest:

Thus the tradition was born that crowned the desires and hopes with which for centuries generations of Greeks were nourished and gave flesh and bones to the Megale Idea, the national ideal, by which was stamped the character of Modern Greek nationality. One can say with confidence that it is impossible to understand the history of the Greek nation from the Fall of Constantinople to our own days without sounding the meaning of the traditions that were created immediately after the ill-omened day of May 29, 1453.[8]

It was this magical, non-logical world that retained fragments of the Megale Idea, whether or not they were identified as such. "The Red Apple Tree" is a case in point. According to R. M. Dawkins, mention of the Red Apple Tree is first found in

7. N. G. Politis, *Meletai, Paradoseis,* No. 33.
8. Megas, "La Prise de Constantinople," p. 131.

Bartholomew Georgevits's *Prognoma sive Praesagium Mehemetanorum*, where he includes a prophecy current among the Turks. In Dawkin's translation it reads:

> Our emperor will come, he will take the kingdom of the Infidels; he will take the Red Apple; he will seize it; after seven years, if the sword of the Infidel be not drawn, he will be their master; he will take his pleasure; he will plant vines; he will fence gardens; he will beget sons and daughters. After twelve years the sword of the Christians will be drawn; it will drive the Turks back again.[9]

In the course of this extremely interesting essay, Dawkins accepts the identification of the Red Apple as a symbol of world domination on the part of the Turks, but he sees a contradiction with its meaning in the Greek world, where it is associated "with the final overthrow of the Turks and their withdrawal to their original home, far away from the Christian world into which they had intruded."[10] He solves this contradiction to his own satisfaction by interpreting the prophecy in Georgevits as a confusion of the two ideas: "the [Turks'] conquest of the Red Apple and their final defeat and expulsion":

> This transition ... was made all the more easily because in earlier days at the time of the Taking of the City the place to which the Turks would at last have to flee was also called by the name of a tree. They were to go their way back to the mysterious Solitary Tree, to the Monodéndrion, of which we

9. R. M. Dawkins, "The Red Apple," *Archeion tou Thrakikou Laographikou kai Glossikou Thisavrou*, 6 (Athens, 1940), p. 401.

10. *Ibid.*, p. 405. References to the "Red Apple Tree" can be found in Politis's *Eklogai apo ta tragoudia tou Ellinikou Laou*, p. 178, and 180, in Barba-Pantzelios's *To Tragoudi tou Daskaloyianni*, ed. Basil Laourdas (Heracleion, Crete: Mourmel, 1947), p. 15, lines 10-14.

14

read in "The Lament of Constantinople" and of which Doukas tells us that it was at the borders of Persia.[11]

The identity of religious imagery and ethnic ideals, of Byzantium and the Megale Idea, seemed to continue unquestioned in the folk mind until well beyond the Revolution. Religious and ethnic liberation would result directly from the Turks' defeat.

But other forces emerged to help the oppressed *rayah*, or Christian subject. Though the Greek was to feel the first and most lasting threat of the Turk to his national survival, the European powers, threatened by the territorial ambitions of the Sultans, were compelled to unite to defeat the Moslem — first at sea, in the Battle of Lepanto in 1571, and then on land, in the Battle of St. Gotthard in 1664. These victories over the previously invincible Turk allowed the Western Europeans access to an East that was previously barred to them, and this at a time when interest in classical culture was rapidly increasing.[12]

The Greeks themselves, traveling to study in the West, brought back Enlightenment ideas that tended to weaken the monopoly which religious training had secured after the Fall of Byzantium and the closing of all secular schools.[13] There still remained, however, a strong distrust of the Westerner, stemming from the events of the Fourth Crusade and the consequent and steady pressures to submit to Papal authority that often rendered the West an even less attractive alternative to the power of the Sultan.

Though the rise of nationalism began to draw the imagination of the Greeks away from the restoration of the Byzantine Empire

11. *Ibid.,* pp. 405-406. The quotation can be found in Michael Ducas, *Historia Byzantina.* ed. Bekker, I. (Corpus Scriptorum Historiae Byzantinae) Bonn, 1834, p. 290, line 4.

12. Terence Spencer, *Fair Greece, Sad Relic* (London, 1954), p. 2.

13. See G. P. Henderson's *The Revival of Greek Thought, 1620-1830,* (Edinburgh and London, 1971) for a thorough treatment of this.

and toward the establishment of a modern nation-state on the European model, the increase in national fervor corresponded to an almost universally recognized deterioration of the once-supreme Ottoman Empire. The Megale Idea was merely a Greek version of a common European pastime: virtually every European monarch or political theoretician had his own plan for the partition of the obviously crumbling Ottoman Empire, alternatively called "The Sick Man of Europe" or, more vaguely, "The Eastern Question."[14]

Quite simply, what came to be called the Megale Idea provided the newly established Greek Kingdom with foreign policy objectives which, for a number of reasons, it found itself unable to ignore. For most of the nineteenth century, the free Greek state was limited to the least productive regions of the Greek world and contained fewer than a third of the population of the Greek people. In an age of irredentism and territorial expansion, it was natural that the Megale Idea would lose its exclusively religious and cultural content and take on economic and strategic considerations that very few European peoples have the right to condemn.

Greece, all the Greeks felt, was to be a small state only temporarily. The Megale Idea was a promise of Greece's future greatness. The alternative to it, though sarcastically expressed, was nevertheless the only real one: the draining of Lake Copais.[15] As long as vast areas of Unredeemed Greece continued to exist, therefore, the populous and wealthy Greeks of Anatolia

14. Aside from I. A. Marriot's *The Eastern Question, A Historical Study in European Diplomacy,* 4th ed. (Oxford, 1940), a number of other books treat the various plans for partition, among them, William Miller's *The Ottoman Empire and Its Successors* (Cambridge, 1936), pp. 38-39, Spencer, pp. 178-179, and L. S. Stavrianos's *Balkan Federation: A History of the Movement toward Balkan Unity in Modern Times,* Smith College Studies in History, 27, Nos. 1-4 (1941-1942), pp. 5-6, 38 and 45-46.

15. Yiannis Kapsis, *Hamenes Patrides* (Athens, 1962), p. 50.

would wait their turn. By the beginning of the twentieth century, however, the headlong decline of the Ottoman Empire meant that the time was nearing for the Megale Idea to be realized.

As the Ottoman Empire showed that it could not respond to the crushing challenge before it — losing Libya and the Dodecanese to Italy, parts of Asia Minor to France, and Syria, Palestine, and Arabia to Britain — the Greek state, under the stewardship of Venizelos, began to realize the Megale Idea, gaining Crete first, and then with the successfully managed Balkan Wars absorbing southern Epirus, parts of Macedonia and Thrace, and the Aegean Islands.

The coming battle between Greece and Turkey, the Near Eastern "detail" of the mosaic that was the struggle between the Entente and the Central Powers, was to be a mortal one. Turkey was in the process of losing all her possessions in Europe, Africa, and the Middle East, while the total realization of the Megale Idea would demand that she lose most of Anatolia as well.

The Great War, as Venizelos clearly understood, was the decisive historical moment at which the Megale Idea might be realized. Turkey's entry into the war on the side of the Central Powers determined Greece's position: her interests, because of her position as a merchant naval power, belonged with whoever controlled the Mediterranean and whoever was against Turkey. The Entente was the obvious choice. Because Venizelos disagreed with King Constantine over Greek entry on the side of the Entente (the king was accused of pro-German sentiments because he favored neutrality), he was dismissed, and his decision to create a Revolutionary Government in Salonika (1916) led to the destructive period in Greek political life known as the Dissension (*O Dichasmós*), which played a major role in the tragedy that was to occur in 1922.

Greece's entry into the Great War on the side of the successful Entente would have attained for her the status of a major power

17

in the Mediterranean and the Balkans and might have realized for her the dreams of the Megale Idea if it had not been purchased at the price of a Dissension whose tragic results in Greek political life have never been totally effaced. Nevertheless, the Treaty of Neuilly (November 17, 1919) deprived Bulgaria of frontage on the Aegean and of Western Thrace. Bulgaria, for two decades the major enemy of the Greeks at their northern frontiers, was thereafter "to be de-Prussianized."[16]

The Treaty of Sèvres, moreover, signed on August 10, 1920, ceded the rest of Thrace up to the Chatalja line to Greece. Turkey renounced to Greece all rights over Imbros and Tenedos, two islands of great strategic importance, since they commanded the entrance to the Straits of Dardanelles (which would be open to all and placed under an International Commission); but it retained the islands in the Sea of Marmora, Constantinople, and a strip of territory in Europe. Smyrna and the Hinterland went to Greece, and this area with its great Greek population was to have a local parliament. In five years the residents would have the right to ask "for definite incorporation into the Kingdom of Greece" to be decided by a plebiscite overseen by the League of Nations.[17]

Catastrophe, as in tragic drama, was shortly to follow the deliriously happy but deceptive moment of triumph. Venizelos had doubled the size of Greece in less than a decade and had "title" (though this was to be disputed by Italy), by the Treaty of Sèvres, to most of the lands the Greeks had for centuries dreamed of with the Megale Idea. In May 1919 the Greek army landed in Smyrna and took up defensive positions throughout the predominantly Greek province of Aidin. Constantinople, the Imperial City, was not to be Greek at once, but it would merely be a

16. Miller, *The Ottoman Empire,* pp. 540-541.
17. *Ibid.,* p. 541.

matter of time, Greek nationalists believed, before the pressure of Hellenism from Thrace in the West, from Anatolia in the south, and from within the City itself would unite it with Greece. The Christian Greeks and Armenians of Trebizond began campaigning in 1919 for an independent republic, invoking the "self-determination" clause of the League of Nations.[18]

There were several problems on the horizon. The first was the "national" movement of the Turks at Ankara, led by Kemal Ataturk, that opposed the feeble remains of Ottoman power in Constantinople, which was controlled by the Allied Commissions. The second was the diplomatic hostility of the Italians, who claimed Smyrna had been promised to them at the Conference of St. Jean de Maurienne in 1917, and of the French, who saw Great Britain and the United States dominating the oil-rich regions of the Middle East.[19] The third was, ironically, the obstacle to the fulfillment of strategic objectives which democracy, because of its demand for periodic elections, made on the Western powers. Of the governments of France, Italy, the United States, and Great Britain, only the last, the Coalition Government of Lloyd George, was still in office in 1922.

Venizelos had revolted against King Constantine and been de facto prime minister of Greece for four years without having received a mandate from the Greek people. The Greeks had been at war for eight years, since 1912. The elections, called for November 1920, were considered safe for Venizelos

18. The "Ligue Nationale du Pont Euxin," founded in Paris in 1918, published its claims in a 42-page pamphlet entitled *Greek Republic of the Black Sea,* 1919.

19. Hints of this are seen in Edward Hale Bierstadt's *The Great Betrayal* (London, n.d.). It is treated in a thorough manner by Nikos Psyroukis in his *I Mikrasiatiki Katastrophi* (Athens, 1964) from the Marxist point of view.

and necessary to show the Allies that a parliamentary Greece would be infinitely preferable to a corrupt Turkish Empire in the postwar world.

Venizelos, for a number of reasons, "the prolonged mobilization, his long tenure of office, his inevitable absence at Paris while unpopular subordinates governed and made enemies in his name," was routed at the polls.[20] The sudden death of the young King Alexander left a vacancy in the throne, which meant that the election had become a personal struggle between Venizelos and ex-King Constantine. Besides this, the assassination on July 31, 1920, of the brilliant Ion Dragoumis by security units of the army in retaliation for numerous attempts on the life of Venizelos had removed this most interesting and capable man from a role in the right-wing politics of Greece. Rhalles became Prime Minister only to discover that the former allies of Greece were relieved to gain a pretext for withdrawing from their treaty obligations.

By the time Gounaris had succeeded Rhalles as Prime Minister, the die had been cast. A plebiscite showed an immense majority favoring the return of King Constantine, and he was recalled to the throne on December 5. His "pro-Germanism," which the Entente powers had detested, might have been forgiven if Greece were still useful to them. The Central Powers had been defeated, however, and the Allies had only themselves and their competing interests to worry about.

The plight of Gounaris was pathetic. He was a man of little stature who during the days of Venizelos's triumph had waged a purely negative campaign against him, criticizing his landing of troops in Smyrna, implying that the Expedition was imperialistic, and urging peace and a return to the reality and values of a "small but honorable Greece"; he now found

20. Miller, *The Ottoman Empire,* pp. 541-544.

himself opposed by his country's former allies, committed to Asia Minor by the presence of a large army, confronted by a Venizelist Ecumenical Patriarch, and suspected by two and a half million Anatolian Greeks of wanting to abandon them to Kemal Ataturk. His allies cut off funds needed to pursue the war, a fact he kept secret upon his return from London, and the Treaty of Sèvres was revised at the Paris Conference of March 1922, returning Smyrna and its Hinterland to Turkish rule.

It would be foolish to blame Gounaris for behaving like any ordinary Greek premier and replacing, with men loyal to him and Constantine, most of the General Staff and higher echelon officers who, over the years, had been characterized as Venizelists. Certainly the Greek army needed to be at peak efficiency to overcome all the disadvantages it faced in Anatolia, but these disadvantages would have defeated even a much larger and better equipped army. The Greeks had been at war for eight years and were now deep in Anatolia, without supplies or reinforcements, unsupported by allies, waging a conventional war against guerrilla forces, and led by a Prime Minister who was on record against the very expedition he now desperately urged the newly appointed General Staff to win at all costs.[21]

The military defeat of Greece was a rout, and given the existing ethnic and religious differences, as well as the "New Turk" persecution of minorities, it was to result in the total eradication of Hellenism in Asia Minor.

It should not be doubted that this eradication suited many of the Western interests in the Near East, since any economic

21. Along with five other ministers, Gounaris was executed on November 15, 1922, at Goudi by the decision of the Revolutionary Council. The best historical study on the expedition and its aftermath is A. A. Pallis's *Greece's Anatolian Venture – and After* (London, 1937).

competition for tobacco and oil would come from the only bourgeoisie native to the area, the Greeks and Armenians, who held almost total control of all Anatolian assets. It would be too cynical to say that the Western consuls expected what actually happened: the brutal imprisonment of all males between the ages of 18 and 45, the barbaric mistreatment of many of the women, the burning of Aidin, Proussa, Smyrna, and hundreds of other towns and villages, the total destruction of Greek and Armenian property, and by conservative estimates the slaughter of at least a million people. But it is documented beyond a doubt that these men, with the honorable exception of George Horton, the United States consul in Smyrna, did virtually nothing to save the Christian populations from the horrible fate that awaited them.[22]

The effect of the Disaster on all aspects of Greek life was overwhelming. The future, which before had beckoned with the promise of national greatness, now offered the Greeks a bleak prospect. All the sacrifices of a decade were wasted, all the dreams of centuries were seen to be delusions. "The young men of 1910-1920 ... are a sacrificed generation," wrote George Theotokas in *The Free Spirit* in 1929:

> Perhaps the best of them, those who today could have been our intellectual leaders, fell in Macedonia and Asia Minor before they could show their abilities. The moral

22. The interested reader can refer to a fairly rich bibliography, so I will mention only a few titles. In English, there are Bierstadt's book, as well as George Horton's *The Blight of Asia* (Indianapolis, 1926), Lysander Oeconomos's *The Martyrdom of Smyrna* (London, 1922), and Marjorie Housepian's *The Smyrna Affair* (New York, 1971). In Greek there are Christos Angelomatis's *Chronikon Megalis Tragodias,* Yiannis Kapsis's *Hamenes Patrides,* and the extremely valuable sourcebook, *Mikrasiatiki Katastrophi* by Kostas Triandafyllou; for publication data, see the Bibliography.

impact of the defeat was and remains overwhelming. Not only their abilities, but also their ideals and self-confidence were lost to us in the port of Smyrna. From then until today our country has lived without grand and noble sentiments, without the need to surpass itself, without any exaltation. The Disaster stifled every idealism. . . . What need is there to attempt [new things], to struggle, to solve, when "Nothing [important] can be achieved by the Greeks"? (Τίποτα δέν μπορεῖ νά γίνει στό Ρωμαϊκο.) This is the lesson to be learned from the words of the majority of our intellectual leaders. . . . I have no desire to criticize them. It is natural for men who have seen all their struggles and their dreams humiliated in the Disgrace of 1922 to expect nothing from the future.[23]

After the Disaster, Unredeemed Greece ceased to exist. The vast wealth and culture of the Anatolians were destroyed, along with a million lives. The million and a half penniless and terrified refugees who arrived within the borders of the Greek state had to forget their previous existence in Asia Minor entirely, just as the race had to forget the millennia that had been eradicated in August 1922. Instead of increasing her boundaries to embrace the site of Hellenic colonies, Hellenistic civilization, the Byzantine Empire, and four centuries of expectant servitude, Greece was compelled to receive within boundaries created for her by the whims of history the last hunted remnants of Hellenism in Asia Minor.

The age-old Greek world had disappeared. There was now only the small, mountainous Greek state, economically poor, predominantly agrarian (though without particularly rich land), culturally backward, and riddled with political rivalries that even the passage of decades would not erase.

23. Orestes Digenis (pseudonym of George Theotokas), *Elefthero Pnevma* (Athens, 1929), pp. 102-104.

It was to this Greece that the refugees had come to be saved, the Greece that in some measure had been responsible for their fate, a humble and defeated Greece now stripped of the Megale Idea, a Balkan nation struggling not to remain financially solvent – for it was bankrupt – but only to believe that it had a purpose. Now, almost exactly a century after its Revolution, its ideals, or its illusions, were utterly destroyed.

The Asia Minor Disaster of 1922, as Greek historians of varying political orientations agree, was the most important historical event for the Greek people since that other "disaster," the Fall of Constantinople in 1453. It is the impact of this historical watershed on the creative imagination of the Greek – that is, its impact on the subject-matter and treatment of Greek fiction – that the rest of this study will attempt to assess.

The Culture of Greece Before 1922

A cultural tradition as old and as splendid as his is an overwhelming burden for the contemporary Greek. He must not only close up a gap of four hundred years (during which Europe developed from Renaissance to Romanticism), but must also resist the definition of himself and his past that the interested and educated European wants to impose upon him. More than the citizen of any other nation, the Greek and his tradition has been subjected to the study and assessment of foreigners. This honor, more often than not an imposition, began even before the nineteenth century, and certainly in every decade of the modern Greek state's existence, foreigners have pursued, criticized, and compared the Greek, rarely favorably, to the small facet of his past with which a particular discipline is concerned.

More than any other people, therefore, the modern Greeks have developed with two standards of assessment, their own and that of foreigners, and the latter has frequently been considered the more important. His ethnic credentials have been doubted: his right to call himself a "Hellene" has been questioned, and his language has been labeled "corrupt" by authorities who have spent their lives studying a small fragment of the vast and complex mosaic of his past.

Of the two standards of assessment, the one employed by the foreigner and classicist tended at one time to be more coherent, because it was arbitrary and supported by a more impressive bibliography. For non-Greeks, the identity of the "Greek" was the identity that existed in Hellenistic times. Any variation from that was in the direction of decadence and corruption, particularly since, as Fallmerayer strove to prove in his study of the modern Greek, the person who called himself a "Hellene" was apt to be a Hellenized Slav. The presence of a Fallmerayer in Greece in 1830, challenging the belief in racial continuity of a people who had barely won their political independence and for whom this racial heritage was a precious possession, was a threat of major proportions.

It did not take long for the Greeks to react. The two major answers to Fallmerayer's theories are to be found in Constantine Paparrighopoulos's five-volume *History of the Greek Nation* (1860-1872), which traced the Greek lineage back to pre-Homeric times, and in Nicholaos Politis's studies of Greek folklore. The systematic study of the mores and traditions of the Greek folk — that population least influenced or changed by Western fashions, expressions, or attitudes — was to have a direct bearing on Greek literature. By studying the village in all its "purity," it was thought, the organic development from ancient Greek religious beliefs to modern

Greek folk customs and traditions would support the descent of the modern Greek from his ancient ancestor.

George Drosinis, a member of the Generation of 1880, says of Nicholaos Politis: "[he] led us to the as-yet unexplored treasure of [Greek] traditions, folk tales; superstitions, and customs of the Greek people, and exhorted us to study and use [in our writing] these national heirlooms."[24]

Organically involved with the issue of identity is that of language. Unlike the Greek, most cultures solve their language problem early in their modern careers and develop within a century or two a body of literature that makes impossible any retreat to an earlier form. But *diglossia* has been an issue in Greek since the language became the *koine* in the Mediterranean in Hellenistic times. From that era on there has been a demotic form — a vernacular which developed according to historic linguistic principles — and an archaizing and literary form, which always tried to approximate, with greater or lesser success, Attic Greek.[25]

Of course, it was not only prose that confronted this problem. Poetry, too, encountered the language issue, but at least demotic verse, one of the glories of Modern Greek culture, had a great tradition and could claim verse romances like *Erotokritos,* verse drama like *Erophile* and *The Sacrifice of Abraham,* and the literally thousands of folksongs, a great

24. Quoted in C. Th. Dimaras's *Istoria tis Neoellinikis Logotechnias,* 3rd ed. (Athens, 1964), p. 356.
25. See Manolis Triandafyllidis's *Stathmoi tis Glossikis mas Istorias* (Athens, 1937). As of this final revision (1976) the use of the demotic language in all aspects of Greek life seems to have been agreed upon by all the political parties in the country and initiated by the government of Prime Minister Karamanlis. If there is no political change, this would mean that the language problem in modern Greek culture will soon become an historical issue solely.

proportion of them composed before the establishment of the Greek state in 1830.

With a rich and complex heritage such as this, a poet who wanted to write in the demotic would, for a number of reasons, be spared the problems of the writer of prose. Folksongs, first of all, were written down only by scholars who wanted to preserve them. As a rule, they were composed anonymously by the folk, in their own living diction, as an expression of a powerful emotion. They are, moreover, a coherent and compressed statement of the values of the Greek people without the self-conscious awareness of what these values are. Besides this, since they are by and large without foreign influence, they come to us as one of the few aspects of modern Greek life that have maintained a link with the Greek tradition, a link that prose could never pretend to have.

The unlettered folk have also expressed themselves in prose with folk tales and "traditions," but these – for all their intensity and power – are not extended or complex pieces of work. Unlike verse, whose recitation or singing was always aided by mnemonic devices, long and involved works of prose have always been written down and have thus remained difficult, if not impossible, for the uneducated to transmit. Greek prose, because it had been the medium of the educated, therefore, had always been confronted by the language issue in its most difficult form.

Prose is written by individuals (it is rarely anonymous) to be read, usually in privacy, by other members of society, in a language selected so as not to interfere with clarity in order to express ideas of importance and utility. Prose is employed for "use" more often than for "beauty" and "power," and since it is the province of the erudite, it is much more vulnerable to the strictures of approved grammatical usage. For the Greek language this has meant the use of archaizing grammar and the rhetorical principles of the Hellenistic world. Its very self-consciousness, its very concern with maintaining links with the Greek tradition, had robbed prose of its organic development.

A universally accepted form of prose, therefore, did not exist to serve as a vehicle for the expression of the social, political, religious, and philosophical values of the Greek people at the time of their independence. Since the archaizing tendencies were too rigid and the demotic speech considered too simplified and lexically poor, a compromise was found in Korais's purist grammar, the *katharevousa,* which was influenced by Western, and specifically French, grammar.[26] This linguistic problem was to condemn the first half-century of Greek fiction to virtual oblivion, for it is written in a language either theoretically or in fact incapable of immediacy, vividness, and power.[27]

But these were problems inherent not only in the language issue but in the makeup of Greek society as well. When the Generation of 1880[28] made their bold revolt against the use of *katharevousa,* they gained more than linguistic authenticity

26. See Yiannis Psycharis's "Cabinet de lecture," in *To Taxidi Mou* and the Constantinopolitan Elisaios Yiannidis's *Glossa kai Zoi,* first published in 1908, and *Glossika Parerga,* both republished recently by Kalvos, Athens, the former in 1969, the latter in 1970.

27. Certain important texts emerged during this period, however, notably the *Dialogos* and *Woman of Zakynthos* by Dionysios Solomos, and *The Memoirs of General Makriyannis,* which hinted that demotic Greek would not always be barred from prose expression.

28. This Generation included Yiannis Psycharis, Grigoris Xenopoulos, Alexandros Pallis, George Drosinis, and Kostis Palamas. They were the first to make a conscious use of the demotic in their work. Papadiamandis was the only one who did not make a change during his career, while Ioannis Kondylakis, after a lifetime of writing in the *katharevousa,* wrote his last work in the demotic.

and vividness. By following the advice of Politis and going to the folk for their themes, the writers – using a language with little prose tradition – were enabled to describe characters and report conversations without the difficulties they would have encountered had they wanted to write about an urban or cosmopolitan class.

The demotic linguistic tradition had existed without a break in the Ionian islands, where the writers, influenced by Cretan literature, had employed the vernacular in prose as well as in poetry. The significance of the Generation of 1880, however, was that its members, despite their origins and residences, were published in Athens, the stronghold of classicism and the purist. It was in Athens that Nicholaos Politis was professor and in Athens that he published his *Modern Greek Mythology* in 1871. It was in Athens, moreover, that the school of ethography – the description of the manners and morals of the Greek folk – began and reigned for at least half a century, until it became, in the words of Apostolos Sachinis, a "sickness" from which Greek fiction needed to be healed.[29]

Ethography and Demoticism, therefore, are twin phenomena that begin in the latter half of the nineteenth century

29. Apostolos Sachinis, *Anazitiseis tis Neoellinikis Pezographias stin Mesopolemiki Eikosaetia* (Athens, 1945), p. 70. The same author defines ethography as "the simple and faithful copying of the manners, the morals, the customs, and all those specific characteristics of the peasant and, generally, the provincial way of life. Ethography is that prose that concentrates on the village, that shows obviously the author's intention to express and emphasize the facets of peasant life and that, without attempting to disguise the fact, places greater importance on these than on the complete outline and the total development of character, in the expression of sentiments and passions, or in the rendering of a rich interior life. Ethography is the prose writing that does not go beyond the appearance (of things), beyond the external confines of locale, ignoring the essence (of things) either out of design or, more frequently, out of inability." *To Neoelliniko Mythistorima, Istoria kai Kritiki* (Athens, 1958), p. 139.

With the emergence of Politis and the study of folklore, the first scientific attempt was made to store and assess the slowly disappearing Greek oral tradition. The folkloric studies were precisely those that needed to be carried on in the villages, where the Greek people lived and had lived for centuries, and this required the active cooperation and contribution of the folk. Its raison d'être was the very conservatism of the Greek folk, who conserved and retained their oral treasure from generation to generation.

The other phenomenon, Demoticism, though it promoted the use of the language of the people and should have had strong popular support as a result, was on the contrary a demand of the bourgeoisie who lived primarily in the Unredeemed lands or in the West. It can be said to have begun when Yiannis Psycharis (born in Odessa and educated at the Sorbonne) traveled to Constantinople, where his family then lived, as the representative of the French Ministry of Education to a conference sponsored by The Literary Club of Constantinople. While in the City, during the summer of 1886, he spent much time in the Library of the Metochi of the Holy Sepulchre, studying Greek medieval manuscripts that sound "the depths of folk fantasy" in linguistic as well as mythological, political, and religious terms. From Constantinople he traveled to Pyrghi, in Chios, where he "considered the need to study all of Greece from the point of view of linguistic geography."[30]

In linguistic terms, therefore, Psycharis did much the same thing as Politis, but the conclusions he drew led him to a direct confrontation with the official language of the Greek state, a head-on collision first seen in *To Taxidi Mou* (*My Journey*), published in 1888. Politis, as a professor and thus

30. Emmanuel Kriaras, *Psycharis* (Thessaloniki, 1959), pp. 95-101.

an employee of the Greek state, had felt compelled to study and assess folk material in demotic through the filter of the *katharevousa.* Psycharis, as a Greek from abroad, was able to confront the Greek establishment without the compromises dictated by dependence on the machinery of the Greek establishment.

Psycharis both represented and led the bourgeoisie that lived outside Helladic Greece. "The Hellenism of Europe and the Turkish-held centers," George Valetas has written, was "commercial, creative, and up-to-date." In cities like Paris, London, Trieste, Leghorn, Odessa, and Alexandria, "this Hellenism lived under the direct influence of European civilization and saw the problems of modern Greece in a radical manner." In the urban centers of Asia Minor, the Greeks were the predominant middle-class and were imbued with the characteristic bourgeois drive toward progress and self-improvement.[31] The major support for the thrust of Demoticism came, in moral and financial terms, from men like Alexandros Pallis, Petros Vlastos, and Argyris Eftaliotis.[32] By helping *Noumas,* the combative journal of Demoticism, men like Pallis contributed directly to the final triumph of the demotic in arts and letters.

The major opposition to Demoticism, in fact, came from within Helladic Greece, from a coalition of the academic intelligentsia representing the machinery of the Greek state, and the very folk for whose liberation Demoticism struggled. It was this overwhelming popular support for the conservative

31. George Valetas, *Anthologia tis Dimotikis Pezographias,* Vol. III (Athens, 1949), p. 6.
32. Dimaras justly remarks that since these men lived away from Greece, they approached the language problem with a single-mindedness not always attuned to the more complex Greek reality. See *Istoria tis Neoellinikis Logotechnias,* pp. 370-371.

31

parties that consistently defeated attempts to liberalize the attitude toward language. It was the university students in Athens who rioted *against*, not *for*, Pallis's translation of the Gospels (1901) and Sotiriadis's translation of Aeschylus into demotic Greek (1903).

Prose fiction, to recapitulate, had to fulfill two demands: it had to assert the ethnic and cultural descent of the modern Greek from his ancient ancestor, and it had to do this in a form of the Greek language about which there was great disagreement. It could fulfill neither demand, however, until it thoroughly documented the basic unit of Hellenism, the village. Ethography, a fusion of folklore and linguistic concerns, was an attempt to begin a modern Greek literary tradition organically, from the village, the most basic unit that can be taken to represent national life.

The writers of fictional narrative in the early years of the Greek state, men of great learning and ability, wrote books influenced by the romantic and historical fiction of Sir Walter Scott. These novels, aside from the language barrier that makes them, if not unreadable, at least unread to a great extent by contemporary Greeks, treated characters by and large not as individual people beset by unique problems, but generally as representatives of their nations, with plots drawn from frequently lurid historical events. They concentrated on situations of conflict that stemmed from stereotyped relationships between nations – the Turks and the Greeks, usually – that were in a superior-inferior position, and ignored the conflict that arises from the clash between an individual and the expectations of his own society.

Satisfied to be surface narratives of adventure and information, these novels did not pretend to serve as critical views of the failings and foibles of the writer's own community or people. In Western European fiction, the stage that Georg

Lukacs has termed "critical realism," which begins with Balzac, followed closely upon the historical fiction of Scott, [33] but Greek fiction did not develop into this stage. The language itself placed an obstacle between the reader and the described fictional event, while the lack of sophistication in character analysis, which demands delineation and complexity, and the lack of depth, which is provided by the mature elaboration of fictional conflict, made the novel in *katharevousa* incapable of presenting anything but surface tensions. If the *katharevousa* writers had had talent and serious philosophical concerns, these problems – including that of language – might not have been as thorny as they were. But they did not. [34] They were derivative and reflected literary concerns that had no relevance to the Greece of their time.

But what did have relevance for Greece of the nineteenth century? Iakovaky Rizos Neroulos cited the virtual nonexistence of social life in Athens and the still subordinate role of women, while Alexandros Rangavis – a novelist himself – believed that the orientation of the Greeks toward the classics and whatever was utilitarian tended to make fiction unnecessary as a literary genre. Whatever was important could be said either in didactic or in poetic terms.

> If literature, during the first decades of the nineteenth century, went parallel, generally, to classical studies or journalism, and if, for the informed men of the time, the work of the writer, the philologist, and the journalist was considered identical, we can clearly imagine the difficulties that would confront the development and cultivation of

33. See Lukacs's *Studies in European Realism*, (New York, 1964) *The Historical Novel,* (London, 1962), and *Theory of the Novel* (London, 1971).

34. Alkis Thrylos, *Morphes tis Ellinikis Pezographias,* Vol. I (Athens, 1962), p. 10.

the novel, a relatively new literary genre with a small tradition and few examples even among the great nations of the West.[35]

For the first century of national freedom, the society of the Greek state was basically agrarian and its most representative unit was the tightly knit, tradition-bound fishing or agricultural village. Even if there had been no language issue to complicate the conception of literature, fiction as a mirror of its own national society could not describe any but the most narrow human relationships, particularly since the only crucial political and religious problems had been solved with independence from the Turk. It was either the village, then, or the historically surpassed subject matter that preoccupied the writers of the nineteenth century, who with few exceptions took a simplistic view of the moral world in which their narratives took place. Very few were interested in the contemporary subject matter that was the product of tensions current among the various groups vying with each other in the new Kingdom. To see what life was like in the middle third of the nineteenth century in Greece we must read memoirs like those of the Revolutionary warriors or the anonymous *Soldier's Life in Greece*; the novels, with the exception of Pavlos Kalligas's *Thanos Vlekas* (1855-1856), usually concern themselves with previous eras.

The turn to ethography was facilitated by two developments besides Politis's folklore studies. The introduction of naturalism in 1880 with Kambouroglou's translation, into simplified Greek, of Zola's *Nana* made the Greek writers aware of the necessity for a close observation of reality. For obvious reasons, urban fiction, though it might be attempted at

35. Sachinis, *To Neoelliniko Mythistorima*, p. 22.

this point, could by no means be established, since urban life in Greece was obviously still in the embryonic stage. The other development, the establishment of stability in rural areas previously controlled and terrorized by bandits, promoted the emergence of social patterns that enabled the writer to study individual characters against a clearly outlined background.[36]

Greek fiction, after the eclipse of the historical novel, was true to its most accepted role as the mirror of its society by concentrating on the dominant village. It may perhaps be faulted for not describing the life of Athens, but Athens in the nineteenth century was little more than a village clustered around the Acropolis. A critic must, to be fair, defend ethography as a valid view of Greek society. That this school of writing has been attacked in recent years as limited and outmoded should not obscure the fact that its reputed failings are not inherent in itself but derive rather from the lack of complex social tensions in the village society it treated; more critically, its failings are those of the individual writers who were satisfied merely to describe interesting local characters and to provide a sense of village atmosphere, to which their attitudes were usually predictably approving.

Complex social novels that take village life as their province are rare in Greek ethographic fiction, not only because the writers of the time were ideologically unwilling to admit that social tensions – aside from the simplistically and sentimentally viewed clan-feuds – existed in the idyllic village, but also because the major source of tension – the rebel, the outsider, or the non-Christian element, the Turk – is conspicuously absent. The *klepht* or bandit, as a matter of fact, is

36. *Ibid.,* pp. 136-137.

frequently viewed not as an outsider whose existence is a negation of the writer's contemporary society, but as one who emerges as symbolic of the best in Greek society and history. The attitudes of the Greek novelists toward their subject matter, certainly because of their recent national history, are more like those of the folk poet than those of the writer of contemporary prose.

The Greek village, after all, was the incubator of the modern Greek because its population was by and large composed exclusively of Greek Christians; in most cases, its geographical position was deliberately chosen with a view toward guaranteeing ethnic survival. Since there were few basic economic differences in the average Greek village (except for a rich province like Thessaly, which was dominated by Moslem landowners), there were few social tensions left that could be exploited by writers. Even the rich subject of the individual pitted against his past — the Greek tradition — was effectively barred because it was this very overwhelming past which was considered the ennobling and distinguishing characteristic of the Greek and which, consequently, had to be affirmed.[37]

Under these ideological strictures, ethography could not contribute unique, or even interesting, characters to Greek fiction, let alone representative or towering figures. That it was the dominant school of Greek fiction until the Generation of the 1930s — that is, until the men and women who grew to maturity and published after the Disaster of 1922 — is proof that the writers could not overcome its presuppositions; they could not do so because the society itself had not sufficiently developed out of its agrarian,

37. If I am not mistaken, the first work of fiction that shows a critical attitude toward the excessive "ancestor-worship" of the Greek is Andreas Karkavitsas's *O Archiologos*, first published in 1904, seven years after the War of 1897.

but more importantly, its uncritically affirmative, character even to demand, let alone execute, a change in literary orientation.[38]

By the early years of the twentieth century, however, a new and much deeper view of the possibilities of ethography became evident. Andreas Karkavitsas (1866-1922) and Constantine Hadzopoulos (1868-1920), both from Continental Greece, viewed Helladic rural society in a careful and critical manner, while Grigoris Xenopoulos (1876-1951) and Constantine Theotokis (1872-1923), both from the Ionian Islands, consciously attempted to write fiction that described a complex social world. Although he is a controversial figure in Greek letters, Demosthenes Voutyras (1871-1956)[39] also has undoubted social importance in that he wrote hundreds of short stories and novellas about the lower classes of a gradually urbanized and industrialized Athens and Piraeus. There are others, of course, but these five writers reveal the subtle changes Greek prose was undergoing before the Disaster of 1922 irrevocably changed the concept of fiction.[40]

Xenopoulos, a prolific writer of fiction and drama, was one of the first novelists to attempt the trilogy form, in itself perhaps an index of the emergence of a more complex view of society. His

38. Sachinis, citing the development of a working and middle class in the early years of the twentieth century, believes that Greek writers could have surpassed ethography sooner than they did. The writers, he says in *Anazitiseis,* p. 70, "should have made an effort to renew themselves." I find it difficult to agree with him on this point. Given its "patriotic" bias, I believe ethography could not have been surpassed until 1922. Individual writers of great talent, or great ambition, can make efforts to renew themselves, but they will succeed only if the conditions are right.

39. I am using the dates given by G. M. Politarchis in "Voutyras," *Megali Enkyklopaidia Neoellinikis Logotechnias,* Vol. 4 (Athens, 1969), pp. 327-334.

40. What is immediately evident is that all five of these men were conscious demoticists, regardless of their social and geographical backgrounds.

work documents — seldom deeper, unfortunately, than at the popular level — the tensions and conflicts of the peasants, *popolarii,* and nobility that made up the Italianate world of the Ionian Islands.[41] Theotokis, from the same Italianate world, might have provided Greek fiction, after the work of Xenopoulos, with a coherent and complex view of men and women living together in a variegated society; but he died just as he was beginning to chart the outlines of his world view with *Slaves in their Bonds* (1922).

Xenopoulos and Theotokis are the most notable exceptions to the ethographic school of fiction because they emerge from a civilization that is an amalgam of Venetian feudalism in the process of breakdown and an Italianized Greek population, *not* from the closed and unmixed village society that had by necessity and tradition been egalitarian.

It is instructive to contrast these two socially oriented novelists with the greatest writer of his time, Alexandros Papadiamandis (1851-1911). From the poor and backward island of Skiathos, which certainly had none of the tradition, wealth, social complexity, or inherent interest of the Heptanese, Papadiamandis surpassed this and other more personal disadvantages to create a body of work that has still not been adequately recognized by Greek criticism.[42] In his greatest work, Papadiamandis describes life in the simple Greek society he remembered from Skiathos, and not the "cosmopolitan" world of Athens he so obviously rejected. He can thus more accurately be described as an ethographic writer, unlike Xenopoulos and Theotokis, whose fictional

41. For Xenopoulos's interest in socialism, see Yianis Kordatos, *Istoria tis Neoellinikis Logotechnias,* Vol. I (Athens, 1962), pp. 423-426.

42. Of the historians of modern Greek literature, Ilias Voutieridis and Aristos Kambanis consider Papadiamandis a great writer, while Dimaras and Kordatos, from their opposing ideological positions, view him negatively.

society is complex because it reflects an older and hierarchical communal system that is unrepresentative of Greece as it was then.

Besides this, Papadiamandis is a traditionalist in religion and social values, and thus not interested in showing the usual fictional conflict between individual morality and social values. [43] Neither his world view nor his traditionalism would have made Papadiamandis a source of controversy — as he was until recently — if these had not been complicated by his rejection of the principles of Demoticism and his use of a personal form of *katharevousa*. This inability to sympathize with the forces of renewal and take part in the rebirth of Greek culture that Demoticism represented meant that Papadiamandis would, rightly or wrongly, henceforth be identified with the forces of obscurantism and reaction. Yet it would not be amiss at this point to describe Papadiamandis not only as the greatest prose writer of his time, but, because of the ethographic elements in his fiction, as the novelist who accurately described while transcending the life most characteristic of Greece in his era.

Before prose fiction in the contemporary sense could emerge in Greek letters, therefore, the problems of language and identity, which are intimately related, had to be solved. Their solution, however, was logically connected to the development of ethography, and ethography, given the nature of Greek society, could not provide the basis for the further development into critical realism, the kind of fiction that carefully analyzes the tensions

43. As in most serious fiction, Frangoyiannou, the leading character of *I Fonissa* (1903), is in conflict with the values of the society she lives in, but Papadiamandis places the reader in the unusual position of identifying, not with Frangoyiannou, but with the society whose moral codes she violates. That the novelist is able to convince the reader of the reasons for her behavior and the importance of her quest for a justice only the most glib can formulate, is a proof of Papadiamandis's greatness.

and inadequacies of society by posing a strong and individual character against it.

The War of 1897 provided the great shock to the esteem of the Greek, a blow that was to be the great spur to the Demotic movement, since it resulted in the greatest effort at self-renewal Greece has yet experienced. Demoticism, represented by the Educational Association (*Ekpaideftikos Omilos*)[44] fused both the linguistic and social issues in the early years of the twentieth century and worked for the liberalization and modernization of Greek institutional life. In this group were men and women who, regardless of their political orientation, desired the renewal of the life and culture of modern Greece. Though there were always elements of reaction and resistance to its goals,[45] by the second decade of the twentieth century the Educational Association was well on its way to solving the problems that confronted Greek culture, but not Greek society. One would expect some of these problems to emerge unmistakably in imaginative fiction, but this did not happen. The theater, influenced by Ibsen and the natural-

44. Founded in 1910 by Ion Dragoumis, Dimitris Glinos, Manolis Triandafyllidis, Alexandros Delmouzos, Nikos Kazantzakis, Markos Tsirimokos, Lorenzos Mavilis, and others. Its principles were accepted by the Venizelos government, 1917-1920, rejected during the Populist government's two years in office, and reinstituted, 1922-1925. In 1927 the Association split and many old members, liberal in orientation, resigned. The Association was disbanded in 1936.

45. The *katharevousa* was declared the official language of the Greek State by Parliament in 1911 under the prime ministry of Venizelos. Article 107, moreover, forbids the use of any other language. I personally find it impossible to believe that this would have occurred under Dragoumis's leadership. Venizelos made up for this however, when in 1917, after his triumphant return to Athens, his government, with Dimitris Glinos as advisor to the Minister of Education, not only made demotic the national language, but also laid the foundation for a radical educational reform, a foundation that was not built upon because of Venizelos's electoral defeat in 1920. In English, another view of this can be found in Peter Bien's *Kazantzakis and the Linguistic Revolution in Greek Literature* (Princeton, 1972), pp. 177-180.

ists, and the combative periodicals — as forums — may have been full of social concerns, but only gradually and in scattered examples did these problems surface in the novel.

The reason is clear. The Greek novelist, always excepting Papadiamandis, does not seem to be in basic disagreement with his own intellectual society or with the broader society. He is a Demoticist, which means that he writes in the demotic and that in temperament and politics he is in favor of progress and renewal. Demoticism as a label can characterize men as different as George Skliros, the Marxist, and Ion Dragoumis, the conservative and Royalist. There was, until 1915, no division between monarchic principles, as symbolized by King Constantine, and bourgeois liberalism, as represented by Venizelos. Everyone subscribed, actively or passively, to the validity and the eventual realization of the Megale Idea as the justification for the existence of the modern Greek.

Though there may have been social problems in the Greek state, there does not seem to have been any great disagreement as to how they could be solved. In fact, sometimes it appears as though their solution was being postponed until the realization of the Megale Idea, an event that seemed imminent. Riots in the street were staged and bullets fired into crowds, not because of the usual type of "social unrest" but because of an issue that in other cultures would be considered peripheral: the translation into the vernacular of the New Testament and of ancient tragedy. It was not peripheral, however. The riots were crucial skirmishes in a war for renewal that was just beginning, a renewal that everyone certainly believed would be concluded triumphantly when all the unredeemed *rayahs* became free citizens of a Megale Hellas.

Even the era of the Dissension, which destroyed the tense balance in Greek political life between the monarchic and the parliamentary forces, did not seem to harm immediately the

41

organ of progressive change, the Educational Association. Those important figures who remained uncommitted or even hostile to Demoticism after 1916 were anachronisms, and not at all typical of Greek culture in the second decade of the century. Even the more conservative professors of law, medicine, and the natural sciences begin to feel the attraction of Demoticism.

But there loomed in the future a historical event that would reshape and polarize Greek society by destroying the ideological unity that characterized the intellectual class after 1897. The Asia Minor Disaster of 1922 changed overnight the character of modern Greek culture and society by introducing the elements of dissolution that the almost universally accepted Megale Idea had kept suppressed or unified. The elections of 1920 showed that the dream of the Megale Idea was not strong enough or attractive enough to persuade the average Greek that it was worth an indefinitely maintained mobilization; but if the defeat of 1922 had not occurred, the Idea would have continued to exist. With the events of 1922, however, the Greek people suffered an ideological, social, and emotional dislocation that changed the course of modern Greek civilization. Fiction, as the mirror of this civilization, could not help but reflect that cataclysmic change.

Suddenly, deep cleavages became apparent in a society whose problems had previously seemed to be manageable. The most obvious result was the division into warring camps of the class that articulates and elaborates ideas – the intellectuals. The murder in 1920 of Ion Dragoumis, one of the few right-wing intellectuals in the Demotic movement, meant that from then on linguistic simplification, progress, and Venizelism would be considered identical.[46] Certainly the Russian Revolution preceded the Asia Minor Disaster by five years, but this merely buttressed

46. Yet the attitudes of Venizelos about the language issue are not at all clear.

the more radical forces associated with Demoticism – without, however, threatening or alienating the bourgeois elements. The Disaster of 1922 and the consequent military revolution in Chios and Mytilene swept the Royalists out of power and eventually pitted Venizelists against one another. Marxists like Dimitris Glinos came into conflict with liberals like Markos Tsirimokos, Manolis Triandafyllidis, and Alexandros Delmouzos, and this conflict resulted in the fateful division of the Educational Association in 1927.

The destruction of the Megale Idea, however, was removed from the purely ideological sphere by the destruction of Hellenism in Asia Minor and the arrival of a million and a half refugees in the Greek state. It was not solely the intellectual disorientation that the Disaster wrought but the accompanying dislocation of the Greek state, its economy, and what many people continued, even after 1897, to view as its "idyllic" society, which overnight was overwhelmed by problems that other nations had had decades to confront. The problems were legion: overpopulation, fiscal bankruptcy, unparalleled human suffering and degradation; the arrival of an urban proletariat, much of it previously middle-class, violently, and for good reason, suspicious of official authority; the break-up of a governmental system and its machinery; the execution of six ministers, including Prime Minister Gounaris, accused of moral responsibility for the Disaster; the institution of the First Republic; and, finally, the destruction of the underpinnings of a national ideal.

It was this world that fiction sought to document as an event in history, an event that could be described and assessed. The limited success of this effort in the novels and short stories that deal exclusively with the Disaster of 1922 must not lead us to the mistaken conclusion that this cataclysmic event went virtually unrecorded; Greek literature has been irrevocably marked by it. It is the immediate impact that must first be assessed. The fact must never be forgotten, however, that the real gauge of this impact is the vast change the events of 1922 wrought on the composition of Greek society and thus on the image of this convulsed society within its mirror, Greek fiction.

By the time the events of the Disaster exploded upon Greece, the language issue was well on its way to solution. Greek society, moreover, with the rapid development that began to be noticed in Greece at the turn of the century, was becoming urbanized. The first examples of attempts to describe tensions within a complex social world began to make their appearance in the first decade of the twentieth century, with men like Xenopoulos and Theotokis. Fiction, therefore, as a genre capable of treating ideological issues in a complex society with a commonly accepted language, had already appeared by 1922.

The Asia Minor Disaster came at the precise moment when a new way of looking at man and society was beginning, faintly, to emerge in Greek fiction. The great majority of writers had encountered in the events of 1922 and their consequences an experience that destroyed the certitudes that consciously or unconsciously supported them; they were overwhelmed by the very problems they had previously ignored. It was the lack of real issues that had made much of Greek fiction seem so shallow before and made its escape from the fifty-year-old "sickness" of ethography so problematic.

The convulsions that Greece underwent as a result of the Disaster were to reorient and disorient older writers like Kostas Varnalis and Nikos Kazantzakis (men whose temperaments required ideological thought), while these traumas would create the conditions which would nourish the writers of the Generation of the 1930s, who were by and large from the urban and the middle class. It would be these younger writers who would use the scattered examples of social and urban fiction that preceded them and establish the form of the novel in Greek letters.

Ethography did not cease to exist in Greek fiction after 1922, but it was no longer the exclusive interest of most writers. The world to be described by fiction after the Disaster would be distinct from that of the village or countryside. Besides, the Greek people, at least until their resistance to the Italian invader in 1940, could no longer expect the unquestioned admiration of the Greek intellectual. Not after the elections of 1920. It is this rejection of the dreams of the Megale Idea by the very people in whose imagination it had lived for four centuries that complicated the attitudes toward democracy of men like Kostas Varnalis and Nikos Kazantzakis.

2 The Theme of the Asia Minor Disaster

The "theme" or subject matter of the events of 1922 and their aftermath, as directly treated in prose, is usually and erroneously considered the only impact the Asia Minor Disaster has had on Greek fiction. Viewed from this perspective, however, the way fiction, and the novel in particular, has matured and developed after the Disaster and as a result of it is necessarily either ignored or confused. Consequently, works written in the 1950s and 1960s and inspired by the subject matter of the Disaster have been seen by critics merely as more recent manifestations of the same theme; the totally different world (and issues) from which these works emerged, as well as the greater maturity the Greek novel has attained as a result of the foundations laid by the Generation of the 1930s, have been ignored.

The Asia Minor Disaster has had a double impact. The first is its "theme," the direct representation in prose fiction of the events of 1922 and their aftermath. The second is the impact made on the life of letters and thought in Greece, including the result of this impact on the development of the novel. By the time the Civil War was concluded in 1949, the greater resources of conception and execution at the disposal of the writers of the 1950s and 1960s allowed them to view the Asia Minor Disaster (to *review* it, rather) in a totally different way.

The actual subject matter, the first impact of the Disaster, falls into fairly clear categories. Though there is some overlapping, the "theme" develops in three major stages, all unavoidably influenced by the impingement of historical events and ideological issues on the psyche of the writer who feels he must communicate his experience or vision.

The classifications would have varied greatly if the fate of Greece from 1922 to 1940 had been different, but fiction is not written in a vacuum. Even countries further removed from the maelstrom of history than Greece reveal, in their imaginative prose, the movements and agitations of the whirl. Added to our interest in the subject matter and the treatment of a particular work, therefore, must be a concern for the date of its writing and publication, since the preoccupations of the Greek writer in 1923 are bound to differ greatly from those of writers in 1935 or 1939.

A critic could legitimately challenge the coherence of these categories only by disagreeing that the Disaster was, in its first and most important phase, a mid-war phenomenon. Granting that the Disaster theme is an essentially historical experience and thus subject to the impingement of specific historical events, he is compelled to accept the fact that the works of fiction inspired by the theme — though many transcend the limitations of a specific time — can be subjected, more than most novels, to the process of historical development. Since much of the imaginative literature about the Disaster in the "theme's" first phase has been written by men and women who were themselves uprooted from Anatolia, it does not seem difficult to accept the conclusion that the fiction they have written has depended, to a large extent, on the adjustments they had made to life in Greece.

For the first decade, the major concern of the refugee was to survive and establish himself in his new home. If he had the leisure and the need to write a work of the imagination, it would concern events that had definitely been concluded. The important works of this period, therefore, deal with the recently experienced imprisonment. All of the examples treated in this first category, Narratives of Captivity, rest to a greater or lesser extent upon actual experiences.

By the mid-1930s, the majority of the refugees had been settled, despite the international monetary crisis and the political instability that characterized that time. At this point, writers — native, as well as Anatolian Greeks — began to be interested in the process of establishing roots in the new environment. Accordingly, the second category, The Refugee Experience, will review the works inspired by the presence of the Anatolian in Greece and his efforts to sink roots into the earth to which he had been "repatriated." For the first time, moreover, a vague, groping attempt to understand the ideological significance of the vast human migration is evident on the writer's part.

By the late 1930s, the writers who had come from an "Unredeemed Greece" that was now forever lost began to review their youth with nostalgia. The Sounds of Another War (the third and last category) that began to be heard immediately before and during World War II revive old memories and stir the imaginations of the Anatolian writers. The fictional statements made at this time are, with only a few exceptions, the last the writers of this group will make about Asia Minor. When they go on to other concerns, and when the war, which continues in Greece until 1949, is over at last, the Asia Minor experience will be taken up by new writers who, as heirs to the fictional and linguistic achievements of their elders, will use the events of the Disaster and its aftermath to illustrate and express values more relevant to their own time.[1]

1. For another view of the stages of the refugees' absorption, this time from the political, economic, and sociological perspective, see Dimitri Pentzopoulos, *The Balkan Exchange of Minorities and its Impact upon Greece* (The Hague, 1962), p. 225.

Narratives of Captivity

For reasons that are readily understandable, the memoir of imprisonment is the first to emerge after the Disaster. As a form it has severe limitations in the hands of the less able; thus we find stereotyped relationships between the guards and the guarded; constant and thus undifferentiated psychological tension; an almost total dependence upon external stimuli to create incident; and the removal of free will from the major characters, which tends to limit the amount of self-knowledge they can attain. Instead of probing the complexity of man, who is both perpetrator and sufferer, these narratives by their very definition are compelled to divide characters neatly according to the roles of tormentor and tormented and, in the less ambitious literary efforts, to employ lurid and melodramatic incidents to support moralizing of a smug, simplistic, and nationalistic sort. Obviously, these characteristics exhaust all possibilities for esthetic elaboration and make the narrative of captivity a short-lived form. In the proper hands, though, this type of narrative has great potential for emotional depth, psychological authenticity, and philosophical comment. Though its great works were created early (Stratis Doukas's *Narrative of a Prisoner* was published in 1929 and Ilias Venezis's *The Number 31,328* in 1931), this form produced, in the half-century of its existence, a highly valuable substratum of factual information and psychological analysis that has been used by younger writers not involved personally in the slave-labor battalions.

The first work of this kind, a superbly precise and intelligent memoir entitled *From the Captivity* by B. K., an officer in the Greek Air Corps, was published in 1923, one year after the Disaster and within no more than a few months of his release.[2]

2. *Apo tin Aichmalosia* (no publisher, Athens, 1923).

B. K.'s narrative has the profundity and perception that in many other cultures would have made the book a minor classic, an integral part of a nation's memory of its physical and psychological sufferings by a man who — though we know virtually nothing about him — must be accounted as one of the noblest warriors in a doomed cause. Though *From the Captivity* cannot be classified as fiction, the author's strategy of hiding his identity in order to tell a truth he could not otherwise tell makes the book the precursor of the works of Doukas and Venezis, since at the core of all three is the interest in the nature of man's appearance and his reality.[3]

B. K.'s imprisonment begins when his airplane crashes on a reconnaissance mission and continues until his release from the horrors of captivity. Between those two events, Basil K. (we learn his Christian name indirectly when he mentions his name day) provides the reader with an unsparing account of the panic and brutalization of a once triumphant army. As an officer he is saved, somewhat, from the rigors that the enlisted men are subjected to, but only until the front collapses and the Turks no longer fear and thus respect his countrymen. Then, whatever protection the Greeks may have had is stripped from them and they are defenseless, unable to resist any mistreatment that their captors, even the lowest ranking guards, decide to visit upon them. Serving as an even darker background to the slow deterioration of prisoner discipline, national cohesion, and individual self-respect is the wholesale persecution and massacre of the Greek

3. From the text we learn that he is a Venizelist, an only son, and of Spartan background; possibily he was acquainted with Penelope Delta, for of the two copies I was able to locate — both in Melpo Merlier's Center for Asia Minor Studies — one copy bore Miss Delta's signature on the title page with a note reading: "To my beloved Melpo, with the wish that she give it [the book] to many to be read." *From the Captivity* is mentioned only in Nikos Milioris's invaluable Bibliography in "I Mikrasiatiki Tragodia stin Logotechnia kai sti Techni," *Mikrastiatika Chronika*, 13 (Athens, 1967).

civilian population. This extermination the reader sees described within the text, but the many silent towns and villages, plundered and fire-blackened, attest to the already concluded annihilation of the Armenians, who by then no longer exist in most regions of Anatolia.

From the Captivity is a tour through a timeless Greek Asia Minor which ceases to exist as soon as he stops looking at it. The vignettes, the brief views he gets on his imposed travels further into the interior from the front, are the final inventories before Doomsday. He and a group of Greek prisoners are herded onto a train at Ikonion and there, silently, without a trace of recognition, without a gesture of friendliness except their presence, scores of Greek women and children appear, gazing at them in a mute solidarity. "As the train pulled out a Greek girl waved to us with her kerchief, was followed by the other women and children, and the whole crowd begin to wave at us," an act that called in the guards, who pushed and kicked at the demonstrators.[4] On his "odyssey" through the circles of his own "inferno", B. K. provides the reader with unforgettable views of a world about to be destroyed: of the rising strength of Bolshevism among the hitherto inert Moslem peasants; of political and ideological discussions with anti-Kemalist Turks who are hoping for a different outcome to the war; of the breaking of Greek ranks into Venizelists and Monarchists which presages the destruction of unity among themselves; of the crypto-Greeks, who have lived as Turks among Turks for centuries but have maintained their religion and sense of nationality, who speak to him furtively in the few moments when they are unobserved, then lose themselves again in the Turkish mass when the encounter is over. *From the Captivity* is a steady and sure gaze at a precious terrain before an earthquake has disfigured it for eternity, a document — forgotten

4. *Ibid.,* p. 72.

as so many others in Greek letters – that claims to be nothing more than a memoir of imprisonment.

On his release, during the train ride to Smyrna, this cultivated man sees his more shallow companions gradually forgetting the experiences they had undergone and withdrawing from "the depths of the abyss" into which their fate had plunged them. "May God protect a man from all he can bear," he repeats the proverb, nourishing a secret contempt for men who refuse to accept the fearful wisdom they have been granted:

> It is truly unimaginable what man can bear. . . . Only up to a certain point can he remain a man . . . a point beyond which social conventions lose their hold, where the eye of one's fellow man cannot reach and support him, where every human vanity and pretence is removed. . . . At that point, the thin layer of humanity peels off and he is left with his primitive inheritance. . . . From that point, every attempt to appear human is forced affectation, every attempt to resume a previous life false and mimetic. . . . When a man returns (to live) among others again, in cities, he'll be compelled to hide all the disgrace he has undergone, to play-act, to wear a mask, to play the human being and to disguise, with craft and terror – as a leper his leprosy – the hated beast inside his clothes.[5]

The reader can only marvel at the tireless observation, the descriptive powers, and the austere self-control that B. K. evinces in a narrative that records his gradual despair and near brutalization. One must not forget, certainly, that he was a trained reconnaissance pilot and that, as such, his role was to observe and record, as accurately as possible, reality as it existed beyond himself. Yet *From the Captivity,* appearing and disappearing as it does without the slightest mention in Greek literary histories,

5. *Ibid.,* pp. 236-237.

should convince the critic that humility must never be abandoned when dealing with "unknown" writers. Besides all his other qualities, this mysterious B. K. is that rarity in Greek writers of the memoir — a man from whom not a paragraph can be deleted without removing an important or interesting perception or fact. He is broadly educated as well, without the narrow-minded certitudes, the justifications of self, the copious and dull stretches of shop-talk, or the personal animosities that mar most works of the genre. Moreover, B. K. knows his audience and wants to interest, inform, and communicate with them at all times about important matters.

For whom, then, is B. K. writing? For people like himself, clearly, men and women accustomed to the acceptance of responsibilities, to the making of important decisions, people for whom emotion and rhetoric appear not as comforting, patriotic gestures but as the confusing and even threatening techniques used by demagogues and incompetents to befuddle the decision-making faculties of free men. Without wanting to make *From the Captivity* a mere partisan document, one can describe it as the assessment of the effects of the Dissension in the army and among the Hellenism of Asia Minor, written by a republican and a liberal who comes to the personal understanding that it is the very democracy he believes in that will lead to a frightful "disaster."

Seeing the Turkish soldiers herded and pushed about by their NCO's, B. K. wonders if this "flock, without conscience and decision, will ever conquer" the Greeks. "We, on the contrary, are a people full of energy," he says with a bitter irony. "The Turks would never be able to do what the Greeks had done, "overturn within a moment the tyrant who always led them to the difficult, uphill climbs." The Turks are as slavish as the Greeks are free.

In the consciousness of our freedoms we surpass all of the people of the world. What is freedom? Many rights and few responsibilities. The leaders who do not follow this principle are suspected of tyranny, and that is why we shall always prefer those leaders who speak to us of our rights but do not annoy us with responsibilities. Except that on this particular occasion [the elections of 1920], we blundered somewhat. Without wanting to we are paying more than we expected to pay. If that hated exile [Venizelos] were still in Greece the war would have been over, perhaps. Kemal had no hope for success and before long he would have sued for peace. But who dares say the majority was wrong? Every evil is preferable to that confession.[6]

B. K. would have been too diffident to consider his memoirs as art, which entails some elaboration upon and manipulation of reality, but his book has more in common with the literary works to be discussed in this section than it has with the memoir as the form is usually practiced in Greek letters. Like *Narrative of a Prisoner* and *The Number 31,328*, it exhibits an intimidating honesty, an absence of bombast and rhetoric, a clarity of thought, a precision of expression, and, finally, a commitment to the demotic that is astonishing when it is recalled that B. K. is a military man, though probably a reserve officer. Unlike those two other works, however, *From the Captivity* makes no attempt to shape the outlines of the narrative according to the Aristotelian demand for a beginning, middle, and end; it offers nothing more elegant than the order provided for by real events.

The first conscious effort to turn the events of the Disaster into "fiction" was by Stratis Doukas, whose deceptively simple *Narrative of a Prisoner* disguises the complex ambitions of its author.[7] Like many of the Anatolians from the area of Aivalik, Doukas spent some time during the first persecutions in Lesbos

6. *Ibid.,* pp. 19-20.
7. *Istoria enos Aichmalotou* (Athens, 1929). I consulted the second edition, that of 1932.

(1914), and in the final uprooting he went there again briefly. In the literary circle that included Fotis Kontoglou, Stratis Myrivilis, Ilias Venezis, and George Valetas, who named the group, the "Aeolian School,"[8] Doukas found himself sharing a highly conscious attitude toward the demotic language and the folk arts.

Narrative is related by Nicholas Kazakoglou, a man whom Doukas met in a refugee village near Katerini while working as a reporter for *Makedonia* of Thessaloniki. Kazakoglou, "the man who acted the Turk" in order to escape death, is a Turkish speaker, though the story he tells Doukas, who knew very little Turkish, is narrated in a Greek heavy with Turkish syntax and vocabulary. Doukas took notes, which he constantly reworked, to produce the first of five editions, each edition being revised for the purpose of "purifying the language of the Turkish diction and syntax" he thought was necessary when he first began to fashion it. *Narrative* is a creative work, then, not a mere transcription of the words of "a good Anatolian narrator," as Doukas described Kazakoglou. It is a creation that uses the basic outlines, the diction, and the spirit of the narrator, but a creation that proceeds out of the author's own esthetic needs and personality. Kazakoglou, in relating his story, ceases somehow to be the narrator; the cadences are still his own and the turn of phrase is that of the Anatolian folk, but he magically becomes a character of a "myth," within it but unconscious of it. He is a primitive, like Theophilos the painter, who knew the folk because he was of it, while Doukas, grounded in the folkloric principles of Nicholaos Politis, respected the folk but was not one of them. He knew, moreover, that he was not working on an epic but on "an episode from an epic."[9]

8. See Valetas, *Anthologia tis Dimotikis Pezographias,* Vol. III (Athens, 1949).

9. All the statements and words within quotation marks are quoted directly from Stratis Doukas and were gathered in the course of four interviews with him.

The "ambitions" of B. K. may have been great – to relate the thoughts, the sufferings, and the despair of a sensitive man in captivity – but they were not complex. He wanted to tell the truth as forcefully and as eloquently as he could, using all of his considerable talents of description and analysis. Aside from not revealing his identity, however, he *is* what he *says* he is throughout his narrative. He hides his identity, rather than disguises it, in order to fulfill his objective, which is to express it more fully and more honestly, without the subterfuges and caution that social obligation would force upon him. It is a "memoir", after all, and the important quality of the memoir is its honesty, its accuracy, and its scope. If the value of *From the Captivity* depended upon the reader's knowing who the author was and from what official position he derived his authority for relating the events of his narrative, its independence as a work would suffer. All that is important is that B. K. is a prisoner of war and a perceptive man. *That* is his authority.

Doukas's *Narrative of a Prisoner,* on the other hand, is "fiction," a creative work, and thus an effort to turn from the strict recording of factual observation and spiritual crisis, caused by the captivity and the Disaster, to the imaginative recreation of the point of view and the diction of a character – not the author – and his experiences. Honesty, accuracy, and scope are also important here, but more important is the conviction that the narrator gives us, not of the reality beyond him, but of the *feeling* of that reality. Unlike B. K. who, for his purposes, obscures his identity, hiding it under a hood, Doukas *disguises* his identity, wearing the mask of someone else, a man less complex than he. *Narrative of a Prisoner* contains a double subterfuge, for Kazakoglou "acts the Turk" while Doukas is "acting Kazakoglou." The objective of each is to present not a convincing reality, as it is in B. K.'s case, but a convincing illusion.

For the time the reader is under the spell of the narrative, he forgets whatever sophistication he may have and becomes again the "listener" to a "good Anatolian narrator" who tells a story of catastrophe, terror, and despair as though it were "fiction," occurring to someone else, a Nicholas Kazakoglou who is wily enough, resilient enough, and enduring enough to surmount every obstacle placed before him and arrive, against all odds, at his destination, free. It is no wonder that *Narrative of a Prisoner* is a well-beloved "classic," for it takes a subject as bleak and forbidding as the destruction of Asia Minor Hellenism and lends it the fascination and charm of an age-old legend.

Kazakoglou is one of two thousand men rounded up near Smyrna, formed into "squares," and marched past joking French and Turkish soldiers on a brutal trek to Magnesia. Robbed, stripped of their clothes, beaten, and compelled to do heavy labor for any Moslem civilian who is able to pay their military guards, Kazakoglou and a friend decide that their chances of survival, despite the daily recaptures and on-the-spot executions, are better if they escape. Living off the land, stealing, hiding by day and marching by night, they return to Kirkinze, their plundered village, and find it unrecognizable. It is then that they separate and decide to "become Turks" until they can make their way to a Greece that neither has ever seen. Kazakoglou's change of identity is successful, though that of his friend is uncovered and he is killed. Kazakoglou jokes with the Turks about the Greeks; he claims to have been in the Turkish army and to have killed, not merely plundered, Christians; he then finds work as a shepherd, quickly learning the customs and prayers of Islam, even fasting, for good measure, for forty days during Ramadan. The major threat to his identity comes when his employer offers him his niece as a bride. If he accepts, he would be posed with a dilemma: either to try to maintain his own identity while making his duplicity permanent, or to willingly submerge his Greekness, doing within his lifetime what his ancestors refused to do for four centuries. Kazakoglou evades the dilemma by asking for permission "to bring his sister" down from Proussa first. Using this excuse, he goes to Smyrna and from there escapes to Greece, to freedom, and to his own personality.

Identity, as B. K. the cultivated European expressed it, is that which lies beyond what "the social conventions" demand and what "the eye of your fellow man" sees. Kazakoglou, of the folk, does not have the pretensions of the sophisticated and is able, then, to "play-act, to wear a mask" without the heavy penalties to which the intellectual, or, for that matter, the urban man, is liable. He is helped in this, of course, by the fact that he has not undergone the brutalization of the others, as well as by the very "identity" he initially possesses, a mixed Anatolian one: by a cleverly acted mimickry, he can *save,* not *lose,* his self.

If, to the literary demands placed upon the genre by *From the Captivity,* we add those inherent in Doukas's *Narrative* – concentration on the individual rather than the general and unspecified, on the episodic rather than the panoramic, and a preoccupation with serious philosophical comment disguised by what appears to be artless narrative – we can define loosely some of the achievements of *The Number 31,328* by Ilias Venezis.[10]

More than any writer in the Generation of the 1930s and perhaps more than most in Greek – if not European – fiction, Venezis has been provided with the material for his greatest work by his considerable personal suffering. His first publication, *Manolis Lekas* (1928), a collection of shorter works, includes – besides the superb "Lios" and the title story – preliminary sketches of the major effort that was to appear three years later. "The Boar Hunt" and "In the Valley of the Kimindenia Moun-

10. *To Noumero 31,328* (Athens, 1931). Hereafter this novel will often be called simply *The Number.* The edition I've used is the Third and definitive edition of 1945, published by Skazikis, Athens, and reprinted in 1952.

tains" draw on experiences of his fourteen months in the forced labor battalions, but they give only a pale hint of the reality he was to describe later. He claims to have written parts of these sketches as early as 1924, immediately after his repatriation. If this is the case, one can easily understand why these two sketches have little of the force of *The Number*. Psychologically, it would have been difficult, if not impossible, for an artist to keep the stark truth of what he had suffered for such a long time — and with death as a constant probability — at the necessary esthetic distance.

By 1931 Venezis, already established in a life of security in Athens, could look back on the terrifying experiences he had undergone almost a decade before and begin the careful process of invention, selection, emphasis, and stylistic elaboration that is the creative process. What emerged from this effort is the most mature and compelling work of the genre in Greek literature. More accurately, by its appearance, *The Number* became the model of a form that barely existed in the West (beginning perhaps with Dostoevsky's *The House of the Dead* and continuing in the works of Maxim Gorki) until two decades later, when the literature of the concentration camp began to appear after the Second World War.

Obviously, Venezis wrote this book to save himself from the nightmare of what he had undergone; but *The Number* is more than a chronicle of man's suffering under man's brutality. It is a clear and unsparing account of the human condition. In it we see people swept up by history — which seems to be written by racial, religious, and national hatreds — suffering without even a hope of salvation, and understanding through their pain that they are bound by a common humanity to the people they hate.

The brutality one sees in *The Number* makes a great impact on the reader because of the usually genteel nature of Greek prose. Only this verbal honesty of expression could have provided the reader with the moral complexity that is so significant a part of the novel's impact.[11] Though the Turks behave savagely to the men and women they control, the Greeks as a people are not themselves blameless. Two examples prove this. In the first, a Greek whose wife was brutally raped by a number of Turks in a stable — really a desecrated church — is seized by an old acquaintance, a Turk, when the labor battalion of which the Greek is part passes through Bergama. The Greek had been a soldier in the army unit that retaliated against the Turkish civilians of the city for the execution of forty Greek soldiers. The Turk's wife, a close friend of the Greek's wife, was killed by a stray bullet during the Greek occupation of Bergama. The Greek is executed, not because of the death of the Turk's wife, which everyone accepts as accidental, but because of his role in the vicious cycle of vengeance. The second example occurs to the novel's central character, the boy Ilias, who is found in a dangerously feverish state by a Turkish doctor and literally saved from death caused by overwork. Ilias learns that the doctor is from Proussa and that his mother was killed by the Greeks there. These events, stated without emphasis, show the universality of guilt.

After the "slaves" arrive in the Anatolian interior and begin working to rebuild what was destroyed during the war, they find that there exists a common bond between them and the Turkish guards, a bond that excludes anyone with power. Both are oppressed by their own people: the soldiers by their officers, the prisoners by the Greek *tsaousides,* a version of the Kapo who

---

11. "Honesty" is the proper word, I feel, because it implies as close an approximation as possible in diction to the thoughts and actions that the author thinks necessary to describe. That Venezis is reputed to have "cleansed" *The Number* to be eligible for election to the Academy — as Renos Apostolidis claims in *Kritiki tou Metapolemou (Post-War Criticism),* Athens, 1962, pp. 16-17 — should not change one's attitude, not even when this allegation is more adequately supported by proofs, because the work as a whole has not been harmed.

became notorious in the Nazi concentration camps. But oppression does not stop at the borders of Anatolia. The "slaves" transcend the exclusiveness of their own torment and identify with the black miners of the Transvaal and those other blacks who were shipped to the New World. It is this extension of moral awareness to a universal brotherhood of the downtrodden that makes the vision of Ilias Venezis so impressive.

The number young Ilias is given — No. 31,328 on the official list of prisoners — attains a symbolic importance, since it is a proof of his existence. The boy has undergone suffering, matured, and "defined" himself as a human being, but as long as he can be killed or starved or "lost" without record, there is no security in this achievement. Given the "number," Ilias still retains his name and identity, but as "31,328" he knows that his existence is recorded and that someone is responsible for him. He does not submerge himself into anonymity, but takes on the number as another attribute of his psychic complexity, a complexity that uncovers for him his kinship with the Moslem guards and unknown black slaves, and the great distance that separates him from men of his own race and religion who would willingly act as overseers to guarantee their own well-being.

The Number 31,328 is unlike anything that came before it in Greek literature, a work of art that said everything that needed to be said about the theme. It is a sounding from the depths, a new view of the human experience, appearing in Greek literature when there were few novels, and those few almost overwhelmingly ethographic. Yet *The Number* is unquestionably a novel, not a "memoir" or a "folk narrative"; it is a convincing fictional experience of a young man, too crazed with pain to notice and describe things precisely as did B. K. and too overwhelmed with fear to charm the reader as did Doukas. Ilias must compulsively relate his sufferings in order to rescue himself from their hold on him.

Everything in *The Number* refers to Ilias because it is felt through his raw nerve ends. He has neither the time nor the energy for abstraction or generalizations. Since every fact and experience impinges upon him in a visceral manner, the novel can be read as the fever chart of a young man ill with a reality that most human beings, mercifully, have never seen. But there is more to his torment, for *The Number* is the narrative of Ilias's growing into manhood. It is a "novel of adolescence" as well, a *bildungsroman* with a vengeance, a fourteen-month long tour through a concentration camp world more than a decade before Buchenwald was built. Ilias would have entered manhood without these torments, but there are things he has learned from them that he would never have known otherwise.

After *The Number,* the other chronicles of captivity, like *Prisoners of Kemal* by A. Pissanos and *Prisoners of the Turks* by Christos Spanomanolis, would only add names, facts, and incidents to the already bulging archives of captivity, not a new moral vision or esthetic synthesis.[12] Stripped of sentimentality, of nationalistic rhetoric, and of explicit ideas, *The Number* is, ironically, one of the most philosophical of Greek novels. Its meaning is implicit, and man's brutality and greatness alike are revealed in a narrative of stark and uncompromising power. Man is petty, comfort-loving, and fearful of death. Over these truths are spread the "ideas" that, when untested, degenerate into no more than hollow sentiments about society, religion, the nation, culture, and man. It is these sentiments that the experience of slavery sweeps aside at once. Those who survive the ordeal emerge into the self-awareness of those tried by fire and are inoculated forever against all the "great ideas." "If we ever get out of the

12. *Prisoners of the Turks (Aichmalotoi ton Tourkon)*, was first published in serial form in the newspaper *Ethnos* of 1932 but was stopped because of a complaint by the Turkish Ambassador. The case is discussed more fully in Chapter Six.

slave labor battalions alive," Ilias thinks, "I hope we'll be the most critical minds in the world."[13]

Clearly, the narratives of captivity brought a new note to Greek letters, a dark, somber vision expressed with an austere elegance never before represented. As though unwilling to risk again whatever had been at stake, the writers in question never approached the power they showed in these works. Though *From the Captivity, Narrative of a Prisoner,* and *The Number 31,328* are all unique texts, their preoccupations are surprisingly similar. The experience of "slavery" had struck all three men in that innermost part of the self, their sense of identity, and the unknown B. K. torments himself with "the hated beast within his clothes," Nicholas Kazakoglou experiments with becoming a Turk, and Ilias "loses" his identity to Number 31,328 in order to save it and himself. Captivity threatened all three, not merely by crushing their sense of freedom but by undermining their identity. They see now what B. K. called "the thin layer of humanity" and know how easily it is peeled off. It is a knowledge not easily forgotten. At one stroke, the events of 1922 made most of the pre-Disaster fiction appear shallow, offering only pale reflections of a naive, optimistic world now morally obsolete.

The Refugee Experience

The Asia Minor refugees very quickly made themselves felt in the social, economic, and intellectual life of the Greek state after the Disaster. Indeed, so great was the population influx that it was difficult to ignore their presence, particularly since their arrival changed the political complexion of Greece, certainly until 1935. That they were to be a force to be reckoned with in every aspect of Greek life cannot be disputed, for there

13. *To Noumero,* p. 179.

emerged among them articulate leaders who expressed their contempt for the monarchy they considered responsible for the military defeat in Anatolia and their hatred for the authorities who had made it impossible for them to defend their villages and homes, in effect condemning their loved ones to death or captivity in the slave labor battalions, and themselves, the survivors, to uprooting, homelessness and poverty.[14] When we consider that, besides the refugees, there were two other groups alienated by the current government – the Venizelists, who thought themselves vindicated by the incompetence of the Populist regime, and the military establishment, which felt a profound humiliation at a defeat of such proportions – we can readily imagine the Disaster's revolutionary effect on national life.

These attitudes do not go undocumented in fiction. The threat of the refugees' republicanism is felt in two novels that deal with the events of that period. In *Star-light* by I. M. Panayotopoulos,[15] the Peloponnesian royalist, Dimitris Petropoulos, whose uncle is deeply involved in the political maneuverings of the monarchist right, argues with the novel's central character, Angelos Giannouzis:

Should a person leave his house to give it to one of them?
Forget the fact that all of them smell, that they're sick and

14. Among these authorities, Aristides Stergiadis was particularly detested. He was the High Commissioner of Smyrna, appointed by Venizelos, and retained by the Royalists. The pervasive hatred of him, manifesting itself in extremely harsh but frequently unsupported accusations leveled by refugee intellectuals like Christos Angelomatis in *Chronikon Megalis Tragodias* (Athens, 1963), pp. 55-69 and 128-152, only serves to warn the reader that these attacks must be more adequately proved before they are to be accepted. Stergiadis died in France in 1951, trying desperately to get people to listen to his side of the story. A new series of articles in *Refugee World* (*Prosfygikos Kosmos*), a weekly newspaper published in Athens, signed by Christos Solomonidis, began August 22, 1971, and seemed to have as its objective the further blackening of Stergiadis's name.

15. *Astrofengia, I Istoria mias Efivias,* 2nd ed., revised (Athens, 1971). The novel was first published in 1945.

penniless. One and a half million people! What can poor Greece do for them! We couldn't even provision our army, and now we're loaded down with all of these. The committees are falling down out of exhaustion. There isn't a school, a shed or a tent left unused. [They are in] theaters, cinemas, churches, coffeehouses – all over Greece. Everywhere! And what people! God protect you from them![16]

But when Angelos reminds the royalist that the refugees were uprooted from their homes and had their families destroyed because of the Greek Army's expedition into Asia Minor, an undertaking embarked upon by a republican government under Venizelos and seconded by a monarchist government under Gounaris (a government that won the elections of 1920 by promising to withdraw the Greek army from Anatolia), all Dimitris Petropoulos can say is, "Let them stay in their home lands." To such obstinancy, Angelos's only reply is "Where?" Their home land is ashes and withered vines. The Aegean is red [with blood]. The fishes cannot keep up with the corpses."[17]

Petropoulos sees in the presence of the refugees the mass force that would destroy the predominance of rural and provincial Greece over the still small and underdeveloped urban centers. The arrival of a vast number of people would wrench Greece – Dimitris and his politician-uncle knew well – from an economy almost exclusively agrarian to the beginnings of industrialization. The refugees, though the great proportion of them may have been agriculturalists and provincials in Anatolia, became urban dwellers on their arrival. The large refugee quarters built in and around Athens – Byron, Kaesariani, Nea Ionia, and Kokkinia – at once became focal points for agitation and resistance, at first of the republican variety, and then with the Metaxas dictatorship

16. *Ibid.,* p. 157.
17. *Ibid.,* p. 157.

(1936-1940) and the German Occupation (1941-1944), agitation of a more revolutionary sort. Politically, as soon as these heavily populated areas of class-conscious proletarians came into existence, the Royalist opposition to Liberal domination "felt that it was functioning under a handicap, the fear of a violent refugee reaction hanging over it like the Sword of Damocles."[18]

One clear result of the threat of the refugee's numbers and their explosive contempt for authority was the notorious "Trial of the Six," in which Dimitrios Gounaris, the Prime Minister, G. Hatzianestis, commander of the Greek Army in Asia Minor, and four ministers, N. Stratos, N. Theotokis, P. Protopappadakis, and G. Baltatzis, were executed. The "Six" were tried by a court martial summoned by Nicholas Plastiras, a leader of the Revolution of 1922, and composed of Theodore Pangalos and Alexandros Othonaios; the men were found guilty and executed by a rifle squad at Goudi on November 15, 1922. I. M. Panayotopoulos describes the emotions at the time:

One party struck at the other with hands full of refugees. [Bring forth] those responsible! [Bring forth] those responsi-

18. Pentzopoulos, *The Balkan Exchange of Minorities*, pp. 182-183. Pentzopoulos draws a convincing portrait of the refugee, not only as a man who wanted revenge for what had happened to him but as someone whose republicanism would have been threatening to a monarchy even if he had arrived in Greece under the most pleasant of circumstances. "The Greeks of the Ottoman Empire elected their chiefs from among the respected elders, worshiped in churches they had built, were educated in schools they had financed." Coming from a society of this sort, where local autonomy and intense Hellenism seemed to be identical, "the highly centralized state, the omnipotent bureaucracy of the capital ... was a foreign concept which [they] instinctively rejected." By and large they accepted the Liberal Party at once, while the native inhabitants of Greece, "more provincial in outlook and lacking to a certain extent in independent political thinking were ... conservative and upheld the Populists," pp. 174-175. "It is debatable," Pentzopoulos quotes Papanastasiou, the first Prime Minister of the Greek Republic, "whether the republican regime could have been established without the fanaticism of the refugee masses in favor of it," pp. 180-181. The Glücksburg dynasty was deposed and Greece declared a republic on March 25, 1924.

ble! Six men paid for all of this Disaster with their blood. Six men for so many thousands of dead and for the [lost] gardens and for the houses and for the boats and for the silver-plated samovars and for the richly-velveted sofas and for the pianos and for the unbearable deprivations to be suffered in the future.[19]

The execution may have caused shock and horror in the very diplomatic circles of Europe that had looked upon the Asia Minor Disaster with apathy, but the acceptance with which it was received by the Greeks themselves is surprising. The view that the Six were scapegoats for the continued survival of the Greek state is supported by Grigoris Dafnis, the leading historian of the period, who takes full account of the threat of the refugees.

> The panic fear [caused by the executions] proved to be a saving one. It was conducive to the discipline of both the citizens and the army. In particular, it restrained the refugees. The Greek leadership feared, and rightly so, that the refugees, in the psychological state they were in, would create disorders. But nothing of the sort occurred. The execution of the Six expunged from them the desire for revenge that oppressed them.[20]

How many Greeks were alienated from the cause of the Revolutionary Government and the refugees by the execution of the Six can never be known; it is clear, however, that there were Royalist and Populist elements who would use the violence by which pre-Disaster Greece had been dismantled by the events of 1922 as rallying points for their return to power. Though there were forces in Greek life sympathetic to the homeless and helpless masses from Anatolia, there were many others, like Dimitris Petropoulos in *Star-light*, whose expressions of impatience and

19. Panayotopoulos, *Astrofengia*, p. 162.
20. Dafnis, *I Ellas Metaxy Dyo Polemon (Greece Between Two Wars)* (Athens, 1955), p. 16.

contempt toward the refugees were bound to have repercussions in the social and intellectual life of Greece.

Another negative view of the refugee (more important than that in *Star-light* since it seems to reflect directly the author's view and not that of a fictional character) is to be found in Andonis Travlandonis's *Plunder of a Life,* published in *Nea Estia* in 1935.[21] The date is significant, for that was the year of the reinstitution of the monarchy in Greece and the end of the Venizelist-Liberal influence.

Using the identical metaphor that attracted Henry Morgenthau,[22] Travlandonis urges whoever did not see "the cataclysm of 1922" to imagine a large ship, heavily laden with passengers of all social classes, sinking into the sea.

> They all want to cling as tightly as possible [to a plank] that represents their last hope for life, and everyone struggles with his hands, feet, teeth, and head to push the other away, to sacrifice him, the servant his master, the friend his friend, the brother his brother, the lover his beloved, the child his father, the mother her child, in order to save his own life. Because all the human instincts, all the teachings of civilization, of religion, of virtue, all have been extinguished at once

21. *Leyilasia mias Zoïs* (Athens, 1966).

22. Morgenthau, *I Was Sent to Athens* (New York, 1929), pp. 101-102. Morgenthau was United States Ambassador to the Sublime Porte in Constantinople during World War I and, after the Disaster, Chairman of the Greek Refugee Settlement Commission. He describes his first view of the arrival of a ship bringing refugees from Asia Minor to Thessaloniki: "I saw seven thousand people crowded in a ship that would have been taxed to normal capacity with two thousand.... They had been at sea for four days. There had not been space to permit them to lie down to sleep; there had been no food to eat; there was no access to any toilet facilities.... They came ashore in rags, hungry, sick, covered with vermin, hollow-eyed, exhaling the horrible odor of human filth – bowed with despair.... And yet I knew that a fleet of nearly two hundred more such ship-loads would need to land before my eyes if I were to see all the human beings who were in exactly their same plight." Morgenthau wrote using the estimated number of refugees available to him at the time. It was, in fact, higher.

with an omnipotent blast from the indomitable, the wild, the hard and merciless instinct for self-preservation.

Let them imagine again . . . dogs, masses of dogs thrown together in a dry well. Raging, moaning, using teeth and claws, each one trying to tear the other to pieces, to live itself, to lengthen for a few hours its own miserable life with the flesh of its companion, its brother.

It was virtually this image that presented itself to the traveler from the port [of Piraeus] to Omonia Square, and in all the squares, sidewalks, streets, alleyways, and beyond, out of the city, from the foot of Hymettus to the foot of Aigaleo.[23]

One need not analyze too carefully a passage of this sort in order to emphasize the connotative words Travlandonis uses to describe the refugees. But *Plunder of a Life* is a novel, not a journal entry or a personal letter to a friend. Travlandonis is writing to communicate to others who, it seems by his manner, would not be prepared to disagree with him. It does not appear as though he needs to defend or justify himself for referring to unfortunate people in this way. Certainly, one cannot doubt that there were isolated examples of members of one family struggling with each other to save their own lives, but these have not been recorded, nor must we ever consider them as characteristic or as representative. On the contrary, the migration of a million and a half people in so short a time and under such frightful conditions was effected without the "dog-like" behavior Travlandonis attributes to the refugees. One can only conclude that the novelist did not actually *mean* for his words to be taken at face value. Instead, writing more than a decade later, he probably meant them to be taken as general comments on a substantial group of people already fully absorbed into Greek life, a

23. *Leyilasia mias Zoïs*, pp. 143-144.

group perhaps even more powerful, proportionally, than it should have been, and not as the immediate assessments of a man strolling through Athens of an evening, or at the port of Piraeus, watching a refugee ship disembark its passengers.

Travlandonis, quick to notice the impact of the refugees on the city of Athens, makes a valuable sociological observation. The refugees are not only the poor, the homeless, and the helpless, for among the Anatolians are the aggressive and commercially minded who will tend to compete with the native Greek for the limited market. Angelis, the narrator of *Plunder of a Life* – who, along with the author, nourishes a deep contempt for the "Leader", Plastiras – tries to find an old friend and benefactor in the Neapolis neighborhood of Athens. But Mr. Tlemonidis's name is not on the mansion's brass plate: the house is now owned by "someone with a name unknown to me . . . something *oglou*." The entire neighborhood, in fact, is populated by refugees, among whom one could hear "all the languages in the world except Greek".[24] Angelis's limit of tolerance is reached when he discovers that a millinery shop, owned by an acquaintance – a Venizelist, for whom he did not feel any particular love – was now owned by a "Zacharias . . . *oglou*: "This *oglokratia* – (you'll forgive my coldness) which in a little while would have dominated our Athens, had begun even then, it seems. The banknotes had done their miracle even in Kyr Alekos's shop."[25]

In truth, ignoring the animus Travlandonis expresses toward the refugees, an emotion uncharacteristic of this otherwise gentle, cultured, and compassionate man, the fact is unmistakable that the uprooted Anatolian totally transformed Greece, and in particular, the capital city. It was "our" Athens, he says, admitting his reader into a cozy familiarity that would doubtlessly have for-

24. *Ibid.*, p. 161.
25. *Ibid.*, p. 196.

given him the "coldness" he made no effort to disguise, but now it is "theirs" as well.[26]

Both Panayotopoulos and Travlandonis hail from Old Greece — the former from Aitoliko and the latter from Missolongi, both in the same province in western continental Greece — and thus provide us with the views of native Greeks toward the refugees. Pandelis Prevelakis in *The Chronicle of a City*[27] does much the same thing for New Greece by describing the influx of Anatolian refugees into Rethymno and the uprooting and "repatriation" of the Moslems of Crete to Turkey, in fulfillment of the Lausanne Treaty. In all three of these works, the interest in the refugee is peripheral, subordinate to the major concerns of the author. Yet each writer senses the unmistakable change Greece had undergone with the events of 1922 and the arrival of the Anatolians. In Crete, where the influx was not as great, proportionally, as in some provinces of the mainland, the events of 1922 were perhaps even more decisive because of the

26. But Athens changed irrevocably as a result of the Disaster, and every work of fiction written after 1922 and set in a contemporaneous Athens must reflect this radical transformation. The population of Athens in the period 1920-1928 went from 292,991 to 459,211 because of the settlement of 129,380 refugees. Piraeus went from 133,482 to 259,659, an increase of 101,185, while Thessaloniki went from 170,321 to 244,680, an increase of 117,041, a figure that does not take into consideration the departure of the large Moslem population between 1920 and 1928. Two other facts must also be borne in mind: first, the figures for Athens and Piraeus do not include the closely connected "suburbs" of Old and New Phaleron and Kallithea, the last having a population of over 25,000 in 1928, of whom 15,516 were refugees; and second, the population figures for 1920 by no means reflect a stable situation, since the capital and its port city were increasing at a phenomenal but unrecorded rate, beginning with the First Balkan War in 1912. For descriptions of the village-like atmosphere of Athens in 1912 see *The Wax Doll (I Kerenia Koukla)* by Constantine Christomanos (*Athens, 1911*). For statistics of the population of Athens, see Charles B. Eddy, *Greece and the Greek Refugees* (London, 1931), p. 116.

27. *To Chroniko mias Politeias,* first published in 1938. I have used the Galaxias, Athens, 1965 edition.

"exchange" of the Moslem minority. A new, unitary Crete emerged after 1922, without racial or religious minorities, joined in a firm union with the Greek motherland, a union that so much blood had been shed to effect. It was, as Prevelakis's "chronicle" documents (and which is treated exhaustively in his major trilogy, *The Cretan,* 1948-1950), the culmination of a historical process that had begun centuries before.

Aside from the narratives of captivity and several other examples, there are no fictional works by Asia Minor writers on the subject matter of the Disaster until the late 1920s. The pain at the death of loved ones had been overwhelmed by other, more immediate concerns; those who had survived imprisonment had returned; the great problem of adjustment to a much less wealthy society, with fewer possibilities, was absorbing most of the refugees' attention.[28]

The first fictional work to confront the problem of the uprooted from the Anatolians' point of view, *Refugees,* by the Constantinopolitan Petros Afthoniatis (pseudonym of Heracles Ioannidis, 1897-1950),[29] does so while deliberately avoiding the details inherent to refugee fiction that were to characterize all later works. Afthoniatis's characters in the three short stories that

28. *Niobe* by Kostas Zoumboulidis and *Like Lies and Like the Truth* by Socrates Prokopiou, though written in the 1920s, will be discussed in Chapter Five. The only other fictional work about the last days of Smyrna, "Chroniko tou '22" ("Chronicle of 1922") a short story by George Theotokas, was published in *Evripidis Pentozalis ki' alles Istories* in 1937, though its date of composition is 1936. For some, the problems of adjustment were too great. Quite a few emigrated, though it is impossible to determine their number since the Statistical Service of the Greek state documents the emigration of its citizens only, and the Anatolians, as Ottoman subjects, would not have been included. One novel, Laura Melamed's *J'ai Cherche un homme* (Paris, 1936), published in Greece in a number of installments in *Athinaika Nea* of June 1936 as *Gyrevontas enan Andra,* tells the story of a Franco-Greek family from Smyrna that goes to France after the Disaster.

29. *Prosfyges* (Paris, 1929).

make up the collection are drawn from a variety of social backgrounds: Yiakoumis is from a relatively affluent Anatolian family; Manolis is a proletarian from Athens; and Captain Mitsos is from one of the islands in the Sea of Marmara. The Disaster, so central to the lives of the three, is peripheral in all, a future event in the first story, and merely mentioned in the two narratives that follow.

Yiakoumis, in the first tale, leaves his Anatolian home in 1915 to escape to Greece, witnesses the British and French repression during the Blockade, gets involved with the Venizelist movement and, finally, heeds the call of the Megale Idea and joins the colors to help "Greece . . . recapture her old Byzantine glory."[30]

In the second story, Manolis, a baker active in his guild's union, is a veteran of the Asia Minor campaign. In the fictional present, two years after the Disaster, despite his lack of education and confidence, he becomes a spokesman for his union on the issue of whether the workers' movement should take an active part in politics. Before Manolis dies of tuberculosis, the reader has thoroughly understood that a new Greece is being described, one where the issues of Venizelist liberalism and Constantinist monarchy are neither interesting nor important. Both men and their parties have erred, harming Greece by their animosities; disputes about the correctness of one or the other are irrelevant.

What is clear and important is the growing power of the labor movement, a theme that emerges again in the third story when Captain Mitsos, a once-poor boy whose education was paid for by a wealthy Rumanian-Greek, finds himself checkmated on the ship *Samos* when his crew, almost totally composed of communists, refuses to break the union rules against moving cargo in the hold before docking. To do so would only save the shipowners money that would ordinarily go to other working men, the local

30. *Ibid.*, p. 64.

stevadores. Captain Mitsos, whose entire family was lost in the Disaster, is on his way up the ladder of success — perhaps he will soon be a shipowner himself — but he has little margin for action when confronted by such a class-conscious crew. The sailors eventually break their rule, but it is clear that authority after the Disaster has been undermined and that the captain is viewed by the workers and sailors as inimical to their interests and as a representative, imbued with the desire to become a capitalist himself, of their natural enemy.

The remarkable aspect of Afthoniatis's collection is the detailed interest in trade unionism, a subject almost totally avoided in Greek literature. The last two sketches, in particular, reveal a knowledgability rare in Greek fiction about the day-to-day functioning — the deliberations and industrial action — of workers' councils, all presented with an objectivity so total that the reader is left ignorant of the writer's political orientation. In these stories, Afthoniatis seeks to avoid being classified himself and is satisfied to present his reader with a character who emerges briefly from his social background, acts out his role, then steps back into the shadows of history. The vignettes are chosen by the writer to illustrate a decade in Greek life that began in hope for the realization of the Megale Idea by the exponents of Venizelist liberalism and ended in the bleak post-Disaster years where Greeks disagreed, not about ideals, but about their inherent economic interests. Tangible, *class* conflicts in Afthoniatis's *Refugees* had taken the place of the reconquest of Constantinople, the New Jerusalem. The gold of Byzantium had tarnished in the gray of the interwar period.

This interest in careful documentation of the economic tensions of Greek society was clearly one direction the Disaster theme could have taken, but the exclusive socio-political interest of *Refugees* seems to be ignored in later books that attempt to describe the refugee experience. Instead, the socio-political theme is either totally bypassed in fiction, being reserved for the ideological disputes that raged in Greece after 1922, or it is absorbed as a subordinate element in the social novel that emerges in Greek fiction in the 1930s. Refugees populate the landscape of a number of fictional works not directly preoccupied by politics, but their presence as focal points of ideology and specific historical events is ignored, at least at this point.

Grigoris Xenopoulos, in a novel also called *Refugees*,[31] would certainly not be the writer to grapple at this time in his career with the more significant and profound issues the title implies. This serial novel is a craftsmanlike treatment in journalistic terms of the arrival in Piraeus of Smaragda Zannoglou, a physically maltreated and emotionally defeated girl who survived the massacre of Smyrna; her rescue from certain suffering, and perhaps even death, by Manos Kyriakidis, a middle-aged businessman; and her gradual recovery. *Refugees* never goes beyond the formula of its author's journalistic fiction, however, and it resembles in more than one respect *The Smyrna Woman,* a novel Xenopoulos wrote under the same pressures of time and with roughly the same content, about Altana, another refugee girl from Smyrna, this one fleeing the persecutions of 1914.[32]

Like much fiction of this sort, *Refugees* begins with a strong sense of the Anatolians' sufferings, reflecting the interest of the Venizelist newspaper in the plight of the refugees who made up a large part of its readership. The writing is interesting but shallow, particularly suited to the reader who needed to spend no more than ten minutes each day keeping up with the remarkably slow pace of the story. The convincing description of the Smyrna Terror and the Fire may be either the result of careful research on

31. *Prosfyges,* published in the Athenian newspaper, *Neos Kosmos,* in 96 installments, beginning Sunday, June 3, 1934, and ending Sunday, September 16, 1934. It was subtitled "An Athenian Novel."
32. *I Smyrnia*, published in installments in *Ethnos*, 1920.

Xenopoulos's part or, more probably, a reflection of the wealth of detailed knowledge current at the time. He seems to be strongly interested at first in the social and ethical issues of the refugees' presence, their poverty and thus their vulnerability, but he skillfully extricates himself from all of these issues and turns the novel into a typical "sentimental romance" full of concern about how the characters will pair off.

There is no depth to the characterization. Kyriakidis, who admittedly never thought about his duty to his fellow man and had, at best, a superficial interest in the events of the Disaster and the plight of the refugees, changes abruptly when he sees this nineteen-year-old girl all alone on the quay at Piraeus, her clothes in disarray, her eye swollen, her leg badly hurt. Though the novel is sentimental and, because of its appearance in a newspaper, morally correct, there is a wealth of sexual innuendo, all of it carefully controlled so that it entices but does not excite. Kyriakidis takes Smaragda to a clinic run by a friend of his – where her astonishingly beautiful leg is seen to be only slightly injured – as a preliminary, the reader is led to believe, to a liaison he hopes to establish with her. But nothing of the sort occurs, because he dutifully tells his silent, strong-willed wife and his family about the girl. Lily, his fifteen-year-old daughter, quickly becomes Smaragda's friend and the story settles down to the slow unraveling of Smaragda's experiences during the holocaust, the discovery of the whereabouts of her family – all of whom are alive, well, and still rich – and the long process which ends with her acceptance of the proposal of marriage made by Andreas, Kyriakidis's twenty-two-year-old son.

It is remarkable that although girls were being raped and killed all around her, Smaragda (who looks as though she has been raped but has not been) suffered no more than a few minor bruises. The only member of her family to perish in the flames was her grandfather, who was already dead and in his coffin when the Smyrna fire broke out. Her brother Michalakis and fiancé Marios are prisoners of the Turks, but Michalakis comes back in fine shape, though a bit weary, while Marios, the betrothed whose existence provided the only obstacle to her marriage with Andreas (and to the story's happy ending), is proved to have been unfaithful, not only to Smaragda but to Greece as well. An electrical engineer, he has been convinced by his Turkish captors during the imprisonment to stay and help them create a new Turkey, which he does, settling down with a Moslem mistress.

The novel hidden deep within *Refugees* and not written by Xenopoulos, either because of the society to which he addressed himself (represented in the taste of the people who read his works and the prescribed form of the newspaper serial) or because of more personal inadequacies, was about a beautiful and helpless girl without relatives or money who could survive only by being supported and befriended by a man in fairly comfortable circumstances whose mistress she becomes. But it was not only Xenopoulos who avoided this theme. It was avoided in all of the literature, though there are allusions to liaisons of this sort in a number of fictional works. It would be unjust to blame only the novelists for this, however, since part of the blame should go to Greek society in general, whose many taboos made it virtually impossible to deal at the time with themes that writers of other cultures have treated with few repercussions.

Xenopoulos, certainly, had none of the ideological interests evident in Afthoniatis's collection, at least not during this period of his life. The Disaster of 1922 occurred when he was 55, when he had already crystallized his fictional interests and established his reputation. Being the kind of writer he was, he was unable to see what the Disaster meant to Greece and was limited, consequently, to surface reactions. There is no sense of personal disorientation in *Refugees,* no trace of the collapse of ideals or illusions that occurred to men like Kostas Varnalis and Nikos

Kazantzakis, who were mid-way in their careers. Xenopoulos and most of his contemporaries who survived 1922 were unmarked by the events of Asia Minor, unable to see the great change the Disaster had wrought on Greece. Afthoniatis, unmentioned in Greek literary histories and no more than a minor writer in anyone's estimation, comes closer to providing a valid and convincing picture of the Greece of his time than the Academician Xenopoulos (he had been elected in 1932), who had been considered by many the social novelist par excellence of Greek fiction before the Generation of the 1930's began to publish.

The Smyrniot Pavlos Floros wrote a number of fictional works about the uprooted Anatolians. His novels, perhaps because their length and comprehensiveness demanded from him a commitment to ideas upon which his fiction could be based, differ markedly from his short stories, which present characters forever marked by the experiences of 1922 and unable to adjust to life in Greece. The events and experiences described in *Colonists* and *A Man of the Times* are about men and women of a higher social class confronting the problems, not of how to survive – since their economic condition spares them the conflicts of the short story characters[33] – but of how to give meaning to their existence.

The sensitive characters in Floros's novels require an ideological support that was hard to come by in post-Disaster Greece. The others are the exploiters and plunderers, men whose only principle is self-aggrandizement. They do not need "meaning"; for them, power is enough, and power is money. These "colonists" are not new characters, for their acquisitive instincts assure

33. Notably Bethlehem, the protagonist of "To Englima tis Vithleem" and Bembo of "To Telos tou Theiou Bembou." The first was published in *I Amaranta ki' alla Diigimata* (Athens, 1938) and the second in *Nea Estia*, 27, No. 321, May 1, 1940, and collected in *Nostalgoi* (Athens, 1943).

the reader that they have been around for a long time. The others, however, the wounded and the troubled, are different, Floros seems to say. Before 1922 and the collapse of Greek values, these characters would probably not have experienced the personal anguish that drives them to seek a satisfactory way to live.

The character Dimitris Valeris, who gets his Anatolian ancestry from his Smyrniot mother, is genuinely preoccupied in *Colonists*[34] with ideological concerns, nourished probably by a German education, and he endows a Foundation for Aristocracy by which, with the aid of a German, Dr. Peters, he hopes to improve the genetic and spiritual stock of the modern Greek. Vulnerable to ideological issues, Dimitris feels, because of the Asia Minor Disaster,

> something like an open wound within him. While this must have been more generally felt, Valeris saw, nevertheless, that most people preferred to ignore its existence, denying it and finally trying to dull it with beautiful narcotic words. Some referring to Darwin's Law, others to social justice and the new cosmogony, others to the right to life, others to the nostalgia for the good old days, when the girls were virgins and the politicians morally pure orators.[35]

Dimos Chlomocheilis, his arch-enemy, who uses ideology only as a means to personal power and wealth, does everything he can to destroy Valeris; by the end of this sometimes lurid novel, he has sold out the welfare of the refugee poor, whom he had manipulated as the owner of a yellow newspaper called "The Rights of Man," for a life of affluence on the Cote d'Azur. He is one of the "colonists," as Valeris calls them, "on this land, who come, who leave, who come again, and are finally compelled to

34. *Apoikoi* (Athens, 1934).
35. *Ibid.,* pp. 161-162.

scatter."[36] Without Valeris's love for Greece, men like Chlomocheilis merely use their homeland, abandoning Greece "after they
have milked her like a cow. She was their colony." Valeris, the
aristocrat, leaves Greece "because of pain, out of the feeling that
my dream would never be satisfied," a poor and broken man,
"out of the great love I had for her."[37]

It is difficult to know precisely how to place the fictional
characters of Pavlos Floros, primarily because the novelist as-
sumes that his political and philosophical attitudes, which are not
clearly defined, are shared by his readers. Certainly, the racial
ideology Floros has picked up in Germany is suspect in our time,
but there is more in this novel to alienate the reader than Aryan
eugenics. There is, for example, the identification of "natural"
aristocracy with money and of opportunism and vindictiveness
with low birth and poverty. Chlomocheilis, a villain in melodramatic terms, personifies a social evil, which he compounds by
manipulating the gullible lower-class and refugee masses for his
own benefit. Without Chlomocheilis, though, the masses would
not exist in *Colonists,* except perhaps as the raw material that will
in several generations be improved by the principles of selective
reproduction as expounded by Dr. Peters.

"Improvement" seems to be the watchword in this novel, for
Valeris wants not only to better the racial stock of the Greek but
to reforest the bare, tawny terrain of Attica as well. He does not
like things as they are; the only way to improve them, however, is
not by political action, but by creating a better man through
eugenics and a better environment through reforestation. In both
cases, progress will be made only because "nature's nobleman"
wants it and only if the masses do not interfere. The great plan
for betterment is destroyed by men like Dimos Chlomocheilis.

36. *Ibid.,* p. 364.
37. *Ibid.,* p. 410.

In the novel's terms, the reader is to accept Valeris as "nature's nobleman." Married and the father of three children, Valeris appears to be plagued by sexually demanding young women, who seem to want him to improve the genetic and spiritual stock of the modern Greeks in more tangible ways than merely by endowing his Foundation for Aristocracy. Ideology is a crucial factor in *Colonists,* obviously, but Floros seems to be as confused about what to believe as any of his characters. This confusion is compounded because he chooses as his central character a man whose obsession with an idea makes him unable to convince the reader of its validity.

This was an error he did not make in *A Man of the Times,* a rich and complex novel that creates a fine, multi-faceted character, Hippocrates Asimakis, a Smyrniot who managed to bring much of his great fortune to Greece after the Disaster.[38] Having tried to fulfill all the heavy responsibilities the Greek family tradition lays upon brothers, Hippocrates is still a bachelor, since he failed to marry off Erato and Xanthippe, now in their sixties. He needs someone to whom he can leave his fortune, but the only male relative, a nephew — Christos Kastoridis — "the man of the times," does not seem particularly interested in continuing the family line. Too preoccupied with his career as an important health official in Switzerland, Kastoridis leaves the decision of whether or not to have a child up to Martha, his Swiss wife, who would rather not be bothered with the cares of motherhood.

Had it not been for Hippocrates, who sensed the threat and sent his sister's son off in time to a European education, Christos Kastoridis would have been lost in the forced labor battalions of Asia Minor. If he feels grateful to his uncle for this and for the comfortable life he has led, the young man does not reveal it. Cold and ambitious, Christos has his own duty, one totally

38. *O Anthropos tis Epochis* (Athens, 1939).

different from that which dominated his uncle's life. He owes nothing to anyone. Unlike the other young people in the novel, however, Kastoridis has a plan for his life, a program coldly subscribed to that saves him from the disorientation they feel. Without ideological beliefs, they fall victims to the romantic love that sweeps them up and destroys them.

Christos Kastoridis is a European viewing Greece only as a place he must visit occasionally out of a family responsibility demanded of him by his mother, who is concerned that Hippocrates, her brother, in a fit of pique at being ignored, will not leave his fortune to his nephew but endow an Asia Minor foundation instead. Greece and Hellenism are not enough for Kastoridis: the national horizons are too limited now that the Megale Idea is dead. He returns to Greece only after his uncle is buried because he has been given what he wanted: appointment as full professor at the University. Kastoridis is the product of great national ambitions gone sour. Hiding behind the mask of scientific objectivity, he never considers that the motivation that drives him to rid Europe of alcoholism – the crusade on which he has built his career – may stem from the humiliation he felt as the son of an alcoholic to whom no one ever refers. Christos Kastoridis gets his power and his momentum from ignoring the wellsprings of his own behavior.

Another character in the novel, however, more reflective than Kastoridis, provides the reader with an opposing view of men's attitudes at a time of rapid national decline. General Liakouras expresses most clearly the destructive lack of confidence he felt when unable to refuse the hand of his daughter to a man he knew was totally unsuitable for her, a man ultimately responsible for infecting her with syphillis and driving her to suicide. "Confronting that man with a demanding smile," General Liakouras says,

I weakened and felt something like inferiority. It may have been the result of that terrible moral crisis that the Disaster of 1922 brought us. Do you remember? The same people who in the name of sacred responsibilities sent us to Russia, proclaimed that Hellenism no longer required love of country but that its destiny was to carry the torch of civilization in the East! You can imagine what that means to a soldier. After the nation, they weakened the family — paternal authority. We fathers felt that we were tyrants, that our values were old, worthless. The slogan was: give way to youth.[39]

The traditional values of Hippocrates are clearly sturdy enough to bear the moral weight of the novel, and these are compared with the lack of values that characterize all of the young men and women of the Athenian-Smyrniot society except the old man's nephew, Christos Kastoridis. The young do not know what they want — a sign of the interwar period — and seem to choose the wrong people to fall in love with. The scion of another wealthy Smyrniot family, Petros Lygeros, a contemporary of Christos's, is totally without the scientist's sense of purpose; he hesitates before Ero Liakouras, the proud and sensitive woman who would have made him happy, and flings himself away on Lillian, a desperately confused girl who gives him only unhappiness. Pipitsa Klismanis, the girl Christos's mother had hoped he would marry, grows tired of waiting and runs off to Thessaloniki with a small-time criminal, is arrested with him for fraud, and spends some time in jail. Instead of confusing the novel's meaning and cluttering it up with unnecessary subplots, however, these characters buttress the philosophy Floros has evolved in *A Man of the Times.*

Even Achilles Zervoyiannis, another "colonist," and his son

39. *Ibid.,* p. 231.

Hermes, are unable to harm the novel by their melodramatic villainy, for their presence is less insistent and thus less offensive than that of Dimos Chlomocheilis in Floros's first novel. Achilles Zervoyiannis is a petty crook who, like a jackal, follows Hippocrates, doing odd jobs for him, stealing as much as is safe "to support his family." He has the morality of a scavenger, while his knowledge of the strengths and weaknesses of others enables him to use them for his own benefit. But unlike Chlomocheilis, he consistently fails. When Pipitsa gets back from Thessaloniki after her disastrous romance, Achilles gets Hermes to propose to her, thus offering her a way back to respectability, because he knows that her mother has a fortune in jewelry. Pipitsa refuses his suit, preferring an honorable job to marriage on his terms. Achilles, not one to be denied, makes other attempts to succeed, writing vicious letters to people and signing himself "an honorable refugee," but nothing seems to work for him. Finally, he gets mixed up in an attempted coup in 1935 and is arrested on the day of Hippocrates's burial.

Hippocrates Asimakis sums up the values of another more gracious, more confident era. Not even the Disaster of 1922 could disorient him from the traditional values of Greek life. The young are either confused and lost, or purposeful and bigoted. When Hippocrates dies, the old world goes with him. He is buried, appropriately, while the noises of a coup-d'état are roaring in the streets of Athens. His death marks the end of the republican experiment in Greece. Behind him, he leaves the broken, like Petros Lygeros; the troubled, like General Liakouras; the cunning, like Achilles Zervoyiannis; and the selfish, like Christos Kastoridis – the man of the times.

The ideological issues current in Greece between the wars are given an important role in *The School-Mistress with the Golden Eyes*, the second novel of Stratis Myrivilis's "trilogy of the war," in which he tells the story of a soldier's return from the horrors of the Asia Minor campaign.[40] The first work in this sequence, *Life in the Tomb*, a classic of modern Greek prose, described trench warfare along the Macedonian Front and sounded a note of bitterness and rage not often heard in Greek letters. Before his horrible death, Sergeant Kostoulas, the central figure of *Life in the Tomb,* had lost the ideals that made him volunteer for battle, and he shared neither the certitude of the older Greeks in the Byzantine tradition nor the faith of the young in rationality and Greek national values.

Leonis Drivas, the protagonist of *The School-Mistress with the Golden Eyes,* is very much like Kostoulas, except that he seems to have lost his firm belief in ideals sometime before the novel begins. Kostoulas speaks to the reader of his doubts through his journal entries, but he is silent about his loss of faith in whatever his comrades still believe in. Drivas, on the other hand, is a survivor of the war, living among people whose smug certitudes are abrasive to his spirit and to the sense of truth he has gained through suffering.

Recalling the military defeat and his convalescence, Leonis Drivas struggles throughout the novel to adjust to the realities of peace, love, and creativity in a postwar world among people who seem to have been taught nothing by the aimless savagery of war. His eventual recovery from the horrible experiences of war, which lasted five years for him (1917-1922) is problematic, and the woman who will ultimately help him triumph over his bitterness and rage, the beautiful Sappho of "the golden eyes," is forbidden to him by his conscious mind because she is the widow of a friend, Stratis Vranas, "a fanatic supporter of the Megale Idea," who stayed in a military hospital with Drivas before dying of gangrene.

40. *I Daskala me ta Chrysa Matia,* first published in 1933. I am using the tenth edition, that of 1956.

Whereas war memories make up the first movement of this tripartite novel, and the love-idyll with Sappho comprises the third, it is in the second — where Myrivilis tries to express the conflicts that Drivas has with the provincial society of Lesbos, — that *The School-Mistress with the Golden Eyes* runs into difficulty. Perhaps this is because Myrivilis does not have political ideas; he has, instead, antipathies toward people who do. His central character and the spokesman for his thought, Leonis Drivas, lives in a state of aggravation within his social environment because he is forced to deal with men and women whose value systems seem to have been left intact by a sequence of historical events that should have either destroyed them utterly or called them into serious question. It is obvious that the people who exasperate Drivas are those who have learned nothing from the Great War and the Asia Minor Disaster, who still cling to the shallow patriotism that should have been exploded with the death of their loved ones and the destruction of their national ideals. The refugees in their midst, who have neither food to eat nor land to farm, seem to have no effect on them.

Dining out with a group of acquaintances one evening, Leonis sees two refugee girls approach their table and beg for scraps, which they receive along with a few drachmas and the advice to return home "because good children do not run about at this time of night." When they leave, however, Mr. Phillipas, the customs inspector, observes that the two will be very attractive when they grow up, particularly the older one. In ignoring the genuine plight of human beings too young to realize their predicament fully and too shy to be more intrusive, Phillipas reveals an insensitivity that virtually sickens Leonis Drivas.[41]

This "moral pachydermy," as Myrivilis calls it, manifests itself in those people who are not open to experiences, who go on as

41. *Ibid.,* pp. 141-142.

though Europe and Greece had not been torn asunder by war, who do not "connect," to use E. M. Forster's word, by learning from what they have undergone. It characterizes the anonymous "retired artillery officer" who is offered as inspiration for Leonis by the local doctor, an officer "who left neither his patriotism nor his manhood in Anatolia" and whose newspaper, *Hellenism*, is a "fount of [national] rebirth in a time of defeatism." Drivas agrees with an irony so sour that it calls into question the realism of the scene:

> He seems to be a hero from what he writes. He was present at all the battles and fought like a titan. So did all the soldiers. When a shell landed in his gun emplacement, he stood at attention and saluted smartly. Afterward . . . we were beaten. He was taken prisoner and underwent all the humiliations by the Turks. But he sacrificed his self-respect and did not commit suicide. For the sake of history. So that he could write his sheet. Otherwise, we would not have had our fount of rebirth.[42]

Drivas lashes out at the mindless chauvinism that ruins for him the memorial for the war dead of Megalochoro and is furious with Sappho for decorating her husband's *kolyva* (the small cakes traditionally given out after a memorial service) in the national colors. "Was it a moral pachydermy," he wonders, "or a school-marmish Spartanism of the worst sort?"[43] He identifies the "cheap patriotism" she exhibits at the memorial service with the instinct that tolerates war and the crimes inherent in it.

> I stood up and volunteered for war myself. I believed in war and its values. Since I believed in its values, I believed in its "justice" as well. [In the] executions of soldiers who deserted . . . in the burning of villages. . . . I justified everything.

42. *Ibid.,* pp. 140-141.
43. *Ibid.,* p. 134.

Because I lacked love. . . . Love . . . for one person, or humanity in general. That which leaves our heart as soon as we
enslave ourselves to any particular system. That which, for
example, the Spartan mother did not have who told her son,
"Come back with your shield or on it."[44]

What saves Leonis Drivas from becoming pompous is his out-
rage at the hypocrisy, the affectation, and the unawareness of the
provincial society of Lesbos. Despite his victories in most arguments or his always triumphant irony, however, he is a confused
young man, and Myrivilis himself cannot be completely exoner-
ated of the same confusion. Evidence of this is Leonis's inability
to see the contradiction he falls into when he argues with a group
of university students, home for the holidays, who consider
themselves Marxists. Drivas seems to have given the Russian form
of Communism some thought, "but every type of dictatorship
was unacceptable for him."[45] He is against systems of thought
taken wholesale by someone who has not himself lived the truths
the founder of that system has articulated. But Communists
"employ the slogan 'war against war' " while declaring "the most
repellant, the most harsh and the most ungodly of wars. The war
of brother against brother."[46]

The contradiction manifests itself when a group of war veter-
ans and refugees squat on an estate once belonging to a repatri-

44. *Ibid.*, p. 167
45. *Ibid.*, p. 191. According to Yiànis Kordatos's *Istoria tis Neoellinikis Logotechnias, apo to 1453 os to 1961,* Vol. II (Athens, 1962), pp. 601-602, Myrivilis was a firm social democrat and a follower of Alexandros Papanastasiou.
46. *Ibid.*, pp. 192-193. In the second edition, 1934, pp. 177-178, Myrivilis concludes this thought with the much more coherent: "But instead of [this war] being between nations it is between economic classes. . . ." This seems to be a much more logical continuation of Drivas's thought than the later emendation of 1956. Except for this brief compari-
son, cited to establish a suspicion on my part, I use the 1956 edition exclusively.

ated Turk, an estate now coveted by a "refugee boss" who wants to acquire it fraudulently from the government for his own exploitation. Starting legal proceedings against the squatters, the "refugee boss" gets the Ministry of Agriculture to send five policemen to evict them. In the heat of the argument, there is some violence and the leader of the squatters is shot. This background information is provided for the reader by Myrivilis without the agency of Leonis, who either does not learn what the reader knows about the "class conflict" he temperamentally rejects or does not care to uncover the causes for the death he finds "here, in his idyllic village. Without war, without a battle. Still, it was obviously the same. Man raised his hand and killed another man. The red disease of Cain, inherited by ancestral means in the skull of the human race like incurable epilepsy." [47] This contradiction is left unresolved and unexplained by Myrivilis, but it is clear that by the middle of the 1930s the serious novelists, whether equipped or not, were ready to grapple with the important ideological issues facing Greece in their time.

Excluding purely literary considerations, Myrivilis's fiction has the advantage over much of the previous fiction (that of Pavlos Floros, for example) in that Sergeant Kostoulas and Leonis Drivas are men with whom most readers could identify quite strongly. They represent consciously and fully the sense of violation and disgust that men felt during the interwar period at the collapse of ideas that proved to be illusions. Floros attempted to replace these shattered ideals with others, but this is more properly the role of philosophy, and *Colonists* fails as fiction because of this. Myrivilis is on surer ground when, attempting to clear the rubble of his previous ideas, he arrives at a belief in nature and in man. That even his belief in a "world soul" and his pagan pantheism do not succeed in convincing the reader loses its importance before

47. *Ibid.*, p. 259.

the power of his graphic description and his insistence on humane values. Myrivilis's works – his novels, particularly – gained the popularity they did, not merely because of his considerable talents, but also because his eloquent rejection of excessive patriotism and nationalism was responded to by many Greek readers. His satire of General Balafaras in *Life in the Tomb,* his anticlericalism, his contempt for the various jingoists in *The School-Mistress with the Golden Eyes,* all of these indicated that criticism of certain established forces in Greek life was beginning to emerge. In Myrivilis it is checked somewhat by his political philosophy, which became more conservative and nationalistic in the 1940s. For other writers, such as Kostas Varnalis, as we shall see later, social criticism, allied to a political orientation that sought to overturn established values, became the instrument for brilliant intellectual satire.

Ideology became an important part of fiction in the 1930s. It had appeared earlier in scattered works like those of Theotokis and Hadzopoulos, but by the decade of the 1930s the novel began to act as a forum for the ideological issues facing the Greek people. We see this most clearly, perhaps, in *Argo* by George Theotokas, a large-scale work that can be considered the political novel par excellence of Greece after the Asia Minor Disaster. [48] How conscious Theotokas was of the plot structure and the effects he wanted to have on the reader is made abundantly clear in *The Notebooks of Argo and The Daemon,* in which he provides a fairly careful analysis of the novel from its germination in London in 1928 to its fruition in Athens in 1936, and even beyond, to the opinions of critics about it in 1938. [49] At first

48. *Argo,* 3rd ed. (Athens, n.d.). For this study I have used the 3rd edition, which is based on that of 1936 but was printed after World War II. The first part of *Argo,* as Theotokas mentions in a note, was published in 1933, while the first complete edition was circulated again in 1939 "with the date of 1936 . . . on account of the censorship of the time."

49. *Imerologio tis Argos kai tou Daimoniou* (Athens, 1939).

Argo was to document the sense of ambition and duty in men that leads them to sacrifice women for a higher idea. Later, however, Theotokas understood that *Argo* had other aims, more specific and "political." It was to describe "the drama of contemporary Greece: the weight of the great name, the shame of present smallness, the urge for a Renaissance." In *Argo* he would describe the crisis of the postwar generation, which he considered "a cosmopolitan theme" since Greek youth was similar to that of the rest of Europe, "needing ideals in the wreckage of war."[50]

There was little in the Greek fictional tradition that would have helped him realize his complex ambitions. Theotokas drew great support, however, from his knowledge of British and French novels; the conscious infusion of ideas into his fiction is what makes *Argo* such a unique work for its time. Despite its uneven quality and its weak and wordy conclusion, *Argo* generates an excitement not usual in Greek fiction. Theotokas's university students, in particular, are convincing portraits of youth in a time when the ideals of their fathers have been shattered and the great task of discovering others has fallen on their young shoulders. There are, moreover, a number of interesting and believable characters in the novel whose brief appearances convince the reader that *Argo* is a realistic view of the Greek society of its time.

A central figure — and possibly the most vivid one — is a refugee from Constantinople, Damianos Frantzis, a member of "The Argo," a discussion group composed of "dissatisfied and unhappy [university] students . . . who wanted linguistic, educational, political, and even social reforms." A microcosm of Greece after the Disaster, "The Argo" was modeled on the Students' Company (*Foititiki Syntrofia*), the auxiliary of the Educational Association; in the novel it provides a meeting place for dedicated Communists

50. *Ibid.*, Entry No. 4, Zagora, July 30, 1933.

like Frantzis, and for apolitical poets like his friend, Alexis Notaras, as well as for political conservatives and monarchists.

We follow Frantzis through his short, eventful life from the teeming proletarian quarters of Constantinople to the post-Disaster refugee slums of Athens. Left to his family, young Damianos would have been uneducated, living submerged far below the level where ideas have any relevance. But his uncle, Isidoros Frantzis, a priest at the church of Galata, seeing in him a fierce desire for learning, enrolls him in a school where "a young Macedonian teacher named Pavlos Skinas taught." There is about Skinas that same fresh idealism that Damianos will later express, but the teacher is less grounded in dogma and more inclined to improvisation and a desire for personal glory. "He dreamed of becoming a leader of Hellenism and conquering the City." Skinas, however, is exposed by the Turkish secret police as a Greek spy and is forced to flee Constantinople.

After this separation of teacher and pupil, Damianos goes to the Theological School at Chalke, where his brilliance impresses his teachers but cannot convince them that his religious vocation is genuine. The lonely boy loves the religious life, but his attitudes toward Christianity are complicated and perhaps marred by his inability to distinguish between Orthodoxy and Hellenism. There is much of the Megale Idea mixed up in Damianos's religion, and when the disastrous awakening occurs in 1922 and the Megale Idea perishes, his religion dies as well. "Saint Sophia was still Moslem. The bright plans of 1918 were optical illusions, hallucinations, dreams. The return to reality was, in truth, very painful. It had not come then, the fulfillment of time, the historical moment, the hour of the Megale Idea, which everyone waited for with such faith and longing for five tormented and tear-stained centuries. It was all lies!"[51]

51. *Argo,* p. 154.

92

He leaves the Theological School for Athens and law studies, slowly breaking away from "all the traditions of the race, the wreck of the Megale Idea, [stories like] 'The King turned to Marble'," confronting a void he found hard to fill. He had lived a life of illusion. Religion for him had been a means of keeping alive the national identity, but "without these national passions Orthodoxy lost its meaning and purpose." Christ was no longer the "warrior god" or even the "sweet and consoling god, as he was termed by the other peoples" but a "defeated general, with broken sword, who followed his army in despair on the road of retreat."[52] Not only national and ideological bankruptcy, but also the physical uprooting from his environment totally alienated Damianos from his racial past. In Athens, he wakes up to social problems by seeing the differences between rich and poor.

But thinkers who could have given another interpretation to social injustice, men like Theophilos Notaras – the father of Alexis and a professor of law at the University – are unable to inspire Damianos and his generation with their dry legalisms and cold logic, though they can command respect and silence from "the least disciplined audience in Greece," the students of the Law School. "The wars had ended, the Disaster had abruptly and rudely closed the first century of modern Greek independence. The second century was beginning in anarchy and discontinuity. Greece had suddenly found herself without a form of government, without a constitution, without institutions or state organization, without ideologies, because all had been bankrupted in the conscience of the nation."[53]

Unconvinced by Professor Notaras, a representative of the bankrupt Greek establishment (whose wife even rejects him to go off with an itinerant piano player), Damianos Frantzis chances upon a "red pamphlet," *The Communist Manifesto,* and sees the

52. *Ibid.,* p. 166.
53. *Ibid.,* p. 40

world and all its problems fall neatly into place. "For every question there was now an answer."

It is as a member of the Communist Party that Frantzis meets Skinas again. His former teacher, now Minister of the Interior, calls the young Marxist into his office, having seen his name on a list of radical students compiled by the police. Skinas offers Frantzis vague assurances of protection if he will inform on his fellows, which Frantzis immediately rejects.

Skinas, too, has had his moral adventures; Frantzis has managed to substitute one religion for another, while the Minister is guided only by what is in his own interest. After a German education, Skinas has returned to Greece with his "à priori beliefs in Marxism, in historical materialism, and in socialism generally." But since Greece was a "backward, agrarian, and petit bourgeois" country, the "natural prerequisites for socialism were lacking." Before they could exist, "it was necessary that our society be organized on serious capitalistic bases" until Greece managed to acquire her fair share of "proletarians and economic troubles," whereupon Skinas and his friends "would declare the class conflict." In order to develop the prerequisites for socialism, however, Skinas "entered by necessity the capitalist environment, tasted the sweets of capitalism, became accustomed to them, and after a while had no desire at all to change things."[54]

By far Theotokas's most interesting characters in *Argo,* Frantzis and Skinas are the major actors in the novel's events. They are "public men" whose interests draw the reader into the maelstrom of post-Disaster Greek life, while the Notaras sons (who provide the other story-line of the novel), whether introspective or daemon-ridden, tentative or decisive, drift through their era, more concerned with their personal development or pleasure than with what is occurring to their environment.

54. *Ibid.,* pp. 71-73.

Book One and *Argo* itself reaches its climactic moments in a splendidly described attempted coup by a gang known as The Military League led by a General Tsaveas, whose goal is "the salvation of the nation by any means." This incident, a reminder of the perpetual instability of the Greek state and the constant threat of military intervention (another aspect of which concludes Floros's *A Man of the Times*) exhausts, by and large, the novel's ideological content.[55]

Theotokas implies that the Greece of the refugees, of poverty, of military coups, and of ideological and fiscal bankruptcy can no longer provide an adequate arena for those with great ambitions. Damianos Frantzis escapes from prison, goes to Russia (where he loses faith in the Soviet experiment), returns to the West, and is killed in an attempt to assassinate Mussolini. Pavlos Skinas is emptied of meaning by the introduction of Venizelos, who pushes aside the Minister who might have used the coup of Tsaveas for his own benefit. Alexis Notaras dies, his poetic genius recognized too late, while Nikiphoros, his oldest brother, who himself has literary ambitions, abandons Greece and a pregnant mistress (the wife of Pavlos Skinas) for Paris. He blames Greece for his failure. "Mean, peevish, malignant, wickedness without pride, humility without beauty, sallow-faced, sullen, poisoned, with the most insane ambitions and the sensibility of an envious servant, Greece of the small harbors and the small ships, the small houses, the small deals, the small passions, the small, petty lives. Greece, the inferno of pettiness! Horrors! How can a great force bear to live here?"[56]

Characters in novels did not describe Greece in this manner before the Disaster. It is clear, however, that after 1922, "the

55. For a more complete discussion of *Argo*, see my book, *George Theotokas* (Boston: Twayne World Authors Series, No. 339, 1975), pp. 41-54.
56. *Argo,* p. 377.

weight of the great name" aggravating "the shame of present smallness" made outbursts like this more common. If Christos Kastoridis in *A Man of the Times* were interested enough to question his own motives for not returning to Greece until offered the position he accepts, he would, perhaps, have said roughly the same thing. Even Dimitris Valeris of *Colonists* feels "the shame" in his desire to improve Greece and the Greeks.

This sense of inadequacy is felt more vividly by the refugee than by the native, more strongly by the Anatolian – or, for that matter, by Greeks from other than Old Greece, like Kazantzakis from Crete and Varnalis from Bulgaria – than by the continental Greeks, perhaps because the uprooted saw first-hand the disgrace Greece had suffered, or perhaps because they subjected their fellow-Greeks to a standard that had evolved in separation from the reality. Whatever the reason, Greek society would have been even more the target of criticism if the instability that had manifested itself in 1935 had not been followed by the repressive regime of General Metaxas in August 1936, which effectively put an end to the use of the novel as a means of expressing explicit ideological concerns.

The refugee experience after the events of 1935 is, therefore, rendered without the political background that characterized novels such as *Colonists, The School-Mistress with the Golden Eyes,* and *Argo.* [57] One cannot be sure how much *A Man of the Times* had been influenced by the climate of the Metaxas era, but it seems clear from what Floros wrote that he felt some constraint about expressing his attitudes on the Asia Minor events and the problems of the refugees. [58]

Of the two novels that focus on the refugee adjustment to life in Greece, only Ilias Venezis's *Serenity* (1939) would have been

57. It must be emphasized that the political interest in *Argo* is concentrated in Part One, which was published in 1933.
58. For a discussion of this, see Chapter Six.

at all affected by the Metaxas era, but it shares with Tatiana Stavrou's *The First Roots* (1935) much more than a common subject matter. Both novels seem to concentrate exclusively on the economic, psychological, and social problems encountered by the Anatolian refugees trying to establish themselves in Greece, and never on the political problems, which if viewed in a broader perspective would have embraced all of these. Both *The First Roots* and *Serenity* are by uprooted writers who had previously published impressive works of fiction, and both avoid explicit and implicit references to the political events leading to the Asia Minor Disaster and from that to the fictional present. The lack of depth and resonance that results from this avoidance harms these two novels immeasurably.

Tatiana Stavrou, from Constantinople, had already produced a fine collection of short stories entitled *Those Who Remained,* which treated the lives and struggles of women who continued to live in Constantinople while their menfolk were mobilized or imprisoned during the Great War.[59] In this collection, the gradual but irrevocable destruction of the City's middle class is chronicled. In the relentless economic decline and mobilization, the women are subjected to drastic rationing that leads to slow starvation, the breakdown of mutual confidence, the selling – at first discreetly – of jewelry, furniture, and then of their own bodies, for food, clothing, and security.

It is clear that Mrs. Stavrou was unable to entertain any idea of writing about the refugee's life until she had gained some perspective on it, until she had rid herself of the experiences contained in *Those Who Remained,* and freed herself for her next book. *The First Roots* tells the story of three young refugee women and their "rooting" in the new environment of Athens.[60]

---

59. Stavrou, *Ekeinoi pou Emeinan* (Athens, 1933).
60. *Oi Protes Rizes* (Athens, 1936).

Eva Xenou, the central character, has lost her family in Constantinople during the war and now finds herself tutor for the
children of Alexis Lambikis, a wealthy widower, also from the
City who will eventually marry her. Her life, by far the most
comfortable one experienced by the novel's young women, provides us with only an echo of the problems of adjustment to an
Athens unprepared for the influx of refugees. It is only through
the letters that Eva, living placidly in the Lambikis mansion in
Kifissia, receives from her aunt, at the Kastella of Piraeus, that we
are informed of the Constantinopolitan's amazement at Greece's
backwardness, of the unproductive, barren countryside, and the
lack of water, roads, and sewage disposal.

Her aunt serves Eva as the reminder of a reality she is protected from by her good fortune. "You must struggle," she writes
to her niece,

> to pierce this dry, white earth. You must gouge it with your
> nails, your teeth, with all your might, in order to establish a
> poor, little life, without memories. There are moments when I
> feel I'm not human, but am becoming a tree. I try to . . . dig
> my roots as deep as I can, to suck a little coolness through my
> quivering, thread-like mouths. . . . I consider my children.
> None of them, when he grows up, will imagine our struggle.
> They'll read about what happened in their lives as we learn
> about Noah's Ark. . . . We will be the first roots; they, the first
> blossoms that will flower or wilt, depending upon our own
> agony. If we can hold on, if the sun that burns like a threat
> above our green lives does not scorch us first.[61]

Martha Papazoglou, from the Pontos, provides the second
story-line. Since her father and uncle were hanged by the Turks
for pro-Greek activity and her brother is in the slave labor
battalions, Martha provides the chiaroscuro in what might other-

61. *Ibid.*, pp. 242-243.

wise have been too rosy a view of the middle class's adjustment to Greek life. She, too, eventually marries her employer, but only after a bleak, relatively hopeless life in the refugee district of Pangrati and an attempt at suicide at what she interprets as her lover's cold decision to ignore their affair and force their relationship back to that of employer-secretary.

If the story about Kallio Christodoulou had not been included, *The First Roots* would have run the risk of being unrepresentative of the refugee experience, a modified confection of the Xenopoulos variety for the consumption of people who think of literature as an esthetic escape. Kallio represents the wreckage of the artisan class and her attempt to keep the family together despite her tailor father's inability to function means an acceptance of a position — peddling cigarettes — at the lowest economic level of urban life.[62] She manages to find jobs for her beautiful sister, Flora, and her brother, Kosta, but both go astray. Flora is seduced and made pregnant by a medical student who refuses to marry her, and Kosta is killed in the bed of an occasional prostitute by her boyfriend.

The weaknesses of *The First Roots* are obvious. Mrs. Stavrou tried to construct a synthesis of the refugee experience in a new land without limiting herself to those areas in which her instincts, feelings, and experience granted her depth and sureness. She was cautious and self-indulgent, despite the fact that in presenting the experiences of Eva Xenou and Martha Papazoglou she was dealing with women of her own social class. These weaknesses did not allow *The First Roots* to have the power and explicitness that

62. According to *L'Établissement des réfugiés en Grèce* (Genève: Société des Nations, 1926) the artisan class was the hardest hit of all by the Disaster and the uprooting, because the demand for their products could not possibly rise to the number of artisans and craftsmen who arrived, since all of the handicrafts and retail trade, over an immense territory in Asia Minor, were in the hands of Greeks. See pp. 178-179.

made *Those Who Remained* so successful, which can be seen in the differing attitudes toward sexuality in the two books. When it is not expressed in a wartime Constantinopolitan background of desperation and of force, sexuality must lead – in the homogeneous Greek society of *The First Roots* – to marriage, to disgrace, or to death. (If even male writers felt this way until recently in Greece, the unstated compulsions on women must obviously have been much greater.) Yet, where Mrs. Stavrou was most powerful and controlled, with Kallio Christodoulou, for example, she seemed to feel the least confidence, perhaps because she herself was not of the artisan class.

One might say that in *The First Roots,* Mrs. Stavrou – though concentrating on the lives of refugees immediately after the Disaster (November 1, 1922, to the summer of 1923), which gives her a perspective of more than a decade – is nevertheless writing about a historical process as yet unconcluded. The situation differs, therefore, from that of *Those Who Remained,* which is fixed in historical time by the war and in the author's emotions by her emigration.

This may explain the feeling of oppression, of asphyxiation, that the reader experiences from the confined dimensions of the novel. The characters seem to be crowded into spaces too small for comfort, walking joylessly in a darkened, sunless Athens, condemned to cramped interiors and bleak futures. The author is clearly unable to see anything but the sorry drabness of refugee life. The solutions to her characters' problems are, consequently, limited to three, yet Mrs. Stavrou does not question the popular and conventional attitudes toward sexuality: it leads remorselessly to marriage, disgrace, or death. From these there is no appeal. She accepts completely the moral world as presented to her by the past. It is this timidity, this total subscription to the mores of her society, that makes Mrs. Stavrou's novel so oppressive, not the poverty of the refugees or their sorrow at the death of loved ones.

Perhaps the choice of the realistic, communal novel as a container for the various stories she wanted to tell was the initial error, because this compelled her to attempt a synthesis that a short story collection would not have demanded of her. We see this in the four short stories of her 1943 collection, *The Summer Has Passed.* Viewed as a unit, each narrative is as bleak and unsparing as each story-line in *The First Roots,* but the fact that she was not compelled to weave them into a single work permitted her to break from the compulsive focus that characterizes her novel. There is a sense of creative freedom in "Resurrection" and "The Broom" that is not present in the novel, despite the fact that in both stories the heavy price paid for sexuality is once again disgrace or death. In "Instinct," the drab life of a refugee girl, jilted by her lover, is not enough to drive her to the suicide that appears, superficially, to be her only recourse. The memory of her parents' tenacity in the face of their uprooting, and her desire to have a child, even though it is not by the man she loves, allows her to triumph over her feelings of despair. Finally, in "The Nostalgic Ones," a Constantinopolitan family, preparing for a New Year's celebration in the still-unfamiliar environment of Athens, reveal their gradual acceptance of life in their new city. The two daughters feel the strangeness of their freedom of movement in an urban environment without Moslems. "You hear Greek everywhere," one says. "You speak your own language with everyone."[63]

Because the short story form does not overextend her, Mrs. Stavrou is able to infuse the nostalgia for a past, simple life in a city her characters had grown to love and identify with into

63. *To Kalokairi Perase* (Athens, 1943), p. 149.

narratives that convince the reader with their spare power. It was the *will* of a writer aware of the historical significance of her subject matter that made Mrs. Stavrou undertake a large canvas in *The First Roots,* when she would have been more successful with a series of portraits.

Roughly the same problem arises with the attempts of Ilias Venezis to describe the refugee experience. The Asia Minor tragedy expressed so brilliantly in *The Number 31,328* was also reflected in many of his short stories. "The Sea Gulls," for example, is a story of an old lighthouse keeper off the Island of Mytilene who tries to delude himself into believing that his two sons were not killed in Asia Minor; the truth of their death, however, he cannot continue to repress. The same quality of longing, bitterness, and despair is evoked, with lesser success, in "A Bird," "There is no Ship," "Death," "Resurrectional," and "Mycenae." The best of the group is "Lios," a story that goes beyond melancholy at the death of loved ones and numbness at the uprooting from the Anatolian homeland to show the gradual development, in a man previously full of hatred, of forgiveness for his enemy, the Turk.[64]

The major statement of the refugee experience by Venezis, however, is *Serenity,* which documents the establishment of an Anatolian refugee village, Anavyssos, on a barren stretch of land near Sounion in Attica.[65] It is clear in Venezis's strategy that a few of the events in *The Number* and *Serenity* are simultaneous, since the refugees of Anavyssos are relatives of men in the forced labor battalions. Specifically, Andreas, the sole survivor of his

64. *Aigaio* (1941) and *Anemoi* (1944) in the Kollaros Estia editions contain all these stories, including "Akif," which is interesting in that it relates the other side of the coin: the story of a Turk in Mytilene who is to be repatriated, while his son, Mehmet, decides to embrace Christianity and stay on the Island. "To Lios" and "Manolis Lekas" were written as early as 1928.

65. *Galini,* (Athens, 1957). The novel was first published in 1939.

labor battalion, is clearly Ilias, the boy through whose point of view we saw the identical events in *The Number.*

Besides this interest in narrative documentation, Venezis employs a symbolic strategy — the planting of roses in the barren soil of Attica — to help him show the "rooting" of a people so harshly uprooted. The core of the novel exposes the tense relationship between Dimitris Venis, an ineffectual doctor, and his attractive wife, the embittered Irene, who is considerably younger than he. This unfortunate match was the result of the unsettled economic and political conditions of the century, since Irene, the daughter of the British consul in Aivalik, would never have married the older doctor if the economic crisis had not destroyed her father. Still, she might have adjusted to marriage with a man she seems incapable of loving or respecting if the Disaster had not flung them on the salt-flats of Anavyssos in a condition no less bleak than that of Eleni, a maid in the household of Irene's father in Aivalik.

The tensions of a complex relationship are present, but Irene and her husband do not develop and define themselves through action. They have as much definition when they first appear as they ever attain later in the novel. Nevertheless, Irene has the makings of a major fictional creation because her negative and life-hating attitudes are a convincing reflection of what people — specifically of the middle class — would have been like after having seen their life wasted and their past uprooted.

With Eleni and Glaros, her husband — both of the common people — Venezis is on surer ground, possibly because he knows them better, or possibly because they are outward-looking, unlike the life-denying Irene and her passive husband. It is through their discovery of an ancient statue, a *kouros,* on land given them by the state, that the terrain of Attica, previously used only by nomadic shepherds, will appear more like home to Eleni and Glaros. The *kouros,* even though it is taken from them, connects them culturally to a land that was alien to them before. Doctor Venis's roses can root in any hospitable soil, but the discovery of age-old cultural roots previously forgotten is of major importance to them: "They walked like solitary beings who planned their life in this soil, the earth that created a past in [their] conscience only because it sent . . . a message from its depths."[66]

Even though Eleni is drowned in a torrent halfway through the novel, she has imposed the force of her personality on the reader, while Glaros emerges, in the changed conditions of the refugees' new life, as a clever and capable man who needed only a change of environment to show his native abilities.

Irene lacks the resilience of the others because, without love, she sees no purpose to her life, particularly when she is being pulled into a lower social class by her husband's ineffectuality. Her agreeing to go off with the loud and vulgar road-worker is less out of physical passion for him than out of despair, the same despair that motivates her to pull up the roses that have at last rooted in her husband's garden. These actions she performs consciously, aware that they are dictated by essentially life-negating elements in her psyche, since she views the acceptance of a continued life with her husband in the refugee village as life's brutal violation of her past and its irrevocable end. She returns to her home only after the fortuitous murder of her only daughter.

Serenity fails to convince because Venezis's ambition to design a communal novel, which demanded that he document the establishment of a refugee village, compelled him to control the development of Irene Venis and, consequently, to subordinate the most complex character his imagination had ever confronted. The technical problem this subordination caused is one of perspective. The reader is uncertain what is foreground and what is background, and the confusion stems from Venezis's own uncer-

66. *Ibid.*, pp. 78-79.

tainty. No such confusion exists in *The Number 31,328* because we accept Ilias as our point of reference, and the "communal" aspect of the labor battalions is subordinated but not stripped of its great importance.

The sense of confinement the reader feels would not have been so oppressive if Mrs. Stavrou and Ilias Venezis had dared to express more within the terms of their novels. It is as though these writers had deliberately confined their imaginations to the bleak and defeated world of the refugees in order to reflect their despair more accurately, thus forbidding themselves the perspective they could claim as artists. The major criticism one can make of these two novels is not that their drabness is false, since it is doubtlessly accurate as far as it goes, but that the novelists concentrate so much on the monochrome of refugee life that they misrepresent the polychromatic complexity of reality. This is something Venezis would point out a few years later, but neither he nor Mrs. Stavrou were able to shake free of the sense of drift and helplessness they thought characterized the uprooted. In reality, the refugee was often much more resilient and vivacious, much more aggressive and outgoing, than his chroniclers indicated.

Ultimately, both novels fail because their writers lack the perspective to see the heroic and epic dimension of the experience they set out to document. Neither novel has a strong plot or characters who can develop through action, and the novelists seem to have felt they had to give them definite narrative coherence by imposing melodramatic conclusions. Both works might have been more than the sum of their parts if the writers had been able to infuse their material with a world view. This lack of ideology is particularly obvious since both books are essentially social novels set squarely in a historical sequence of events. Vignettes, interesting characters, and sharply defined scenes were not enough to make them successful works of fiction.

Sounds of Another War

The approach of World War II brought about a radical but understandable change in the attitude of writers from Anatolia, for it was they, almost exclusively, who continued to concern themselves with the experience of what had become "lost homelands." There is a profound instinct at work here, moreover, for the works of these Anatolian writers employ their perspective of time to describe, not the terrible end of Hellenism in Asia Minor, but the beginning of that end, setting the major works of this category – *Leonis* by George Theotokas, and *Aeolian Earth* by Ilias Venezis – in the early years of the century, before the final uprooting.

Theotokas seems to be the first to handle the theme in this way with *Leonis* (1940), possibly his best work of fiction.[67] The novella employs a narrator, Leonis, who from the perspective of an adult recalls the confusions and slow gropings toward comprehension of a boy growing up in Constantinople during the first two decades of the twentieth century.

Constantinople was the Imperial City, the enticing Queen that scores of conquerors had aspired to and many had seized and enjoyed. It was a cosmopolitan city with highly distinct national and religious communities, each with its own extremes of wealth and poverty. Though the Greek community dominated commercial and cultural life, it nevertheless shared the Turkish-controlled city with the French, Italian, and Armenian communities, being much more restrained than the first two by the Ottoman authorities for historical reasons. Constantinople, despite the fact that

---

67. *Leonis* (Athens, 1940). There are indications of *Leonis* rather often in *Neoellinika Grammata*: chapters are excerpted, Theotokas himself is interviewed, but he seems aware that he is in a race against time. He wrote the novella, he says in a "note" to the October 26, 1940, issue of *Neoellinika Grammata,* because "I heard the war approaching." The book had just been printed and bound and was ready to be released. Two days later, of course, the Italians invaded Greece.

the Turks had controlled it for 450 years, had never ceased to be a Greek city. Only formally it was non-Greek. According to the folk song: "Again with years and times they [the lost lands] will be ours." And the time seemed ripe.

The Megale Idea was about to become a reality; the awakening was at hand. With the Great War that threatened as soon as Leonis was ready for school, the centuries-old dream would certainly be fulfilled. The sounds of war, filtered as they are through the consciousness of Leonis, come to the reader only as a distant rumble. He is much too preoccupied with his developing sexuality to be conscious of the threat and promise of the Great War.

After Leonis has been rebuffed by his first great love, Eleni Phocas, and has had his first erotic adventure, one silent day the war ends. His future, and that of Greece, seems clear. When he completes the Gymnasion, he will go to Athens, then to Paris. The affairs of the world seem to be getting settled at last and reasonable men of good will can again begin to make plans. Wilson, Lloyd George, and Clemenceau are in Paris at that very moment establishing the League of Nations. The past will be forgotten with all its problems of war and injustice: the future beckons, full of freedom and comforts.

> Every nation will look to its pleasure, will enjoy its life without restraints, will walk without obstacles on the road to progress. The Greek nation had to make one small effort still, to give one small push to settle once and for all the open business it still had pending in Asia Minor. Afterward, no other problem would arise to disturb the good life and the games of the children of Odysseus. "You are happy," the older people said, "because your life is beginning now. Fortunate generation."[68]

68. *Ibid.*, p. 76.

But the "little matter" still unresolved — the Megale Idea and the unredeemed Greek lands — looms over the horizon. Leonis, being a child of his century, cannot develop in his own way. He must mesh with his time, as Pavlos Proios, the friend he admires, tells him before going off to Smyrna to fight: "The only thing that truly counts [about understanding our century] is to enter into it, to take part in it with whatever forces one has. To involve oneself with the century, that is the issue."[69]

But Pavlos is killed, Eleni Phocas marries a much older man, Asia Minor is lost in the flames of Smyrna, and Leonis and his family leave the Imperial City for Athens — a "dull white city scattered carelessly . . . in the plateau, among rearing stone peaks and the sheer drop of quarries" — where he wanders aimlessly, not knowing what to do with himself, uprooted from his personal past until he discovers another one, an Helladic past this time, and finds his place in it.

Leonis is a brilliant evocation of a "lost homeland" whose significance is inescapable once the coming of war duplicates the external conditions of the author's childhood and unlocks the memories sealed in his psyche. It is an "education novel" in that we see the growing up, with the century, of a young man who learns, along with his limitations, the wealth of his complexity. Unlike Pavlos Proios, Leonis does not involve himself with his century; he mirrors it. By reflecting it, he reveals how much has been lost: an entire Greek world, an Imperial City permeated with racial memories reaching back for two millennia.

Yet there is no despair in *Leonis,* no grinding defeat by history. Life is rendered in all its confusion and complexity, with much of its pain and much of its pleasure. What distinguishes it, essentially, from the novels that documented the "refugee experi-

69. *Ibid.,* p. 138.

ence" is its aura of mystery, the sense it creates of resources and depths hidden in man and waiting for liberation. *The School-Mistress with the Golden Eyes* had some of this quality, as did *Argo* to a lesser extent, but their content helped them overcome the interwar grayness that seems to characterize *The First Roots* and *Serenity*. *Leonis,* despite its focus on a world whose splendor is no more, communicates a quiet but defiant joy. "We lost everything we had . . . we lost all our loves, but we're in love with a thousand things, with whatever dies and whatever begins," is how the young man concludes his story.[70] *Leonis* is not a refugee novel. It is something else, because World War II put an end to the fictional use of the "refugee experience" narrowly conceived. Although short stories would be published that retained the refugee mentality – such as Mrs. Stavrou's *The Summer Has Passed* – most fiction, but particularly the novels, reflected the new world created by the coming of the Second World War.

Theotokas was not alone in wanting to review and reassess his previous life in Anatolia when he heard the sounds of World War II approaching Greece. This was done by virtually every writer who had some ties with Asia Minor. Among others, Fotis Kontoglou published two books during the German Occupation, *Famous and Forgotten Men* and *Stories and Events,* which contain four stories set in an Anatolia infused with longing for the old life and the virtues of heroism and fortitude.[71] The Asia Minor Disaster had disoriented Kontoglou more than most Anatolians. Before the loss of Aivalik in 1922, Kontoglou traveled "in the exotic islands and the seas of cosmopolitanism," as Angelos Prokopiou remarks,

70. *Ibid.,* p. 178.
71. *Fimismenoi Andres kai Lismonismenoi* (Athens, 1942) contains "Papa Yiannis Oikonomos," pp. 83-88 and "Kapetan Rongos," pp. 89-90. *Istories kai Peristatika* (Athens, 1944) contains "O Alexis O Tsombanis," pp. 58-77, and "To Kairo Ekeino," pp. 88-93.

living and working in a Europe that had been born essentially in the Renaissance. Sophia Antoniadou agrees with this assertion, pointing out the strong influence of foreign writers in his first work, *Pedro Cazas* (1917 or 1920?). In fact, in the introduction to *Pedro Cazas,* "Desinit in Piscem," Kontoglou notes the great impact made upon him by Daniel Defoe's *Robinson Crusoe.* After the Asia Minor Disaster, however, "the refugee from Aivalik" requires what he considers sterner stuff, a faith the need for which he reveals in *Vasanta* (1923). Shaken by the Disaster, Kontoglou goes to Mount Athos for study and spiritual concentration and hears, as Prokopiou says, "the sound of the bell of Byzantium for the first time." His style as a visual artist as well as a writer still retains Western influence, according to Prokopiou, and it is only in the latter part of the 1920s that Kontoglou begins to use an exclusively Byzantine style in his painting. [72] By the time of the Second World War, however, the religious element in Kontoglou is overwhelming. During the Occupation, he finds himself oppressed by a sense of guilt "for the dream life of the corsair and bandit he had lived up to then" in his writing. These fantasies make him feel that he bore "a share of the responsibility for the evil that had beset the world." From that point on, "Kontoglou lives totally in the will of Byzantium."[73]

Stratis Myrivilis, too, though technically not an Anatolian, recalls during the German Occupation the common culture that the island of Lesbos shared with the opposite city of Aivalik in his best work, the novella *Vasilis Arvanitis* (1943). It is a rich, powerful work, half legend, half realistic fiction, of a fresh, vital time, an Anatolia beckoning with promise, before the Great War, before Liman von Sanders, before the Young Turks, a time of

72. Prokopiou, "Kontoglou," *Angloelliniki Epitheorisi,* 3, No. 5 (1947), p. 134.
73. *Ibid.,* p. 135.

relative freedom, when Moslems and Christians lived without the intense hatred that was to flare up and consume them both. It is at this time, moreover, that he is at work on the final book of his "trilogy of the war," *The Mermaid Madonna*, which was published after the Civil War.[74]

What was it in the psyche of the writer with an Anatolian background that was reminded by World War II of life in Asia Minor before the Great War? Was it perhaps the unlocked memories of youth; of helplessness before the tide of history; of a world, once part of them, that existed no more and assumed day by day aspects of the ideal?

Aeolian Earth, the novel by Ilias Venezis that concludes this final cycle, was written and published during the German Occupation and is both an idealized product of the refugee experience and a comment on it.[75] Viewed twenty-one years after the Asia Minor Disaster, the subject matter of *Aeolian Earth* is not a story that can be reduced to a chronological plot, but a way of life whose complexity would be distorted by the demands of a linear scheme. The hard-edged clarity of *The Number 31,328* or even *Serenity* would, therefore, have been out of place in this milieu, since the major issues of the novel, seen through the central intelligence of a child, Petros, are as perplexing to the adult mind as they are to his. The motives of man, the well-springs of his behavior, are as shrouded in mystery and as obscure as the natural phenomena that perplex Petros and his sisters.[76] It is interesting

74. That Myrivilis was at work on *I Panaghia I Gorgona* in 1943 is mentioned by Venezis in an article in *Prosfygikos Kosmos,* January 24, 1943, pp. 1-2. The novel will be discussed in Chapter Five.

75. *Aioliki Ghi* (Athens, 1943). I have used the 4th edition (1955) and have translated the Greek title directly since the book, in the same translation, was called *Aeolia* in Britain and *Beyond the Aegean* in the United States.

76. Petros Spandonidis, in *I Pezographia ton Neon (Prose Writing of the Young),* 1934, pp. 26-27, has something interesting to say about "the

that both Theotokas in *Leonis* and Venezis in *Aeolian Earth,* while remembering their Anatolian youth in a present fraught with the terrors of war, choose to tell their stories as much as possible through the points of view of children, the children they were when the "other" war broke out.[77]

Petros gropes toward an understanding of a complex and terrifying world that not even the adults can control or fully comprehend, and he is uprooted with the beginning of the Great War. When the shot rings out at Sarajevo, the patriarchal world comes to an end. The twentieth century comes to Anatolia, and with it matures the "logic" of the nation state. It is this "logic" that results in the break-up of the Ottoman Empire, and Petros, his relatives, and the other Greeks are the awkward statistics that must be tidied up by "repatriation." It is this first "expulsion from the Garden," from what Venezis calls "the blessed land of Anatolia," that the novel documents.

Since *Aeolian Earth* is a story about Petros's growth to pubescence in a patriarchal world deeply rooted in tradition, the novel's action takes place only in the summers that he, his sisters, and his mother spend on his grandfather's estate near the Kimindenia mountains. We are never referred to his life during the winter, which he spends in Aivalik, where his father pursued a mercantile way of life removed from close involvement with the land. The father never appears and, quite rightly, is never mentioned, since his appearance would tend to weaken the patriarchal authority of the grandfather, who is the undisputed pater familias.

---

flooding of clear light of naturalistic reality" in *The Number,* upon everything except "the cause, the source of evil" in man. Venezis, he continues, "keeps the mystery of moral cause" obscure.

77. This applies to Myrivilis as well, for he tells *O Vasilis O Arvanitis* (Athens, 1943) through the point of view of a young boy, who is himself.

In this still "archaic" world, the children's inability to understand the complexities of love and sex, war and death, and
madness vs. reason is matched by that of the grownups; the
animism that imbues everything in the novel is an attempt to
explain what would otherwise be inexplicable. Everything has a
spirit. Inanimate objects have motives and the natural world of
trees, animals, and stones is intimately enmeshed with human
destiny.

Founded in ancient traditions, these folk beliefs have an age-
old coherence. Thus, they are not viewed by the author, or the
reader, as quaint holdovers or survivals, but as beliefs that actually function in people's lives. The grandfather reads auguries from
the backs of sheep, and the grandmother has secret prayers she
will pass on to her older daughter only when she is ready to die.
The patriarchal principle, accepted as natural here, provides the
older people with a direct line to God, Who Himself is the apex of
the patriarchal pyramid.

But it is not only Petros who undergoes change. In a seemingly
changeless society, change is ever-present. We see this in the
challenge that the foreign wife of a young neighbor offers to
patriarchal morality and in the tensions that exist within the
marriage of Petros's aunt and uncle. In this archaic society,
change is more convincingly explained by attributing dissatisfac-
tion with the existing conditions of life to madness, or
"phantasmata."

War is the great, the ultimate madness, and the children slowly
grow to an awareness of its power. At first it is localized in "the
yellow room," where the weapons and ammunition are stored
and from which strange noises are sometimes heard by the children at night. Later, this vaguely understood "war" seems to have
something to do with the hungry jackals beyond the estate's
walls; but man's madness is eternal and universal, as Petros

discovers when he wants to show his love for his unattainable beloved. The lust for killing is not something foreign that has invaded him, but a potentiality that has developed as he grew up. He feels that he must kill in order to show his value as a man.

But it is in the code of the *pallikar*-hero that we see in miniature the behavior that, when raised to the level of foreign policy, leads irrevocably to the Great War. Antonis Pagidas, the noted bandit, smuggling a load of arms from Syra to the Greeks of Anatolia, is informed that his good friend, Stratigos Garmbis, has been compelled to kill Constantine, Pagidas's brother. It is the brother's fault for defying a clearly established pattern of behavior, but his death compels the two men, whose friendship is legendary, to a duel for blood vengeance, itself a clearly established pattern of behavior. There is no avoiding the duel nor, when Pagidas kills Garmbis, of surviving it. As all the Greeks prepare to leave Anatolia for the safety of Greece, Pagidas buries the friend he killed and stays behind to hold back the Turks and die. The way of life the two men represented is finished, as is the Ottoman Empire that provided them with an arena for their actions.

The grandfather senses that his patriarchal way of life has been negated as well, but he accompanies his seed to their new home, to Greece, bringing with him some soil from the estate, to plant basil in, he says, not needing to explain that it will also act as "culture" – the μαγιά – for his own people.

When the Greeks left Anatolia the first time, history began. The drama that began in 1914 was to be concluded, in pity and terror, but without purgation, in the Disaster of 1922.

The Second World War and the German Occupation provided the ideal moment for the Greek writers from Anatolia to view retrospectively the experiences – clustered about the events of the 1922 Disaster — they had undergone and to express them in the hope of being rid of them at last and being able to go on to other themes.[78]

78. It is significant in the light of this that Theotokas in *Astheneis kai Odoiporoi (Invalids and Wayfarers,)* (Athens, 1964) and Venezis in *Exodos* (Athens, 1950) were, with one exception, the only members of the Generation of the 1930s to write major fictional statements about Greece during the War, Occupation, and Civil War. The one exception is Yiannis Beratis, whose *To Platy Potami (The Wide River,* 1965) is heavily indebted to factual experiences. This attempt to deal with the period 1940-1945 (or 1949) was a task that would clearly fall to the younger writers of the Generation of the 1940s and 1950s.

3 The Enemies of Hellenism: The Greek People Themselves

The autumn of 1922 is a watershed in the intellectual life of Greece: before this time, the Greek mind is permeated by a sense of Greece's eventual expansion and greatness. After the Asia Minor Disaster, Greece and the Greeks try to find a place in a world suddenly grown very narrow and bleak.

J. C. Voyatzidis, referred to previously for his study on the Megale Idea, provides us with the ideal gauge for measuring the impact of the Disaster on Greek intellectual life. In "The Origin and Development of the Megale Idea," a 1921 version of "La Grande Idée" later published in the volume commemorating the 500th anniversary of the Fall of Constantinople, Voyatzidis defends the expansionism implicit in the realization of the national goals. It had been alleged, he states, that the Greek irredentist efforts differed from the "liberating struggles of the other Christian peoples of the East" since these needed only to free limited geographical areas, whereas the Greeks found themselves "within the very heart of the Ottoman Empire and were compelled to destroy it in order to fulfill the Megale Idea." Voyatzidis disagrees with this allegation. There is no necessity, he says, "to destroy the entire Ottoman State" in order to liberate "our unredeemed Greek brothers." There are vast lands for the establishment of the Turkish State "beyond the territories that the national consciousness of the [Greek] Race" considers its own. It was on this understanding that the Treaty of Sèvres was signed. This essay, completed on the significant date of March 25, 1921, demonstrates a confidence in the ultimate realization of the profound dreams of the Greek nation. "We can be certain that this ripe fruit" (ὁ ὥρμος αὐτός καρπός) by which he means Anatolia, "will fall into our laps."[1]

By one of those technical mishaps from which no industry — and certainly not publishing — is free, the publication of this essay was delayed until 1923, when all the certitudes expressed by Voyatzidis were proved to be pathetic delusions. It was because of this, perhaps, that both he and George Drosinis, the publisher of the annual periodical, felt it incumbent upon them to print another, more current view of the political situation after the Great War. If the first essay bore a completion date redolent of impressions of national rebirth and religious Annunciation, "The World War and Greece" (dated August 30, 1924) carries with it very different connotations. "National" still, the August days — exactly two years before the essay was written — reflect a tragedy and horror unsupported by religion. Since the Virgin had clearly removed her Grace from the Greeks, the completion date reflects the collapse of the front in Asia Minor, rather than Assumption Day, a fortnight before. In this essay, moreover, Voyatzidis mentions neither the Megale Idea nor his earlier certitude that it would soon be realized.

Instead, Voyatzidis carefully analyzes the geopolitical and economic preliminaries to the Great War — the conflict of Great Britain, France, and Germany over colonies in Africa — and concludes that the foreign policy of Greece had erred after 1918 by pursuing national objectives in Asia Minor. In continuing the

1. "I Archi kai Exelexis tis Megalis Ideas," *Imerologion tis Megalis Ellados* (1923), pp. 161-171.

war against Kemal Ataturk, the Greek leadership ignored the fact that the major issue – economic competition – had been solved essentially by the outcome of the Great War. He sees, from the perspective of 1924, that the war Greece fought in the Balkans in 1917-1918 was essentially a "Third Balkan War" and should have been terminated at the same time that the Great War had come to an end. Greek policy – by which he clearly means that of Venizelos – ignored the fact, moreover, that the postwar climate of Europe and Greece was anti-war. Voyatzidis does not mention the frightful result of this foreign policy blunder. There was no need to do so: in 1924, when he wrote the essay, every third person he saw in Athens would have been a refugee. The only solution left now was "the internal reorganization" of the Greek state.[2] But this, "the draining of Lake Copais," had always been the alternative to the Megale Idea.

The change is vast. From the type of thinking that places a great deal of emphasis on the significance of dates, on concepts such as "national consciousness," and on myth and legend, Voyatzidis expresses within three years a rational attitude that limits him to economic and geopolitical considerations. It is as though, reeling from the shock of the Disaster, he can find stability only in what is clear and provable.[3] The "traditions" of the Greek people are now, in the light of the Disaster's proportions and finality, no more than "fairy tales," and the emergence of a new, more rational way of thinking becomes imperative.

This change was not undergone by Voyatzidis alone. The intellectual life of Greece reacted as a totality. Athens, now that

2. "O Pankosmios Polemos kai I Ellas," *Imerologion tis Megalis Ellados* (1925), pp. 377-390.

3. In "La Grande Idée," in which he rethinks the whole issue, he studies from the distance of a historian the ideas that earlier he had implicitly believed in as a man. In the later essay, therefore, he investigated as a scientist a state of mind in which he had previously shared.

Greek Constantinople and Greek Smyrna no longer existed, was the undisputed intellectual center of Hellenism, and it was in Athens that this fermentation was to be reflected.

At a gathering in The Greek Odeion on May 2, 1923, Sophia Spanoudi, an uprooted Constantinopolitan writer, lectured to her "first-born brothers of freedom," the intellectuals of the Greek capital. She was there to introduce the verse of Homer Bekes, the poet of Constantinople, now, like all Anatolians, "flung . . . for how long?" she asked, "by the most horrible of all cataclysms, on the white and dreamed-of land." Perhaps the "unrevealed demands" of history have "ordered a new creative rebirth of the Race" that will emerge as a result of the "forced embrace in the rubble of our national ruins."[4]

But one did not have to wait until the spring of the following year to see the effect of the Disaster's new historical reality on Greek thought. Almost immediately after the upheaval, another Anatolian intellectual, Dimitris Glinos, a politically important man gifted with brilliance and force, gave a series of lectures, also at The Greek Odeion in November and December of 1922 on "The Crisis of Demoticism." Glinos had been the General Secretary to the Minister of Education under Venizelos in 1917, and had been responsible for the radical reforms in education that the electoral victory of the Populists in 1920 had negated. He was a Marxist as well as a Smyrniot. In fact, by the time of the first lecture, November 27, he had just learned that his family was safe after the Fire at Smyrna.[5]

Glinos saw Demoticism as an effort to renew Greece by first introducing the demotic language into every aspect of the national life, then by refashioning education at all levels, and finally

4. *O Poiitis Omiros Bekes, Vivlio A'*, pp. v-vi (Athens, 1924).
5. It is not clear whether the November 27 date is Old or New Calendar; if the former, the Execution of the Six must have taken place on the morning of the lecture.

by subjecting what he called the "vague, narcotized, dream- and illusion-ridden, childish, primitive, petty, sophistic, intellectually flabby ... Greek thought" to the rigorous examination of criticism and analysis.[6] The goals of Demoticism, he claims, were defeated as much by the betrayal of the position of Psycharis by intellectuals within the Demotic Movement as by its two major enemies – the Greek state and the inertia of the mass of the people. Of its friends within the Demotic Movement, some were careless linguistic "anarchists," while others were "platonic demoticists," men who in principle believed in its goals but who did not want to practice it in every aspect of their lives as writers. Being unwilling to struggle with the demotic in order to mold it into a delicate and powerful instrument for the expression of complex ideas, and by compromising and accepting words and phrases from the *katharevousa,* these demoticists proved their disbelief in the ideal of Demoticism, exhibiting a "weakness that is the hydrophobia of the demoticists, who want to learn how to swim without getting into the water."[7]

These were the friends by whom Demoticism was not adequately defended, while the urge for renewal was straightforwardly attacked "by the old conservative elements clearly supported now by the popular will. One of the many interpretations given to the epoch-making vote of November 1, 1920, was this: that Demoticism be struck down, which with the support of the 'Tyranny' [the Venizelos government] introduced the demotic language into the schools by force, attempting its so-called linguistic-educational reformation."[8]

It should be apparent that the same state machinery that voted

6. "Programmatikoi Schediasmoi" of "I Krisi tou Dimotikismou" in *Eklektes Selides, B'* (Athens, 1971), p. 16.
7. *Ibid.,* p. 37.
8. *Ibid.,* p. 7.

katharevousa as the official language in 1911 was supported by the Greek people overwhelmingly in 1920 despite the "tyranny" of Venizelos. Demoticism, far from being the popular wish, was the target of popular hatred, while its goals were seen and interpreted immediately as political goals by the Greek people and the state. Glinos, therefore, was only stating unequivocally and in public what everyone knew: the language issue was a political one. It had clearly been political in 1911 when Article 107 had been ammended to the Constitution and when Kostis Palamas was suspended from his position in the University.

"I had never imagined," Palamas himself wrote to Penelope Delta on April 10 of that year,

> that the name of a quiet and withdrawn man such as myself, merely because he writes as his literary honor demands, and not as he is ordered to by Mistriotis and his followers, would have been placed on the agenda for months now, [attacked in] parliament, newspapers and [by] students, and subjected to curses and every sort of idiocy. But the "never imagined" reveals a certain naiveness — we must imagine everything, and even more, about our language issue, which has become political and religious and makes fanatics of the mass of the people.[9]

Argyris Eftaliotis, writing to Mrs. Delta a week earlier from Germany, places much of the blame on the behavior of Venizelos. "He should have set his foot down from the beginning . . . and shouted fearlessly that the language issue was not a political one and has no place in the Constitution." But Venizelos, he goes on, who on other occasions was not afraid, if necessary, to resign, backed down from a confrontation. "The evil results of this," he

9. Palamas, *Allilographia tis P. S. Deltas,* ed. X. Lefkoparidis (Athens: Estia, n.d.), Letter No. 41, p. 17.

is certain, "we'll see when the Mavromichalaioi and Company interpret the Venizelist article according to their own mood."[10]

Language and its role in the renewal of Greek culture, clarified by Demoticism and led by the Educational Association, had clearly become a political issue more than a decade before the Asia Minor Disaster. Ranged against this attempt at national renewal were the majority of the people and much of the machinery of the Greek State. The hope of the Demoticists, Venizelos himself, felt no great commitment to the language issue, considering it a dangerous one, which no doubt it was. The linguistic issue paradoxically served to divide the writer and intellectual from the mass of the people, who seemed to reject, through its representatives, its own language in 1911 as well as rejecting, in 1920, the Megale Idea, a vision and dream at the most profound level of the Greek folk. Having borne the Turkish tyranny for four centuries, the Greek people could not bear for four years what the Populists had called Venizelist "tyranny." In rejecting the Megale Idea, the Greek people rejected their own ideals.

The consequences were radical and far-reaching. There could be no "return to the folk" by intellectuals, and — ironically — definitely no return by those who considered themselves Marxists. It was a frightful and untenable predicament for men and women who used ideas in their daily life and whose foundation, intellectual as well as emotional, was a mystical sense of the fortitude, the wisdom, and the grandeur of the Greek people. When Glinos stated that "Greece committed suicide in (the elections of) 1920," he was not being melodramatic, but describing in bitterness a profound psychological truth.[11]

10. Eftaliotis, *Ibid.,* Letter No. 67, p. 184. Eftaliotis views the great Mavromichalis clan of Mani and their parliamentary allies as unredeemable reactionaries.

11. "Two Unpublished Letters of Dimitris Glinos," presented by Dimos Omiridis, *Epitheorisi Technis,* Nos. 122-123 (1965), pp. 203-206. The letter was posted from Korthi and dated August 27, 1922.

Greek society became for the first time a target for sustained criticism. The complex interrelatedness of rural Greece to the embryonic urban center, a bond at first considered a good thing, a guarantee of proximity to the wellsprings of Hellenic values, was seen now to be a retarding force in the development of Greek culture. The village and its values and the overwhelming power of the Greek past were suddenly viewed as stifling, brutal negations of the great dreams of the historic Greek people. Clearly, only the intellectuals had been foolish enough to believe in those dreams, and only the uprooted, the hungry and despairing refugees, were to pay for these national illusions.

At the profound, psychic levels where creativity is nourished, nothing serious seemed to happen to the men of the Generation of the 1880s and later. Xenopoulos, aside from *Refugees,* and Palamas, aside from several poems, seemed to continue in much the same directions in their creative work as they had before 1922, though in their private moments they may have revealed perplexity and shock over the Disaster. By 1920, Kostas Hadzopoulos, Ioannis Kondylakis, and Ion Dragoumis were dead, and by 1923 Constantine Theotokis was dead. Andreas Karkavitsas, a military doctor, died in 1922 after having intervened in saving from service in Asia Minor the poet, critic, and dramatist Markos Avyeris, also a doctor, who later became one of the foremost Marxist intellectuals of Greece. Travlandonis, as seen in *Plunder of a Life,* viewed the refugees and Venizelos with the utmost contempt. Psycharis, the "leader" of Demoticism, who died in 1929 as fiercely devoted to linguistic reform as ever, was in the words of George Theotokas, "a man of the Megale Idea," who "spoke of 'The King turned to Marble' and of the age-old dreams of the Race with a voice full of passion and flashing eyes."[12]

12. George Theotokas, "To Teleftaio Taxidi tou Psychari," in *Pnevmatiki Poreia* (Athens, 1961), p. 203.

The major ideological blow would affect younger writers, men who midway in their careers would feel the ground collapse under them by a defeat of such proportions. Kostas Varnalis (1884-1974) and Nikos Kazantzakis (1883-1957), who are rarely considered to have been influenced by the Disaster, will be discussed here at length because of their importance as well as their interest in the ideological issues of their time. Both men felt the Disaster as a terrible final blow to a slow process of disenchantment with nationalism that began in 1920. For them, however, August 1922 was the dividing line between two parts of their selves. For Varnalis, crossing this boundary meant making a total commitment to materialism and discovering his genius for sarcasm, while for Kazantzakis, the Disaster meant the beginning of his need to express a credo that would help him escape from "ego" and "the nation," a credo that tried to answer what for him was the perpetual question: the relationship between matter and spirit. The Disaster, therefore, struck both men in metaphysical terms. Varnalis accepted the materialistic basis of communism, while Kazantzakis, faced with the same dilemma but temperamentally committed to idealism, expressed the need for what he termed "metacommunism," a spiritualized materialism that few communists would have credited.

Kostas Varnalis had forsaken *katharevousa* by 1904, and between then and the Disaster was a firm demoticist and nationalist. In 1919, awarded a scholarship by the Greek state and championed within the government by Dimitris Glinos, Varnalis went to Paris, was influenced by the intellectual ferment of the time, and became a socialist, determined as Yianis Kordatos claims, "to stand beside the working people."[13] This change is not immediately apparent, however, because in 1919 he wrote "The Pil-

13. Kordatos, *Istoria tis Neoellinikis Logotechnias* (Athens, 1962), Vol. II, p. 476.

grim," dedicated to Nicholaos Politis, a rhetorical and national-istic poem in which the Greeks, "the Great Race," are seen "not [as] beings, but Ideas, who live in combat."[14] By December 1922, however, he reveals how much firmer his ideas had become in a poem entitled "Freedom," in which he attacks Palamas, who had characterized the Bolsheviks as "wolves" in "The Song of the Refugees." It is in 1922, moreover, that he had published his first clearly Marxist poem, "The Light that Sears" in Alexandria. After 1922, Varnalis used the lyric less and less frequently and concen-trated on works of larger scale because of the synthesis the greater length permitted him to make. In 1927, for example, he published his long poem, *Slaves Beseiged.*

The Disaster had clearly shown him that poetry as he con-ceived it and as it was accepted in his time could not fully express his genius for sarcasm, for abuse, and for "unpoetic" and "unex-alted" ideas articulated in the vernacular and rooted in a contem-porary Greek social reality. In 1923, accordingly, Varnalis made his first appearance as a writer of fiction with *The Eunuchs,* a collection that, besides the title story, includes "The Tale of Saint Pachomios" and "The Jails." These tales reveal a tension and an insight into what Varnalis considered the repressive nature of bourgeois society and organized religion. The well-being of soci-ety demands crowded jails, less out of the need for security than as non-industrially competitive concentrations of human beings who must be attended to and provisioned. Religion, too, is seen as self-imprisonment by people who, unable to direct their lives without the spiritual suppression of the monastic life, go to pieces in the secular freedom of a flesh-pot Alexandria.[15]

It is obvious that Varnalis, despite the fact that his career as a

14. Glinos, "Ena Arthro tou Glinou," in Kostas Varnalis's *Pezos Logos* (Athens, 1957), p. 22.
15. "O Laos ton Monouchon," in Varnalis's *Pezos Logos.* This volume contains "The Tale of Saint Pachomios" and "The Jails."

producing poet continued well into the 1950s, found that poetry could not fully express the ideas he had developed as he matured as a thinker. In 1925 he emerged as a critic as well, with his publication of *Solomos Without Metaphysics,* an attack on the interpretation that Greek criticism, from Polylas to Apostolakis, had given to the work of the national poet. But it was not until 1931, with "The True Apology of Socrates," that Varnalis, finding the perfect form for the abuse to which he wanted to subject Greek society, became the writer people know today.

The genius of Varnalis rests upon his ability to reinterpret the Greek past by taking a "fact" that is already permeated with interpretation from history, denuding this "fact" of subjective attitudes presented to contemporary men as objective, and offering his own interpretation. Glinos, in an essay on Varnalis, merely states that "sarcasm and satire, the bitter laugh that disguises within it such an experience of life and revolution, does not appear until 1920," though he does not feel the need to explain this change.[16] One can go further by saying that the bitter laugh does not appear in Varnalis's prose fiction until after the Asia Minor Disaster, and the two "facts" that he reinterprets, the Apology of Socrates and the character of Penelope, are themes that would not have interested him before 1922.

With "The True Apology of Socrates" Varnalis hits upon the perfect vehicle for social criticism, one that allows him to reinterpret a historical fact that has reached us so loaded with interpretation that we cannot hope to understand fully the many factors leading to Socrates's execution.[17] By and large, we accept Plato's view of Socrates and the motives for his execution as stated in the "Apology," until Varnalis takes the same "fact," identifies him-

16. Glinos, "Ena Arthro tou Glinou," p. 20.
17. "I Alithini Apologia tou Sokrati," in *Pezos Logos.* The novel was first published in 1931.

self with Socrates, and places the action in an Athens that is post-Periclean as well as post-Asia Minor Disaster.[18]

Socrates, accused of atheism — a convenient way of directing the excited populace to forget official stupidity and incompetence — attacks the corruption of powerful men, "the great bandits" and the mindless, manipulated people of Athens, the "laos" that is no more than the "plethos."

> Socrates ridicules the gods and turns their omnipotence against the State. . . . If by chance a hailstorm destroyed the seedlings . . . or a fire broke out in some neighborhood and left the poor homeless, or if a storm in the Black Sea lasted two or three weeks and held up the provisions ships, or if the terrible news [arrived] that "our lads" had been defeated at the world's end and the mothers wore black — who was to blame?
>
> Who else but the atheists! If I had not annoyed the Immortals with my philosophy, would they have visited the plague of 430 B.C. upon us? But I wasn't philosophizing then. If the son of Kleinias and his group did not smash the heads of the Hermidoi instead of breaking yours (you who sought after glories!) would we have suffered the Disaster of Sicily?
>
> . . . Thus with my atheism and betrayal I benefited, more than my share, country and religion, [and] all of those who are nourished from the breasts of those great ideas! Politicians,

18. That he feels akin to Socrates is unmistakable. Without keeping this in mind the reader would not understand Chapter III, paragraphs 20-23, in which Socrates abuses a vicious and corrupt military man. "Kyr Thodore, why are you such filth?" he asks the staff officer who, stunned, makes no reply at first, then laughs, attempting to disguise his feeling by taking the comment as a joke. "Mind you," the officer thinks, "I'm going to get you when you least expect it." Obviously, Varnalis is here referring to Theodore Pangalos, an important leader in the Revolutionary Government, who condemned the Six to death and who, in 1925, put an end to the Greek Republic by a military coup. Among the many other backward steps Pangalos's regime was responsible for was the sacking of numerous professors and teachers, among them Alexandros Delmouzos, Panaghis Lorenzatos, Nicholas Bees, Haralambos Theodoridis, Yiannis Apostolakis, and Varnalis himself. See pp. 55-56.

priests, teachers found me responsible for every incompetence and dishonesty of theirs, every damage from natural causes, every trick of Fate. When I am gone, they'll try to find another Socrates to be baptized an atheist and traitor in the holy baptismal font of public opinion. They need someone like him to throw in the teeth of the maddened mob like a propitiatory victim whenever they are in trouble. . . .

All of you complain that the world has gone bad. Which world? The mountains or the sea? They are not afraid [of you]. The two or three atheists? Get rid of them and everything will improve at once.[19]

But "The True Apology" is also a self-accusation: Socrates, like Varnalis, finds that he is guilty of a belief in the ideal, which he no longer accepts. That is why he demands payment from the state: he has proved that the soul is immortal, that to be unjustly treated is better than to be unjust, and that there should be no punishment for wrong-doing because there is no evil. By promulgating these ideas he has served the state by molding better — that is more pliable — citizens and protected the rulers of the state, "the bandits," from a punishment they deserve.

Thus my philosophy supported the regime of inequality: "the interests of the stronger." Of course, I should not be executed for this. The states of the future will know how to do their job better. Pulpit, school-desk, newspaper, and social club will work consciously to separate the citizens into the well-fed and the foolish and to smooth over the unsmoothable with the [gospel of the] "harmony of the social classes." It was of this harmony that I was first master.[20]

But he is found dangerous to Democracy, which he considers astonishing, for neither is he dangerous, nor do his condemners

19. *Ibid.,* pp. 63-64.
20. *Ibid.,* p. 67.

represent Democracy. "The dangerous, O Athenians, are not judged. They are, instead, worshipped in the manner of *rayahs* or killed by plot." If he were truly dangerous, he would have been stabbed long ago by paid assassins, for no court would have dared try him. On the contrary, if he were dangerous, *he* would have summoned the court. Democracy, it is clear, is on trial, not Socrates, and Democracy is corrupt, the rule of bandits. The Thirty Tyrants at least killed and seized without pretence, he claims, while the "false Democracy" that condemns him is no more than a "disguised tyranny." The Thirty "obstructed freedom of speech and the teaching of rhetoric, whereas you are trying to obstruct freedom of thought and the teaching of philosophy."[21]

"The True Apology" is set squarely in its time, the years between the Asia Minor Disaster and the beginning of the decade of the 1930s. Varnalis's major target is the liberal democracy that in 1929 voted in the "self-named" law, Article Number 4229 (ἰδιώνυμο), which made it a crime to hold ideas that have as an object the overthrow of the social system. This democracy, a Venizelist democracy, obviously did not feel certain enough of itself, the stability of its institutions, or the force of its mandate to allow the freedom of expression or thought that Varnalis demanded. Since he cannot be defeated in argument or bought with bribes, "Socrates" can be dealt with only by craft. Since he is not liable to the ordinary Athenian weaknesses of nepotism, bribery, threat, or blackmail, he must obviously be an agent of a foreign power.

> Of course, I never took my political rights seriously. I never voted: to choose freely which bandit would rob me and which executioner would cut my throat? That's what I told the Sophists so that you would get angry and I would laugh. The

21. *Ibid.,* p. 44.

Sophists got paid very well. . . . Five minae: 52,500 of today's drachmas, which means that their wisdom was worth that much. It's from its price that one understands the value of an item. My poor knowledge I gave away for nothing and no one wanted it. Which means that it was worth nothing. But this meant something else. Some enemy of yours must have been paying me for me to insist on forcing this poor knowledge on you, in danger of my life. Propaganda! The Slavs were paying me to dismantle the idealistic machinery of the State! For me to be able to make the all-encompassing wisdom of the Sophists look ridiculous did not mean that I was right, merely that I was more clever and aggressive. I could make black, white. A sign of the times. . . . Because with the various changes of regime and betrayals you befouled every sense of justice, you wanted to put the blame on me. I, with my teachings and my ridicule, sapped every confidence in the laws within the souls of the citizens.[22]

"The True Apology" cannot be seen as anything but a show-trial in which a scapegoat, Socrates-Varnalis, confesses his errors in believing, and teaching a belief, in a bourgeois democracy he knew was corrupt and masked the tyranny of the stronger class over the weaker, a tyranny based upon an illusion to which he himself had once subscribed. In exposing himself, he exposed Athenian democracy, a democracy that in the name of freedom of thought and of speech was condemning him to death, a democracy that gained its mandate from the people, the *laos,* the mass which it had, according to him, kept drugged by religion, school, the press, and social organizations.

With "The True Apology of Socrates," Varnalis took a hallowed figure from the Greek tradition and, in contrast to the idealized version promoted by the aristocratic and conservative

22. *Ibid.,* p. 54.

Plato, presented the reader with a materialist turncoat who confesses his role as a propagandist for the regime and who decides to give the hypocrites who judge him a piece of his mind before he dies. With this device Varnalis is able to condemn the liberal democracy for the disastrous Asia Minor Expedition as well as show his contempt for the "mob" that returned the Populists with such a stunning majority. The democracy that condemns him is little better than the Thirty Tyrants. At least *they* were sincere. That he places this unmistakable thrust against what he considers the worst aspects of post-Disaster Greek society – by which time the championing of an uncompromising vernacular had been abandoned by the non-literary bourgeoisie and thus awarded as a gift to the Left – in a brilliantly comic and racy demotic, which could not fail to infuriate his "judges" and confirm their worst suspicions, is proof of Varnalis's happy inspiration.

"The Diary of Penelope" is an all-out attack on Greek society which again reinterprets an image hallowed in the Greek tradition, the modest, faithful wife of Odysseus.[23] Queen Penelope, left in Ithaca by her royal husband, who has gone off to plunder Troy, is faced with the problem of keeping her kingdom stable and secure. The choice of subject matter is again suited to Varnalis's genius, for it permits him to discuss issues of statecraft in the legendary era of the Greek heroic age by using the principles of historical materialism.

As in "The True Apology of Socrates," the Greece is a contemporaneous one. The fact that Varnalis, again consciously using anachronisms and puns, is in the direct linguistic tradition of the pioneer demoticists, however, is more clearly evident here because of the employment of Alexandros Pallis's devices to render

23. "To Imerologio tis Pinelopis," in *Pezos Logos*. The novel was first published in 1946.

in neo-Hellenic terms the many Homeric elements. To the pure genealogy of his linguistic descent, Varnalis adds ridicule and satire of the "hallowed Greek tradition" by overturning the unexamined interpretations of the past: the Trojan War is an aggressive, imperialistic venture on the part of the Greeks and Lenio, middle-aged and sexually starved, very conveniently provides her kin and the other Greeks with a pretext for the profitable war by forcing the young and modest Paris to "abduct" her from her repellent husband to Troy.

"We'll not only reclaim your honor," Menelaus tells the malleable Greek people, who have been convinced by him that it is they who have been insulted by his wife's abduction,

> [but] we'll enrich you, besides. Unending fields and meadows; rivers with golden sand; caves full of pebbles; herds of innumerable cows and horses, flocks of sheep. Beautiful, fat women who do nothing all day but bathe, eat sherbet, and suck gum-drops, and go wild for foreign men. They pull them by their sleeves into their rooms.... Every one of you will become a sultan with his own seraglio and his own harem.... That's how we'll save Greek civilization, which is endangered, and save ourselves, too.[24]

The most unmistakable reference to the Asia Minor Expedition occurs when "Agamemnon I" speaking directly to "the people of Asia," promises them all of the wealth of their "foreign king and nobles" if they will help the Greeks.

> We did not come to your land as conquerors, but as liberators. We know that you, too, are Greeks and our brothers. Your ancestor was Tefkros, a fine broth of a Cretan with breeches, a waistband, and a black kerchief on his head. We have the same gods and the same language. But over the centuries you forgot your noble lineage. We've come to make you Greeks again.

24. *Ibid.*, p. 114.

From slaves and stepchildren of Priam we're going to make you free and pure sons of Deukalion. We'll rescue you from the clutches of your evil stepmother, Troy, and fling you into the warm embrace of your real Mother, the Mother of God [Θεομάνας], Greece![25]

The significance of this view of history is that it is told to Penelope by Varnalis's version of Homer, a minstrel willing to pervert his poetic talents in order to serve the aristocracy. In relating to the corrupt Penelope the "true" events of the Trojan War, which he himself has glorified, Homer — who is no more than a cynical propagandist of royalist values — presents himself to her as the perfect agent for the improvement and promotion of her "image," as the "deification of womanly sense and faith". [26] He deliberately tells lies because he believes art should be used in the service of the ruling class, whose members want to disguise their motives and ennoble their actions and statements in order to be glorified by men of the future. Art, for Homer, is merely a means of inculcating values of subservience so that the state may be kept stable. "If for one moment I denude war and its royal heroes of beauty and ideals," Homer says, "there will be nothing left."[27]

For this reason, Homer chooses Thersites — the ugly, outspoken, and often punished opponent of the "establishment" of his time — as the enemy of all he and Penelope hold dear. It is a non-Homeric Thersites who complicates Penelope's plan to play off the fifty nobles (her eventual suitors and, each in his turn, her lovers) against the *laos* that, pliable as ever, allows itself to be manipulated. "The mass of the *laos,* the pure *laos,*" Penelope

25. *Ibid.,* p. 147. The differing outcomes of the two expeditions obviously compel Varnalis to subdue the rest of the story.

26. *Ibid.,* p. 82.

27. *Ibid.,* p. 137. One wonders how much Varnalis had Kazantzakis's *Modern Odyssey* in mind when he wrote "The Diary of Penelope."

notes in her Diary, helped the police and the nobles subdue "this madman." She learns from an informer that Thersites is "not a local man [but] a foreign agent. Always thrown in jail and never learns any sense."[28] But Thersites, "a mason, an atheist, a Bulgar" cannot be subdued; he constantly reappears, inciting the "slaves" to revolt, a revolt that is drowned in blood. Homer tells Penelope of Odysseus's plan, before the sacking of Troy, to crush the pacifist mood of the Greek army by first seizing "their leader, Thersites." But Penelope stops him; there must be some mistake. She had already hanged this troublemaker. This is another one, Homer tells her. "Every traitor and anarchist is called Thersites."[29]

Before the novel's unfortunate lapse at the conclusion (to be discussed later), Varnalis brilliantly substitutes the Homeric resolution with the arrival of the "false-Odysseus." The "real" one, the "one turned to marble," never arrives. The pseudo-Odysseus, a boar Circe kept in her barn, learned that there was more to life

28. *Ibid.,* p. 114.
29. *Ibid.,* p. 150. The accusation that Thersites is a "Bulgar" can be found on p. 130. It is the "slaves" Thersites speaks to, never the "laos," for the people are beyond hope. "Laos" is used in the pejorative sense throughout "The True Apology of Socrates" and most of "The Diary of Penelope." At the precise moment when "The Diary" begins its unfortunate fall from credibility – in the parable-like section when Penelope and the Pseudo-Odysseus find themselves in the war between the Wolves (Nazi Germany) and the Jackals (Great Britain) – the "laos" is immediately invested with good qualities. The emotional content of "laos" in Varnalis, however, remains pejorative, since throughout his great work "laos" and "plithos" – on which "false Democracy" is always built – have similar connotations. Though a generalization of this sort deserves, and could easily be provided with, more thorough textual proof, "laos" in the work of Varnalis remains easily tricked, foolish, ignorant of its own interests, quiescent under tyranny, and easily manipulated by demagogues. This is clearly a legacy of the events of 1920 and 1922. The good people, mistreated but always defiant, are not the "laos" but the "sklavoi." It is they who deserve freedom. "Laos" obviously changes its connotations because of the heroic resistance of the Greek people in 1940. See Chapter Five.

from his surprised companions, the men of Odysseus who had been turned into hogs by his mistress. In the confusion caused by Odysseus's possession of the herb-charm ($\mu\tilde{\omega}\lambda\upsilon$) that rendered him impervious to Circe's magic, the pseudo-Odysseus was turned into a man by mistake along with the others. Though he will always bear with him a barnyard odor, the boar-man is the "messiah" Penelope has waited years for, the tyrant who will finally bring peace to Ithaca and keep the troublesome island orderly and secure. "The less an enslaved people comprehend and the more pig-like they become, the happier they are. Upon this first axiom I shall build our kingdom. If Thersites were present he would say: 'Struggle to break your chains and devour the Wolves.' That's why I shall hang all the Thersiteses."[30]

Given the goals of the false but hoped-for Odysseus, who intends to realize both the "dream of so many generations, the dream of a Great Ithaca" as well as the "miracle of the Third Ithacan Civilization," the reader understands that Varnalis has succeeded, to his own satisfaction, at least, in equating Venizelist liberalism and the fascism of John Metaxas.

Had Greek society changed so much after the Disaster of 1922, or was it rather that for the first time the Greek writer — and at this point one must insist, *the writer of prose* — could use it as a target for his attacks? Greek society had certainly changed considerably as a result of the Disaster, but more importantly, the Greek writers themselves had changed. They were liberated by the Asia Minor Disaster from the patriotic bias that the ideas of national expansion and progress had always imposed on them. It is in order to prove this point that we have described the work of Varnalis at such length; in him we have the perfect example of a man who turned with brilliant ridicule against everything he had believed in before the Asia Minor Expedition and Disaster —

30. *Ibid.,* p. 174.

against shallow patriotism, idealism, and the unconscious belief in racial superiority, against all the supports of a tradition-oriented society he later considered characterized by hypocrisy, inertia, and greed. The character type of Thersites is none other than the Marxist whose inability to stop himself from expressing the unpopular truth turns the fury of the state and the people against him. Thersites and Socrates are fictional representations of the Greek intellectual who at one time identified himself and his values with those of Greek society. Because the rest of society continued to believe in these ideas — even after they were shown to be no more than illusions — the writers were able to see the men and women around them for the innocents, the smug fools, or the hypocrites they were.

But what happened to a writer whose primary interest was philosophical or religious rather than social and political? Into what ideological dead-ends was a writer led whose vision was a heroic one in a time of appalling defeat and demoralization, whose instincts led him toward metaphysics or theology in a time when materialism seemed to pose the most challenging questions and offer the most interesting solutions to these questions, a writer whose demands for an affirmative world view were constantly overwhelmed by a nihilism that permeated the world about him? What happened, in other words, to Nikos Kazantzakis as a result of the Asia Minor Disaster?

What for Varnalis was a reorientation of vast proportions, a complete reversal of philosophy in the space of three years (1919-1922) was for Nikos Kazantzakis a disorientation that lasted in his creative life until the Greco-Italian War and the German Occupation, during which he wrote *Zorba*. It is not the province of this study to decide whether or not his disorientation was a totally negative one, for it is in this crucial time that Kazantzakis began the years of exile during which he wrote the travel books that range in value from the interesting to the profound, the many poetic dramas whose value cannot be considered as anything but minimal, the significant statement of philosophy entitled *Saviors of God: Askitiki,* and the major work he claimed should represent him after his death, the modern sequel to *The Odyssey.* It is during this period, moreover, that Kazantzakis tried heroically to become an "European" writer by publishing *Toda Raba* and *Le Jardin des Rochers,* and attempting *Kapétan Elia* and *Mon Père* in the French language, works that did not win for him the fame he had hoped. As brilliantly described for us by Pandelis Prevelakis in *The Poet and the Poem of the Odyssey* (1958) and by Kazantzakis himself in *Letters to Galateia* (1958) and *Four Hundred Letters to Pandelis Prevelakis* (1965), these are his years of torment and alienation, of poverty in exile, of sporadic returns to Greece, of bitterness at the failure of his marriage with Galateia, of a sojourn through a bleak, interwar Europe that could only impress on him the efficacy of a Marxism that he was by temperament incapable of accepting.

But how did Nikos Kazantzakis come to this? The early years of the century saw him living with, and after June 1911 married to, the talented and attractive Galateia Alexiou; he was friendly with a circle of people who would eventually become famous and distinguished, and assumed a fairly important position, not only in literature and education, with frequent publications in *Noumas* and in newspapers as well as through commissions for translations of school texts, but in public life as well, where he had strong connections – as a Cretan – in the liberal establishment of Venizelos, with whom he does not seem to have had a smooth relationship.

These connections can be seen in his appointment by Venizelos as Director, then General Director, on May 8, 1919, of the newly formed Ministry of Welfare. Two months later, Kazantzakis left on his first mission, the repatriation of what he later estimated as 150,000 Greeks from the Caucasus. With a number of aides (including George Zorbas, the model for the character who would bring Kazantzakis back to the novel in Greek), he went to the Soviet Union, reporting to Venizelos in Paris during the latter part of August in a meeting he himself described as "cold, abrupt, hostile," then returned to Greece — Macedonia and Thrace — in order to oversee the establishment of the refugees.[31]

The reasons for the expulsion of the Greeks are never made totally clear, but the motive on the part of the Soviet government probably had something to do with Venizelos's dispatch of Greek army units, in conjunction with other military forces of the Entente, to crush the Red Army after the October Revolution. While his contacts with Venizelos are characterized by coldness, Nikos Kazantzakis at this time is still part of that establishment, though his intellectual regard for and friendship with Ion Dragoumis, an enemy of Venizelos, would certainly have acted as an irritant in his role as member of the Liberal Government.[32]

The assassination of Ion Dragoumis on July 31, 1920, by members of the Security Battalion of the Greek Army, still a Venizelos stronghold at that time, was a major shock to him, and the electoral defeat of Venizelos three months later left him

31. *Tetrakosia Grammata ston Pandeli Prevelaki,* "Biographical Material" (Athens, 1965), pp. 10-11. Some of the ideas expressed about Kazantzakis in this chapter have been seconded by Peter Bien in the course of a number of conversations I had with him while both of us were writing our books, he completing his *Kazantzakis and the Linguistic Revolution in Greek Literature* (Princeton, 1972) and I writing *Disaster and Fiction.*

32. Elli Alexiou in *Yia Na Yinei Megalos* (Athens, 1966), p. 88, says that Nikos Kazantzakis, owing to Galateia's insistence, was not sent to the front in 1912-1913 but given a position in Venizelos's private office. At that time, she writes, Venizelos respected and liked the couple, though he later grew cold to Kazantzakis, perhaps influenced by his nephew, Saridakis, who hated Kazantzakis and called him "the disgrace of Crete." Kazantzakis's father, Michalis, was an anti-Venizelist and a follower of Prince George, the husband of the important Freudian psychiatrist, Marie Bonaparte, to whom Kazantzakis dedicated *The Last Temptation of Christ.*

without a means of livelihood. But it was not only these events that served to alienate him from Greece, for his numerous trips without Galateia were symptoms of a crisis in their relationship of a basic and irrevocable sort. The "letters to Galateia," later published in book form, document his loneliness, his inability to live with his wife, his growing interest in Marxism, his estrangement from Angelos Sikelianos and from the circle (composed of Markos Avyeris, Galateia's second husband, Kostas Varnalis, and other Marxists) that his wife began to frequent more and more; they expose, in effect, his estrangement from Greece.

What was seen in Varnalis to be an immediately creative reorientation was in Kazantzakis a great disorientation that began at once. The value of the poetic dramas, the travel books, the French novels, *The Saviors of God,* and *The Modern Odyssey* may not be disputed by their admirers, but no one can seriously maintain that the fame Kazantzakis had secured for himself would have been established without the extraordinary novels he produced at the end of his life.

The letters he sent to Galateia begin on November 27, 1920, and end sometime after March 1924. During these years Kazantzakis saw the ravages of postwar Europe, lived through the destructive monetary inflation in the Weimar Republic, met the numerous Communist intellectuals with whom he became friendly, experienced the skin disease that caused his face to swell hideously,[33] and, from afar, read of the Asia Minor Disaster. It was during this period that he felt the earth turning under his feet and "liberated" himself from the "old Kazantzakis," who was rooted in the Greek-centered universe, to become the "new Kazantzakis," the wanderer who roamed over the world, like the

33. See *The Saviors of God,* ed. and trans. Kimon Friar (New York, 1960), pp. 6-11, and *Epistoles pros tin Galateia (Letters to Galateia),* Letters No. 14 and No. 33.

Odysseus he was to write 33,333 verses about, at home nowhere. Those who know his work know him best as the novelist, the "third" Kazantzakis, whereas at this time the "second" Kazantzakis is becoming better known. Few know the early years of the writer, for they are shrouded in a mist that is pierced only occasionally by biographical studies like the valuable though one-sided *He Wanted to Become Great* (1966), by Galateia's younger sister, Elli Alexiou; by the poet Nikiphoros Vrettakos's excellent *Nikos Kazantzakis: His Struggle and his Work* (1960); and by Peter Bien's careful *Kazantzakis and the Linguistic Revolution in Greek Literature* (1972).

The "first" and "third" Kazantzakis, though influenced by Nietzschean nihilism, were, if not ultimately affirmative (because of an equal belief in Bergson's *élan vital*), still grappling with issues that might have granted him peace and liberation. The "second" Kazantzakis lives in a welter of confusion and personal despair, hating a defeated and chaotic Greece with the hatred only an idealist could muster.

"The news reaching us here about Greece is frightful," he writes to Galateia from Berlin on September 9, 1922. "Will the miserable Greeks get some sense into them now?" he wonders. "Will this catastrophe mark the beginning of a rebirth?" It is in this spirit that he accepts the fateful news "with gratitude," for he feels that it would have been "disastrous for Greece if the current regime had gained the victory" in Asia Minor, since "it would have established" the power of the Populists, whom he considers dishonorable "and would have drugged the people, who want nothing more." Because of "catastrophe, Russia and Germany were reborn," while through triumph in the Great War, France "arrived at the peak of dishonor, because that victory merely strengthened the capitalist regime that governs her." Though he could not have known as yet the frightful human cost of the defeat he hoped would be instructive for his countrymen, he concludes his thought by considering that "the bitter trial of our Greece today increases our responsibility and makes even more indispensable a strong propaganda" for Marxism.[34]

He continues to reveal a passion against Greece and the Greeks that must be tempered in the reader by the insight that these are the first impressions of a man rebuffed by everyone, including the wife to whom he writes, and that the letters he sends her are not meant by him for publication but are passionately felt thoughts expressed in the heat of the moment about historical events over which he had absolutely no control. Anyone reading these quotations from the letters as only outbursts of "hatred" will miss half of their significance, for the other half is permeated with an all-consuming love for Greece. No matter where he travels or what ideas he seizes upon for the moment, it is Greece only that consumes him. Eight days previous to this, on September 1, he had written to Galateia about *Nova Graecia,* a periodical he considered publishing in order to "enlighten as much as possible the [intellectual] darkness of Greece."[35]

A month later, after the military coup that removed the Populists, he instinctively senses the magnitude of the events in Asia Minor by unconsciously comparing them to that other "Disaster" that submerged the Greeks for centuries, the Fall of Constantinople. He says:

If the Greeks again disappear, because they are unworthy, then blessed be the hour of their disappearance. Let them empty that bright corner of the sea they befoul and let others come to honor the name of man. I don't know, but for good or bad, I have surpassed the borders of the Greek homeland. Yes, I am of the Greek race and its decline is my decline — because the

34. *Epistoles pros tin Galateia,* ed. Aris Diktaios (Athens, 1958), pp. 77-78, Letter No. 32.
35. *Ibid.,* pp. 71-72, Letter No. 30.

elements which it affords and to which I am limited [as an artist] in working with on earth, are decadent. But I feel that our Cretan stock is not Greek. The Cretans, of course, are also frightful, but [only] because they have been corrupted by the Greek wretchedness. Deep down they are sturdy, barbaric, pure, and creative. I am battling to escape.[36]

Influenced at this time by Oswald Spengler's *The Decline of the West,* Kazantzakis sees the Asia Minor Disaster and the crisis of postwar Europe as proofs of an inescapable decadence from which he cannot hope to be spared, at least not until he begins dissociating himself from "the Greeks" and dwells more and more on the "intermixture" of barbaric races of which he believes the Cretans to be products.

Greece — the Greek state — had been unable to succeed in realizing the dreams it had dreamed, and it was the Greek people themselves who were to blame. The Greece of Kazantzakis is "a few, very few people" and "the value of Greece is comparable to their value." The mass, the *plethos,* "is used only as ciphers are used in arithmetical figures."[37] Those few, "those who are alive" (he uses Ion Dragoumis's phrase, ὅσοι ζωντανοί) will show who they are. In the midst of this overwhelming historical event, Kazantzakis nourishes a secret hope that somehow the Greeks will be improved by their suffering. He condones the execution of the Six, unhappy only that "the people" did not have a hand in the killing but needed a Plastiras "to utter the brave word." After all, he thinks, "It's better that we die performing a tragedy than live playing an operetta." It was only in this way, perhaps, that the Greeks ("terror is always useful for such a people") would be made aware "that something important has occurred." Since "the loss of Smyrna, Constantinople, and Thrace" did not seem to

36. *Ibid.,* pp. 104-105, Letter No. 41.
37. *Ibid.,* p. 86, Letter No. 35.

matter very much to them, perhaps the fact that "their shepherds" were "killed like this, like dogs, will astonish and frighten them."[38]

Greece is a *lost cause*[39] because the Greek mentality cannot function within the confines of a state machinery, and is in fact crushed by it. In this comment he reveals a suspicion of organization that is evident throughout his literary work, poetry as well as fiction, in which "the letter killeth but the spirit giveth life." We need only think of the concept of the Church in *Christ Recrucified*, of cenobitic monasticism in *Zorba* and *Saint Francis* (*The Poor Man of God*), and of civilization as a general force in *The Modern Odyssey* and *The Last Temptation of Christ.* "The virtues of the Greek race are expressed only outside the governmental machinery (κρατικά καθεστώτα). As a state functionary, the Greek is terrible; as an Odysseus, wandering, working, trading, thinking, without his own governmental system, like the Jews, he is unique in the world."[40]

He commends Galateia for refusing to sign a protest against the Turkish slaughters of Greeks in Asia Minor, believing that "the dishonorable conduct of the Greeks" in Anatolia "was equal to that of the Turks." As a humanist, "interested in Man without [national] labels," he thinks that man, "in Asia Minor was dishonored by both Greeks and Turks."[41] Accordingly, two months later, while he is writing *The Saviors of God,* he declines his wife's suggestion that he return to Greece to press for the return of the refugees to Asia Minor. He does not feel "the inner need" to do anything of this sort.

A civilization is always born from horrible events like this, mortal uprootings. If we must state a goal: *we must transmute*

38. *Ibid.,* pp. 114-115, Letter No. 44.
39. *Ibid.,* p. 111, Letter No. 43.
40. *Ibid.,* p. 140, Letter No. 49.
41. *Ibid.,* p. 97, Letter No. 38.

matter into spirit. This misfortune of the Greeks will bring, after many generations, one of two results: either the destruction of this Hellenism or the sounding, the flowering, from the blood and tears, of a Cry. Both are good. We must break the easy habits, to deny ourselves happiness is an indispensable prerequisite of every ascent.

You will say: you are far away and view with insensitivity the humans who are being lost, not seeing the dishonor, the hunger, the streets full of human wrecks. Yes, I am far away and that is why I see a broader radius with greater clarity. If we allow ourselves to be led astray by the daily details, the blood-splattered images, it would be impossible for us to place this great adventure of the Greek race in a time dimension greater than that of our short lives. I see all of these waves of people outside of my time, beyond my heart's cry, and I know that Greece has always been able to shoot out the blossom of art and intellect from such violent movements back and forth and from such admixtures of Europe and Asia.[42]

The crisis the Greeks went through during 1920-1922 did not decisively reorient Nikos Kazantzakis as it did Kostas Varnalis because there was in the Cretan's psyche a need for a code of conduct and an unshakable belief in the primacy of the spirit that no inadequacy in the Greeks themselves could submerge. If in his greatest works Varnalis reveals such a complex attitude toward the very *laos* that he, as a Communist, would look to for leadership, we must not demand greater consistency from Nikos Kazantzakis. His belief in the spirit, in the ideal, was only aggravated by what he considered the inadequacy of the clay, the "matter" from which bourgeois man was moulded.

It is precisely during the last months of Asia Minor Hellenism that Kazantzakis began to suffer from the skin disease — a grotesque swelling of the face, accompanied by pus sores — that

42. *Ibid.,* pp. 128-129, Letter No. 47.

Wilhelm Stekel, who by chance happened to see him in the Opera House in Vienna — had diagnosed as "the saint's disease."[43] That this great writer, who tried desperately to be a Marxist in the era during which "the decline of the West" was a foregone conclusion, should be embarrassed, in Stekel's words, by "a body that was suffering from a remorse of spirit" was an irony too profound to be merely bitter.

The Saviors of God (and *The Modern Odyssey,* which follows it), presents a strategy by which man is to free himself from illusion. Written three months after the Asia Minor Disaster, between December 1922 and March 1923, it is a credo whose expression was meant to mark Nikos Kazantzakis's "battle to escape" from the limitations of nationality and the falsehood of hope that had confused and misled him during the first forty years of his life. Twenty days after finishing his "credo," he wrote to Galateia: "I've been a purist, a nationalist, a demoticist, a scientist, a poet, a socialist, a religious fanatic ($\theta\rho\eta\sigma\kappa\omega\mu\alpha\nu\dot{\eta}\varsigma$) an atheist, an esthete — and none of these can now trick me."[44] The Asia Minor Disaster proved to him that Greek nationalism was a snare. The countless rebellions of the Cretans against the Turk to join with a Greece that everyone had been confident would eventually take her rightful place in the family of nations, succeeded after frightful cost of life, not in liberating the unredeemed Greeks who lived in the borderlands of Digenis Akritas, but in Kazantzakis's mind, only in "corrupting" the Cretan stock.

The "meta-communist Credo," as he called it in Dimitris Glinos's journal, *Renaissance,* is also a confession of his inability to accept the most basic precepts of Marxism. As "the first lyrical attempt, the first cry" of meta-communism, it comes only five

43. See Kimon Friar's "Introduction" to *The Saviors of God,* pp. 3-11. It is in Letter No. 14, pp. 23-25, in *Epistoles pros tin Galateia* that Kazantzakis first mentions his illness.
44. *Ibid.,* p. 184, Letter No. 62. Dated April 10, 1923.

years after the Bolshevik Revolution, in the very storm center of Soviet Russia's initially creative period. Communism had hardly been established when Kazantzakis, declaring his requirement for a *meta*-communism, found the need to "express the spiritual agony and hopes of a communist circle" in Germany "that could not breathe comfortably in the narrow, backward, materialistic attitudes of the Communist Idea."[45]

Varnalis was consistent. He accepted Marxism, rejecting philosophical idealism, and accepted materialism as well, while Kazantzakis, finding his old theories and tenuous personal adjustments shattered by historical events, tried to adopt "communism" by rejecting its materialistic basis. It is this tension between the ideal and the real, between the realm of ideas – to which his commitment is never questioned – and the realm of matter – which he perpetually wants to transmute into spirit – that is the basis of Kazantzakis's great creative achievement.

This philosophical tension is rarely presented dramatically in his writing, not even in his theatrical works, which he paradoxically did not want considered as performable drama but as something to be read; on the contrary, this tension is always stated, seldom shown in action. The plot of the great majority of his works rarely develops through direct confrontation. The heroes seem to move in a world of events as personages who are more spectators than active participants, viewing the brute matter of the world and their selves as so many obstacles to be surpassed before their transubstantiation can be effected. Even in *Zorba* (written 1941-1943), which marks the beginning of a direct confrontation with the world, one sees few direct conflicts between the "I" and the world about him, which "the professor" seems passively to accept. It is only with *Christ Recrucified,*

45. "Salvatores Dei; Askitiki," in *Anagennisi,* 1, Nos. 11-12, July-August (1927), p. 599.

which is set, significantly, in Asia Minor, that Kazantzakis extricates the complex of tensions and motives from within himself and places them in a setting where they can lock in a life and death struggle. This novel will be discussed thoroughly later, but for a number of reasons it is only in the novel form and it is only after the Greco-Italian war that we find conflict expressed dramatically.

This tension is most clearly found in *The Saviors of God,* for it was written at a time when the issues Kazantzakis had lived with all his life demanded immediate expression. "Kazantzakis had been considering [writing] the book eight to ten years earlier," Pandelis Prevelakis notes, continuing that he found "proof of this in his Notebooks that were found among his effects."[46] But why had the book not been written then? If we are to accept *The Saviors of God* for what it is, a statement of liberation from "ego, race, mankind, earth, theory and action, God — all these phantoms made of loam and brain,"[47] we see that Kazantzakis, though he may have conceived his credo, was not ready to *believe* in it himself until he had actually freed himself — or thought he had — from "ego" and "race," to say nothing of the others.

At the time, his domestic life with Galateia was, if not "happy," at least outwardly conventional, while the Greek nation in 1913-1915 was progressing to the point where its ideals — focused in the Megale Idea — seemed about to be realized. Kazantzakis, however, might still have produced his credo by ignoring all these affirmative "obstacles" and concentrating on the ideas he had distilled from books — Nietzsche, Bergson, Spengler. What he says in *The Saviors of God,* though it may have existed in 1913-1915 like a seed beneath the snow, could not be

---

46. Prevelakis, *O Poiitis kai to Poiima tis Odysseias* (Athens, 1958), p. 300, fn., 101. See also Kazantzakis, *Tetrakosia Grammata,* pp., 12-13 of "Biographical Material," and p. *xlvi.*
47. Friar, "Introduction" to *The Saviors of God,* pp. 127-128.

expressed without being out of time and place – in other words, without being impossible psychologically. Otherwise, why was the book written in a matter of four months, between December 1922 and March 1923?

Quite simply, the conditions were ripe. The assassination of his good friend, Ion Dragoumis, had embittered him; the strained relationship between "the disgrace of Crete" and Venizelos had been severed by the shocking and humiliating electoral defeat in 1920. But this severance was by no means a liberation. Its effects were devastating for the couple: Kazantzakis himself was no longer at the Ministry of Welfare, their friends were no longer at the Ministry of Education, for which he and Galateia wrote and translated many educational texts; Elli Alexiou, Galateia's sister, was out of a job because the orphanage school where she taught was closed down. His father-in-law, Stylianos Alexiou, became ill coincidentally at this time. Even Vasos Daskalakis, Elli's fiancé and the translator of Knut Hamsun, serving with the Bureau of Military Affairs in Paris, ran the risk of losing his attractive post. Elli was reduced to seeking the aid of the bereaved mistress of Ion Dragoumis, Marika Kotopouli, whose considerable prestige with the new government had Daskalakis reinstated in Paris for another year. It was as Elli's chaperone to Paris that Kazantzakis began his long sojourn away from Greece.[48] He was without a livelihood. His marital relationship – since 1912, in fact – had been undergoing the strain of Galateia's affair with Markos Avyeris. He was now alone, a self-willed "émigré" in a chaotic Germany, and he witnessed from afar the horror of the Asia Minor Disaster. What better time than this to write the credo that had been tormenting him?

38. We are living in a critical, violent moment of history; an entire world is crashing down, another has not yet been

48. Alexiou, *Yia Na Yinei Megalos,* pp. 119-129.

born. Our epoch is not a moment of equilibrium in which refinement, reconciliation, peace and love might be fruitful virtues.

39. We live in a moment of dread assault, we stride over our enemies, we stride over our lagging friends, we are imperiled in the midst of chaos, we drown. We can no longer fit into old virtues and hopes, into old theories and actions.

40. The wind of devastation is blowing; this is the breath of our God today; let us be carried away in its tide! The wind of devastation is the first dancing surge of the creative rotation. It blows over every head and every city, it knocks down houses and ideas, it passes over desolate wastes, and it shouts: "Prepare yourselves! War! It's War!"[49]

With *The Saviors of God,* Kazantzakis sought not merely to express the complexity of feelings he had always had about man's existence as a fusion of matter and spirit in historical time, but also to *order* these feelings, to see clearly where in himself there lurked contradictions, to identify these contradictions, and to take an emotional position on them.

For Kazantzakis the most crucial issues in his private life and in his art are those of paternity, of authority — spiritual and political — and of God, Who is related to all of these. If God, viewed either as a Person or as a force in history, does not exist, then human suffering is meaningless and human aspiration doomed from the start.[50] The strategy by which this despair can be made creative is for the "hero," another Sisyphus, to trick other, lesser men by his affirmation that life has a purpose, that man can *save* God by identifying with Him, by *being* Him, in fact, while constantly keeping in mind the "great, sublime, and terrifying secret: *That Even This One Does Not Exist.*"[51]

49. Friar, "Introduction" to *The Saviors of God,* p. 114.
50. See my essay, "Kazantzakis and the Meaning of Suffering," *Northwest Review,* Winter 1963.
51. Friar, "Introduction" to *The Saviors of God,* p. 131.

Philosophically, is the world illusory then? Is that what Kazantzakis really believes? The fact is that Kazantzakis believed many things in his life and their contradiction with one another provided him with the creative tension that not even the 33,333 lines of *The Modern Odyssey* could resolve. In denying the finality of matter, affirming throughout his life the superiority of the spirit, yet unable — because of the human condition — to prove the existence of God, Kazantzakis was tortured by his conception of history, the tragic interplay of matter and spirit. Matter is the blood, the tears, the muck, the soil in which the seed of the rose, the spirit, is nurtured so that it may bloom. If He exists at all, God *is* in suffering, at the point where matter and spirit prove in their loss of equilibrium that they are enemies. The fact that he needed to wait until December 1922 to chart out the terrifying dimensions of his confusions is proof that Kazantzakis felt the impact of the Asia Minor Disaster.

4 The Generation of the 1930s: The Break from the Greek Ethographic Tradition and the Establishment of the Social Novel

In the absence of definitive or even authoritative works of criticism on The Generation of the 1930s, the present writer is apt to be accused of discussing the members of this group from a point of view too convenient for his thesis. Rather than run this risk, it might be wiser to discuss this classification, cite the difficulties inherent in too loose an interpretation of the category, define the qualities I consider characteristic of the writers of this group, and explain my reasons for selecting some and not others to represent this Generation.

The category itself, despite its frequently arbitrary and inaccurate usage, is for historical reasons a valid one, and not merely a mechanical classification of writers who were born around the turn of the century and who published their first serious literary efforts during or just before the decade of the 1930s. Minor confusions, however, appear once a critic begins to look more carefully at the Generation as it is discussed in various works of literary scholarship. For example, Linos Politis in *History of*

Modern Greek Literature (1969)[1] considers Fotis Kontoglou and Stratis Doukas as members of the Generation of the 1930s while they, on the strength of having published in the previous decade, consider themselves members of the Generation of the 1920s, a category only George Valetas, among Greek literary historians, seems to mention in his *Short History of Modern Greek Literature* (1966). Then again, both Politis and Andreas Karandonis, in his *Prose Writers and Prose Works of the Generation of the 1930s* (1962), include Tasos Athanasiadis in the generation on the strength of his having published a critical work on Fotos Politis in 1936, though his major literary effort does not begin until the World War II Occupation years.

In this chapter, we shall discuss, as members of the Generation, only creative writers in prose, considering the many significant scholar-critics and poets as not being within the province of this study. Aside from the dates of birth and first publication, the category as employed in this chapter will tend to emphasize those writers of fiction whose primary concern is the description of the social, political, and moral realities of Greece in the interwar period, that is, between 1922 and 1940. That these writers continued to publish important work after the Second World War is beyond dispute; by focusing our attention on those who reflect in their imaginative prose the interwar period, however, we hope to distinguish them from writers of the same Generation whose political, social, and moral concerns emerged in important fiction after World War II in issues that became critical then, or whose major work exhibits only a minimal interest in reflecting the tensions of their specific historical era. Writers whose important work was published after World War II are Melpo Axioti (Athens, 1905-1975), Yiannis Beratis (Athens, 1904-1968), Menelaus Loundemis (Eastern Thrace, 1912-) and Pandelis Prevelakis

---

1. Not to be confused with the considerably expanded and much more valuable work published in English in 1973. See the Bibliography.

(Rethymno, Crete 1909-). On the other hand, the works of men like George Delios (Thessaloniki, 1897-), Nikos Gavriel Pentzikis (Thessaloniki, 1908-), Yiannis Skarimbas (Akrata, 1899-), Stelios Xefloudas (Thessaloniki, 1902-), and Alkiviadis Yianno-poulos (Athens, 1896-) show a greater interest in a personal world than in social and historical analysis.

Since in this study we shall focus on the writers of the Generation who reflect more than the above the social realities of Greece in the interwar period, the author's time and place of birth and the precise date of his first publication are of secondary interest, important only insofar as they reveal his coming of age at a specific time in national history. Accordingly, Stratis Myrivilis (b. Lesbos 1892 –d. Athens 1969), though his first publication, *Red Stories*, occurred in 1915, is a part of the Generation, as is Angelos Terzakis (Nafplion, 1907-), though two short story collections, *The Forgotten* and *Autumnal Symphony*, were published in 1925 and 1929 respectively. Thrasos Kastanakis (b. Constantinople 1901 –d. Paris 1967), though his first novel, *Princes*, was published in 1924; Ilias Venezis (b. Aivalik 1904 –d. Athens 1973), though *Manolis Lekas* was published in 1928; and George Theotokas (b. Constantinople 1906 –d. Athens 1966), though his first work, *Free Spirit*, was published in 1929, are all indisputable members of the Generation of the 1930s because of their abiding concern with Greece in the period between the wars.

Added to these writers should be Loukis Akritas (b. Morfos, Cyprus 1909-d. Athens 1965), Elli Alexiou (Herakleion, Crete 1898-), G. Ambot (Athens, 1906-), Pavlos Floros (Smyrna, 1897-), M. Karagatsis (Athens, 1908-1960), Lilika Nakou (Athens, 1903-), Thanasis Petsalis (Athens 1904-), Kosmas Politis (Athens, 1888-1974), and Tatiana Stavrou (Constantinople, 1899-), all of whom published works of fiction in the 1930s.

To conclude this necessary but rather tiring exercise in classifi-cation, the members of the Generation of the 1930s, with a few exceptions, were born within a decade of each other, and saw the Asia Minor Disaster occur just as they were attaining maturity and before they had entered upon their careers as writers. Many of them were directly involved with the events of 1922, and those who were not viewed the Asia Minor Disaster, nevertheless, as a starting point in their lives and their creative work. They would not, therefore, like Kostas Varnalis and Nikos Kazantzakis struggle to attain a new equilibrium in mid-career. Their imbalance would be an organic one. The earthquake of 1922 had collapsed structures that Varnalis and Kazantzakis had partially built, while the members of the Generation of the 1930s were to erect their own buildings on the fiscal, political, and ideological rubble of the 1920s and 1930s, a scarred landscape they would view as normal. They would "grow up with a shadow on their soul," as Constantine Dimaras characterizes them in his *History of Modern Greek Literature* (1948). Their spirits had been tested, he continues, by poverty and refugee status, while the world about them had been dominated by the disgrace of military rout. Besides confronting literary matters with a great sense of responsibility, with a seriousness at times pedantic but always well-intentioned, this Generation would, Dimaras claims, surpass "the spirit of dissolution" that was its historical legacy by its "passion for synthesis."[2]

As a result of the unsettled conditions, a generation emerged that for the first time in Modern Greek literature thought almost exclusively in terms of the novel. Previous to the 1930s, most of the important writers were poets, dramatists, critics, scholars, or more frequently men whose interests were primarily non-literary but who also wrote novels and short stories as an avocation. There are exceptions to this, of course, but on the whole, fiction

2. Dimaras, *Istoria tis Neoellinikis Logotechnias,* 3rd. ed. (Athens, 1964), p. 467.

was considered a lesser occupation by the men of letters and a greater proportion of their life-work was represented by their more serious concerns for verse or drama. In the Generation of the 1930s, on the contrary, were men and women who, though involved in other professions, considered themselves novelists primarily and whose contribution to the other literary genres was secondary. Aside from minor interests in drama, the essay, travel impressions, poetry, or art criticism, these writers were first and foremost novelists who took their art seriously by carefully revising their work, by reading and comparing themselves to foreign authors, by speculating on the problems of their genre, and by dedicating much time and effort to issues inherent in the novel, that most comprehensive of literary forms. If the term did not denote remuneration for work done — for obvious reasons an impossibility in Greece even today — one could, in short, say that with the Generation of the 1930s there appeared an attitude of *professionalism* on the writer's part toward his fiction.

The quantitative difference between the fiction of the young, who were just beginning to publish, and the writers of previous decades was noticed by Kleon Paraschos as early as 1937. Earlier, he remarks, up to 1920 or even 1925, the writing of serious novels was not common. "Except for Xenopoulos, along with D. Kokkinos a conscious, professional novelist, there was no Greek writer who systematically cultivated the novel." He denies Karkavitsas, Theotokis, and others the dedication to the novel form exhibited by Xenopoulos, and compares this attitude to the one shown by the young men and women of the current generation. An event of special significance, he finds, has taken place.

Reviewing the poetry publication of the last ten years one notices, at the most, the names of five or six poets, while in the prose of the same time we would be able to list fifteen or twenty worthy writers. [This is] a very important point, if we keep in mind the fact that this has never happened before in

Greece, that poetry has always been in the first rank, and that the publishing conditions that exist in Greece today, at least, certainly do not aid the development of prose. It means, therefore, that we are confronted by a new event, not superficial or coincidental, but organic, and that the reversal in the roles of poetry and prose in Greece is a fact that has its significance not only for our literature, but for all of our intellectual, even more, for all of our national and social life.[3]

In fact, the unexpected *had* occurred: the center of balance had for the first time in Greek culture shifted from poetry to prose. This had been what Yiannis Psycharis had called for in 1927 when he demanded: "Prose, we want prose," knowing that "the critical time in a nation's culture occurs when prose begins to be written."[4]

Xenopoulos had been writing urban novels for decades without influencing anyone, especially not writers of the age of Kontoglou and Doukas, who might have been expected to seize upon his achievement and build upon it. But they were the least interested in the social fiction of Xenopoulos, and not solely for personal, idiosyncratic reasons. Which society would they have written about, since the only one they knew had disappeared in 1922? Xenopoulos, who had no followers in "the barren decade of 1920-1930," according to Apostolos Sachinis, would wait until "the Generation of the 1930s . . . appeared before his attempt . . . could be brought to fruition."[5]

The increasing importance of prose certainly had social and national reasons, as Paraschos had identified them, and so did the

3. Paraschos, "I Nea Elliniki Pezographia," *To Neon Kratos,* I, No. 1, September (1937), p. 69.
4. The first quotation is from the newspaper *Politeia,* October 16, 1927, and the second is from *Roda kai Mila,* Vol. 4 (1907), p. 254. Sachinis uses both quotes in *To Neoelliniko Mythistorima* (Athens, 1958), p. 225.
5. Sachinis, *Anazitiseis* etc. . . . (Athens, 1945) p. 20.

seriousness with which the young novelists viewed their art. I. M. Panayotopoulos finds that this seriousness was an unavoidable result of the critical importance of the issues facing Greece after the Asia Minor Disaster. The "new generation," as a consequence of the experiences they had undergone, felt a great responsibility to express themselves completely. These young men and women were not attracted by the "love of decoration . . . of the ornamentation that delighted people of quieter eras," but felt a "sense of struggle" and a "concern for others." Greece, between the wars, he continues,

> was tossed about by frightful chaos, demagoguery, a deification of *arrivism*, an endless series of world-restorers (κοσμοδιορθωτήδων), brave hopes that sickened as soon as they began to be effected and, beneath all of these, the awesome struggle of the intellectual who tried but could not find his way and knew that it was not enough for him to do purely and simply his duty so that he would justify his existence.[6]

Although seriousness toward art and life was not a characteristic exclusive to the uprooted from Asia Minor, a sizable proportion of the best writers of the Generation hailed from Anatolia and can be said to have dominated the thinking of the time. The presence of the Anatolian in the cultural life of Greece had always been very strong, but the impact of the Asia Minor artist on the civilization of interwar Greece was unprecedented. A brief list would include Karolos Koun in drama, Ioannis Sykoutris in philology, Dimitrios Kapetanakis in criticism, Manolis Kalomiris in classical music, Thanos Valsamakis in ceramic arts, Fotis Kontoglou in iconography, Dimitris Fotiadis in publishing and historiography, Dimitris Glinos in education, and George Seferis

6. Panayotopoulos, *Ta Prosopa kai ta Keimena*, II, *Ta Anisycha Chronia* (Athens, 1943), p. 35.

in poetry. If we study only publishing in the 1930s we would discover that Anatolians had significant contributions to make in this field. *Kyklos*, for example, was published by Apostolos Melachrinos after his arrival from Constantinople in 1922, and was a periodical that consciously presented the work of the young in the later 1920s and early 1930s. *Renaissance* has already been mentioned as the journal of Dimitris Glinos. George Theotokas had a leading role in *Idea*, and "the three Georges" – Seferis, Theotokas, and Katsimbalis (the last was not an Anatolian) were among the founders of perhaps the most important journal of the 1930s, *Nea Grammata*. Finally, Dimitris Fotiadis took over rather early from K. Karthaios the editorial direction of *Neoellinika Grammata* and made it the major organ of intellectual resistance to the Metaxas dictatorship.

The arrival of the Anatolians changed the balance of Greek cultural life, according to I. M. Panayotopoulos, by displacing the previously Helladic dominance of the culture. "For about forty years the intellectuals of Roumeli" – men like Palamas, Drosinis, Vlach'oyiannis, Travlandonis, Malakasis, and others – "dominated the literary life of Athens," he states, after they had supplanted the Ionian School. The Asia Minor Disaster, which he calls "the great migration, the uprooting and replanting in the primeval fatherland of such a mass of Greeks," not only changed the social composition of Greece "but contributed to the spiritual and intellectual transformation that found its frequently authoritative expression in literary art."[7] A decade later, Constantine Dimaras agrees, using much the same diction. He finds the Anatolian elements in the prose of George Seferis "totally different from Roumeliot harshness" and concludes that "the contributions of the intellectuals who have come to us from the eastern shores of

7. *Ibid.*, p. 23.

the Aegean . . . valuable for the cultivation of Modern Greek diction."[8]

An impromptu discussion in *Neoellinika Grammata* in 1936-1937 will serve to prove the conscious commitment to the demotic made by the Generation as a whole, as well as the strong role of "the intellectual from the eastern shores of the Aegean" in this commitment. Angelos Terzakis, one of the foremost novelists and thinkers of that group, in a series of articles, said that the writers of this Generation were the first to take a definite stand, as a group, for demotic as the language for literature. George Theotokas, agreeing with him, repeats a suggestion made by George Seferis that all the young writers agree, again as a group, on linguistic usage, though Theotokas wonders if a conference is the ideal body to do this. He would prefer something along the lines of a style-book, written under the guidance of Manolis Triandafyllidis, the major authority on the demotic after the death of Psycharis seven years before. New writers and those fairly indifferent to language (those who out of a lack of genuine commitment to demotic would be apt to fall into a "mixed" diction) would probably be influenced by a style-book of this sort. Seferis, writing from his diplomatic post in Korytsa, Albania, agrees with Theotokas and suggests that the stylebook be published in *Neoellinika Grammata*. A committee, he continues, composed of two linguists and three writers should be formed to examine the introduction of new and foreign words into the Greek language. A month later Manolis Triandafyllidis replies, agreeing with the position taken by Terzakis in his series of articles that Demoticism had lost its combativeness because, essentially, it had won the day. The first volume of his grammar,

8. Dimaras, in his review of Seferis's *Treis Meres sta Monastiria tis Kappadokias,* in the newspaper *Vima,* June 12, 1953, p. 2.

he informs the readers of the journal, is ready for press. The spontaneous discussion on language is brought to a close by a letter from Ilias Venezis, who agrees with everything said so far and informs the readers that Stratis Myrivilis had broached the very subject to him two years before but it had somehow been forgotten.[9]

The seriousness that is revealed in the dedicated cultivation of fiction and the disciplined adherence to the demotic is the result, as many critics had pointed out, of the social and political upheaval of the time. The Generation of the 1930s came to maturity in a Greece totally different from the predominantly rural, pre-Disaster Greece. Before the arrival of the refugees, Greece seemed to I. M. Panayotopoulos "a stifling, narrow-minded and petty" place.

> A depressing spririt of localism was clearly evident. Life seemed to be dominated by a mean, small-time logic, by the stultifying logic of "two and two make four." After 1923 and once the first difficulties had been surmounted . . . all of us felt the blowing of another wind, a wind that brought a broader attitude toward life. The Greeks of Asia Minor . . . dug roots of renewal and added to the Greek totality, not only their weaknesses, but more importantly, their valuable virtues, their diligence, their tireless activity, their patience, their flexibility, their many-faceted cultivation, their sure linguistic abilities, and their broader and more mature awareness of the outside world.[10]

Besides growing up in a different, more challenging environ-

9. Terzakis and Triandafyllidis, of course, are not Anatolians, and Myrivilis qualifies only as "an intellectual" coming from "the eastern shore of the Aegean." The Terzakis articles ran from late 1936 to early 1937. Theotokas entered the discussion with "Linguistic Order," January 30, 1937. Seferis's letter is dated February 3, 1937; Triandafyllidis's is March 6, while Venezis's letter is published April 17, and dated March 12, 1937.

10. Panayotopoulos, *Ta Prosopa,* pp. 23-24.

ment, the young men and women of the Generation were, for a number of reasons, unusually well-prepared for careers as writers. For the first time in Greek literary history a generation emerged that was predominantly urban and of the middle class.[11] Their parents were landowners, bankers, professionals, or tradespeople who were able to educate their children well. As we saw at the beginning of this chapter, of the twenty-three writers in this group, fifteen were born in large urban areas (Constantinople 3, Smyrna 1, Thessaloniki 3, and Athens 8), five in provincial towns, and only three in villages. After beginning their careers, all except Skarimbas and Kastanakis (who lived in Paris) quickly established themselves in either Athens or Thessaloniki, in occupations that allowed them to continue to write. Of this group, virtually all knew another language fluently, many knew two and three languages besides Greek, a great number had studied abroad, and several had lived in Europe for as long as a decade, and more than a few had, at one time or another in their careers, translated works from other languages, either as a livelihood, or a supplement to it, or out of a serious desire to add to the fund of knowledge available to their countrymen.

Predictably, this interest in and travel to foreign countries exerted a strong influence on the attitudes and creative work of the Generation. They were not the first to have studied and lived abroad, for a long list of Greek writers would quickly show the contrary, but they were the first to have done so in such great numbers and with such great dedication. Previously, moreover, Greek writers had concentrated on and taken their models from the French and, to a lesser extent, the German literatures. The

11. Chrysos Esperas points this out: "The themes of contemporary Greek novels," he says, "are virtually always about the bourgeois or the worker of the cities, where the writers themselves live. Greek urban writers do not usually know the countryside, except perhaps in its external, ethographic aspect." See To Mythistorima, (Athens, 1940), pp. 85-86.

Generation of the 1930s, though, was dissatisfied with this limitation of their sources of intellectual sustenance. English and Russian literatures, which had exercised only a peripheral influence before, usually through the French language, suddenly became of greater interest to the Greek writer. Norwegian literature, particularly the works of Knut Hamsun and Ibsen, became the exclusive concern of Vasos Daskalakis, who taught himself the language and corresponded with Hamsun, thus introducing him to a large and favorably disposed readership in Greece. Italian literature, since its hiatus after the heyday of the Ionian School, again became a subject of intense interest, Spanish fiction became available, and for the first time American fiction began to attract a following.[12]

Post-Disaster Greece was thus open to foreign influence more than at any other time in its first century of free life. The narrow Helleno-centric culture had disappeared along with the belief in the Megale Idea. Now that Asiatic Greece was only a memory, Greece was part of Europe, and the question of what was Greek emerged with the improvement of the means of communication which began to threaten the Greeks with seductive ideas they could not absorb at once and make their own. If nothing else did, the virtual identity of postwar moods made Greece an undisputed part of Europe.

If the destruction of the Megale Idea and the divorce of the intellectual from the mass of the people had not been enough to break the hold ethography and its patriotic bias had on Greek fiction, the attitudes which the Generation of the 1930s shared with their European colleagues might have provided the added force required for liberation. The qualities of postwar European

12. These trends are reflected through the series of *Neoellinika Grammata.* For a thorough treatment of this important subject see K. Mitsakis's essay, "I Xeni Epidrasi stin Elliniki Logotechnia," *Nea Estia,* 73 Nos. 854-855, Feb. 1 and Feb. 15 (1963), pp. 180-186 and 251-257.

fiction, its anti-war character and its cosmopolitanism, were re-flected in Greek fiction also, but the first was delayed because Greece remained on a war footing until 1922, while the second seemed to attract only minor talents. Perhaps as a consequence of this common European mood, perhaps as a result of the study and travel of the fledgling Greek writer in foreign countries and an abiding interest in their cultures, members of this Generation showed a greater willingness to experiment with literary forms than their predecessors had. This was, after all, the era of James Joyce, T. S. Eliot, Ezra Pound, Pablo Picasso, and Igor Stra-vinsky; would anyone expect the young Greeks to be satisfied with the esthetic orientations of George Drosinis, Kostis Palamas, or Pericles Yiannopoulos?

The anti-war mood was a general European phenomenon. This is proved by the existence of important novels in most European languages attacking the stupidity, the waste, and the meaningless-ness of war, the barbarity that it excited in men, and the callous-ness, the cynicism, and the inflexibility of generals and politicians who manipulated national and patriotic ideals as a means of exploiting the society at large. Whether or not this indictment is a gross exaggeration is not essential. What the strength of feeling reveals, however, is a sensitivity among artists and intellectuals for their own naiveté and excessive patriotism before and during the War. It is doubtful that the reaction against war would have been as great and as universal if the writers had had their consciences clear that they, at least, had not been as swept up by zeal and as misled as they had been.[13] Anti-war novels like *All Quiet on the*

13. Myrivilis, the Greek anti-war novelist *par excellence,* was a member of the Students' Company in Athens when the First Balkan War broke out; he represented the "group" before Venizelos and requested the right for Greeks who were Ottoman subjects to serve in the Greek army. Venizelos assured the students that a law permitting this would be drafted that very day, and Myrivilis volunteered the next day. He was wounded in the Battle of Kilkis in 1913. See Manolis Yialourakis, "Myrivilis," *Megali Enkyklo-paidia tis Neoellinikis Logotechnias* (Athens, n.d.), 10, p. 404.

Western Front, Paths of Glory, The Good Soldier Schweik, Under Fire, Farewell to Arms, and *Life in the Tomb* are imbued with the same spirit: a rejection of official terminology and the "big words" of national idealism, a hatred of war and barbarity, a respect and love for individual men and women regardless of their nationality, a desire to return to nature and the natural values, which are seen as a refuge from the violence and destructiveness of war, an invention of man that denies his own humanity.

Since war was viewed so critically and, by extension, since the attitudes and emotions that led to the destructiveness of war became so suspect, cosmopolitan fiction, dealing with men and women of all national and racial backgrounds interacting with one another in various European cities, emerged as an indication that Western society had surpassed the blindness of international hatreds and strife. In the more superficial examples of this fiction, attention is paid primarily to the externals of postwar life: the fox-trot, the tango, dress fashions, jazz, motor cars, the life and manner of the cabaret, and the loosened codes of behavior of the characters who made up the multi-national society. In the more probing works that employ the cosmopolitan atmosphere, however, the reader is witness to the scrutiny of a novelist for whom all – even the most "sacred" values – are held up to question. Ideas of national honor, religious sanctity, family stability – all received body blows that marked them permanently. The world in which they were deeply and securely rooted was destroyed as the result of the colossal slaughter that the Great War represented, and the only values the serious writers were willing to tolerate or accept were those that were tangible and could be assessed or proved by individuals in their daily lives. Carefully described scenes of personal violence and of sexual freedom, fictional characters who explicitly embodied values of hedonism, who frankly accepted materialism, who cynically pursued selfish goals previously condemned in novels, all of these

164

were used as clubs with which to *épater les bourgeois* who could still, despite everything, try to hold on to the old, exploded, prewar values.[14]

In Greek fiction, cosmopolitanism was a clear reaction against the ethographic school that had dominated Greek prose for too long. Apostolos Sachinis considers it a temporary phenomenon and dates its apogee between 1928-1932, considering it merely a stage in the careers of writers who had been interested in it.[15]

14. The "cosmopolitan" should not be confused with the "international" theme, which is a much more profound study of the temperament and tradition of the novelist's own people, who are compared and contrasted to those of another culture. "International" fiction began earlier, with writers like Henry James and Edith Wharton of the United States, Ivan Turgenev of Russia, and a host of lesser writers from other nations. The usual elaboration of the "international" theme showed a member of a geographically and culturally peripheral nation confronting a culture like that of Great Britain, France, or Italy, which represented for him the wealth, complexity, and tradition of Europe. Both nations, that of the leading characters (and the novelist) and that which absorbs his attention, are seen from the clear perspective of an artist who sees the validities and weaknesses of both. The "cosmopolitan" theme, on the contrary, seems to ignore the ties individuals have with their own nations, societies, and social classes, and views them as rootless and alienated characters, interacting with others like themselves, in a social world devoid of any but extremely personal values. Despite the difference in quality, the fiction of Ernest Hemingway, of Vicki Baum, of Erich Maria Remarque and others ignores the careful study of manners and morals in a world rooted and secure that gave "international" fiction its interest and strength, and is instead the sensitive observation of a world – corrupt or otherwise – in a state of flux.

15. But cosmopolitanism was not a temporary phenomenon everywhere, lasting for definite historical reasons longer in some literatures than in others. The political and economic events of the postwar world had their effects on the careers of writers whose continued residence in their own countries would have been inhibiting, dangerous, or even suicidal. Whereas the Depression brought American writers back to the United States in the 1930s, the Russian Revolution, the triumph of Italian Fascism in 1922, the dictatorship of Primo de Rivera (1923-1930) and the subsequent Spanish Civil War, and the end of the Weimar Republic and the beginning of the Third Reich condemned scores of writers to emigration and rootlessness. The effect of this enforced residence outside their own societies resulted either in an extended life for a cosmopolitanism that would have ended

Only one Greek writer of the Generation of the 1930s suffered the permanent effects of separation from his society, and Thrasos Kastanakis lived in Paris because of his profession, not because of political developments in Greece. Other writers like George Theotokas, Pavlos Floros, Thanasis Petsalis, Lilika Nakou, and Nikos Gavriel Pentzikis lived in only temporary separation from Greece, and the attraction to cosmopolitanism for them was likewise transient. One finds, instead, that certain aspects of cosmopolitanism are absorbed into the body of Greek fiction itself. The novels of Kosmas Politis — who consciously chose his pseudonym in order to emphasize his interests — employ postwar European social and moral values and foreign characters, usually women, in a Greek setting that is only incidentally and externally "Greek."

Ethography could not survive in Modern Greek fiction because it could not be used to represent the world as the Generation of the 1930s saw it. Among other targets, ethography is attacked in George Theotokas's *Free Spirit*, a reasoned argument that is not without a young man's errors of exaggeration, nor his eloquence and power. Discussing carefully the "Greek reality" he saw about him, Theotokas struck at the ethographic school for its inability to handle any more than the surface of life, accusing it of mere "photographic realism." These occasionally pleasing but essentially inferior books, he said, offer their reader very little. "A few superficial sketches of Greek locales and several vague shadows that attempt to resemble human beings, flitting rapidly through our imaginations without stopping even for a moment." How could they have "any impact on our interior life" when they have "no real essence"?[16]

---

much sooner, or in a hermetic art in men like Vladimir Nabokov, Herman Broch, and James Joyce. Unlike that of the others, the exile of the last was not forced, but the result of a personal decision.

16. Theotokas, *Elefthero Pnevma* (Athens, 1929), p. 71. For this, his first effort, Theotokas used the pseudonym "Orestes Digenis."

A continued dependence on ethography would render Greek culture irrelevant, incapable of arriving at a national answer to the problems and issues facing Greece in the years after the Asia Minor Disaster.

We have arrived at a point in our national development where we feel more profoundly the need for a more serious imaginative prose. This is not solely to justify the position we hold in the European family [of nations]. That is a secondary matter. It concerns especially ourselves and how we are to live, how we'll offer ourselves the necessary intellectual diet. Our life is only partially fulfilled without fiction that is equal to the contemporary intellectual needs of Greece. As much as we love our poets, we cannot live in the 20th century by lyricism alone, and the ethographers do not have enough substance to nourish our minds. . . . We demand a real discussion of ideas, a real theater, a real novel. . . . The demands of our generation will be greater than those of previous ones in Greece. . . . It would be vandalism, certainly, to eradicate through blind hatred the fiction of our older writers. . . . This no sensitive person will deny. But it is also indispensible that we break with tradition. A routine has been created in Greek fiction, a system of narrow limitations and clear-cut values. If we permit this routine to continue undisturbed it will prevent new writers from discovering their own selves and tracing out their own destinies. Ethography may even claim them. This is why our first duty is to destroy the conditions that obtain and to overturn the established values. We appear implacable and perhaps ungrateful toward the older Greek writers for our own generation's welfare, because the rights of youth have priority.[17]

This was clearly a manifesto to the writers of his generation, a challenge to them to experiment with new forms, to dare more. Though in several passages Theotokas may appear to deny the

17. *Ibid.*, pp. 88-91.

achievements of past writers too insistently, he needed to do so for his effect. Eight years later, however, Kleon Paraschos identifies the two major goals of what he calls "the Generation" as the development of fictional technique and the "obvious and successful attempt to break [through] the narrow limits of ethography." Attaching a warning to the wholesale condemnation of previous fiction as simple ethography, he concludes, nevertheless, that the character of Greek prose "until 1912, and even until 1920" was basically ethographic, while the world the new Greek narrative inhabits is wider, a "climate where people live the events of their lives in deeper and more essential terms."[18] I. M. Panayotopoulos, writing in 1943, when the Generation had already produced much of the effect it had set for itself, agrees that something unique had happened to Greek fiction after the Asia Minor Disaster. "The abundant cultivation of prose in the last twenty years has many characteristics of an actual rebirth," he finds. "It is a beginning, not . . . a continuation . . . [but] a tireless and often desperate attempt to enrich and mature tradition."[19]

The fact is that Greek fiction could not change so long as the society for which it was a mirror remained the same. Most critics seem to agree that the Greek novel came of age in the 1930s because the change in the composition of Greek society made this development inevitable. The Asia Minor Disaster and the subsequent refugee impact, much of it directed toward the urban centers, effected a fundamental change in the Greek social world. Even without the ideas they had gathered in Europe about the role of fiction or the necessity to experiment, the younger Greek writers could not ignore the upheaval they saw about themselves every day. They were thus compelled by the new make-up of their society to concentrate on the social aspects of their art and

18. Paraschos, "I Nea Elliniki Pezographia," p. 67.
19. Panayotopoulos, *Ta Prosopa*, pp. 20-21.

to document the rapid and far-reaching changes their world had recently undergone. Again, since there are no sociological studies to enlighten us about this crucial era in Greek history, we must depend upon the generalizations made by astute literary critics. Kleon Paraschos writes:

> The strong advance that the writing of novels exhibits in Greece today is not a fashion imported, as so many others, from Europe, nor can it be assigned to the ambitions of a few who long to be read by as large a public as possible, but to a much more organic reason in that it reflects, at a specific time and place, our intellectual and social realities. With a century of free political life behind us, having in our poetry richly expressed our interior life in these hundred years, the time has come, perhaps, to express [as well] ... our external reality: the experiences of thoughts and observations; the problems of the society, the nation and the individual; the Modern Greek society – a grouping with unique features – which is evolving, undergoing a myriad transformations, developing about us at a rapid pace, which has its own characters, its own expressions, its own problems, its own dramas, its own distinctive features. No other form but the novel can express this complex world. ...[20]

The post-Disaster Greek world was an unstable one, however, an urban society that could only with numerous qualifications be considered to have social classes as Western Europe conceived of them. The older ethographic writers had for very good reasons concentrated on the village, one of the four sociological group-ings. The *villager* had a clearly outlined way of life and an established value system. The urban society that presented itself to the Generation of the 1930s, on the other hand, was in its initial stages totally amorphous. The *urban proletariat*, only a few

20. Paraschos, "I Nea Elliniki Pezographia," p. 69.

years removed from the village or recently uprooted from Asia Minor, had not created values of their own, expressions of the life they led and the station they occupied in the city, but retained the rural or Anatolian value systems. The same applied to the *urban middle class* (also composed of natives and Anatolians), though they seem to have come to terms more adequately with the life of the city. Finally, what can be termed either the *grand bourgeoisie* or *haute société*[21] seems to have little if any organic relation to the rest of Greek society. It was the class that had relations with the Palace, whenever Greece was a monarchy; with governmental circles; with foreign embassies; a class whose money came less from land ownership and large local enterprise than from foreign commerce or shipping, which was consequently often unconnected with the life of the rest of the nation, dependent on international business conditions, imitative of foreign fashions, and oriented towards the West and European values.

In effect, the Greek leading class, rather than "leading" Greece, seemed to "follow" Europe. Because so much of its enterprise was dependent, not on the Greek reality, but on international financial conditions, it was more often "absent" than "present" in Greek life. It clearly did not function the way the gentry or the business classes did in Great Britain or Western Europe by continuing to have a voice in the social and political life of the country regardless of international economic developments. Unable to fulfill its historic duty to direct society legitimately by its established presence in Greece, it created a moral vacuum at the top of the social hierarchy, a vacuum usually filled by "world-restorers," usually military men, who kept Greek society in a state of ferment by solving some of its pressing problems at the expense of one or another social class, which in its turn

21. Angelos Fouriotis in *Pnevmatiki Poreia, 1900-1950* (Athens, 1952), p. 23, uses the former term, and Panayotopoulos, *Ta Prosopa*, pp. 27-28, uses the latter.

would look to another upheaval to get its own legitimate interests recognized. In a melancholy observation of the problems of the intellectual life in Greece, the editor of *Nea Grammata* sums up the first year of the journal's existence. In 1935 alone, he writes, the periodical survived "one civil war, a number of attempted coups, a violent political struggle, one military dictatorship, [and] one change of political system," the reinstitution of the monarchy.[22]

Aside from the coherent, though static, social reality represented by the village and reflected in ethography, therefore, the rest of Greek society, by which we necessarily mean urban civilization, was characterized in the 1930s by a chaotically fluid situation where families (perhaps, besides the village, the only unshakable social grouping in Greek life) rose to prominence and declined within a generation or two.[23]

Panayotopoulos frankly states the difficulties a novelist faced in trying to describe such a social reality.

All of these groups, the peasant, the provincial, the aristocrat, the bourgeois, the mass-man do not live organically, fused into a totality, but are constantly moving, as though they stood on perpetually rising and falling surfaces. That is why the novelist

22. "Chronicles-Recapitulation," *Nea Grammata,* Vol. II, No. 1, January (1936), pp. 85-86. The contribution is uninitialed by Andreas Karandonis, the editor, but he has stated to me that it was he who wrote it.

23. It is characteristic that since sociology as a discipline cannot be said to exist in Greece, novelists like George Theotokas have made the most interesting generalizations about Greek society. Except for Solomos and Capodistrias, both aristocrats who emerged from the Ionian social system, all other important Greek figures have come from what Theotokas calls the *mikro-astiki* class (the petit bourgeoisie). The values of Trikoupis, Venizelos, Palamas, Korais, Psycharis, and of movements like the Philiki Etairia, Demoticism, and the Revolution of Goudi have been the values of this class – hard work, thrift, the drive for education, a desire for neatness and order, and – always within measure – the good life. See "Gyro sto Thema tou Kommounismou," *Nea Estia,* 44 No. 512, Nov. 1 (1948), pp. 1334-1339.

is not sure what his point of view is to be. One can understand, therefore, why he turns in toward himself and is sustained by his nostalgia and his personal past, [why he returns] to his village and his childhood and adolescent years ... to be inspired ... envying Balzac, who had before him a provincial life established for many years upon which he could build his masterpieces.[24]

Despite these considerable difficulties, the commitments of the Generation were with the urban middle class, not because most of them had consciously chosen to reflect this new aspect of their nation's existence, but because this class was the only one they knew. The ties of the Greek writers with the village were irrevocably broken, not because of ideological or esthetic reasons, but as a result of the social origins of the new Generation. By far the first group of writers in Greek letters so conscious of the social aspects of fiction, most of them identified with the values of the urban middle class, a few identified with the small proletarian class, and hardly any with the peasants; all maintained an alert interest in the political fate of the country, and most significantly, all devoted themselves to writing in the demotic language.[25]

The contributions of this literary generation to Greek fiction are impressive, for if one can say nothing else about these writers, one must commend them for the way they documented the society in which they lived. No other literary generation left within their work such convincing portraits of myriads of characters; careful studies of complex human relationships; thorough and detailed analyses of families, some of which stretched to

24. Panayotopoulos, *Ta Prosopa*, pp. 27-28.
25. The only exception to this, as we have seen, is Nikos Gavriel Pentzikis, who started as a demoticist but who, sometime after World War II, began to introduce elements of the purist and ecclesiastical language into his work.

three-volume novels; a meticulous attention to areas of human life never before treated in Greek fiction; and an often profound awareness of the impingement of history on the daily life of an individual and his society. Quite simply, with the Generation of the 1930s, the conscious and specific individual emerged from the group. This had occurred before in Greek fiction, certainly, but never to this extent.

The emergence of the individual is also accompanied, for the first time, by the much more careful study of the family unit. Xenopoulos may have written the first trilogy in Greek fiction, but the Generation of the 1930s began to cultivate the long novel with an insistence that implies the maturing of the view of an individual within his family and of the family as a unit within the nation and history. Thanasis Petsalis studied the Parnis family in his three-volume novel, *Strong and Weak Generations* (1935), Angelos Terzakis wrote of the Galanis family in the two-volume work, *Captives* (1932), of the Skleros family in *The Decline of the Skleroi* (1933), and of the Malvis family in *The Violet City* (1937), while George Theotokas concentrated on the unstable Christoflis family in *The Daemon* (1938) and, as we have seen already, provided a careful view of the Notaras family in *Argo*. Thrasos Kastanakis, finally, in his numerous novels and short stories, gives a somewhat lurid picture of Greek families in Constantinople before the Disaster and in France after it.

In focusing on the family unit these writers consciously forced themselves to confront human development within a social context and in an historical dimension. In doing this, they clearly outlined the tensions and changes that individual men and women underwent as moral, economic, political, and social realities. The relationships between man and woman, between parent and child, between siblings, between man and his employer, and between the family and the rest of society were forced to be treated explicitly. In fact, the only area the Generation was incapable of treating, probably because of its social origins and rational orientation, was the relationship between man and God. Severed from the village and the folk traditions, living in an urban world where religion was represented only by an established and highly legalistic church, the Generation, epitomizing the prejudices of its class, saw priests and the religious life not in their mystical dimension but as vestiges of an outmoded world view.

Because disciplines like history, sociology, and psychology were at a rudimentary stage in the Greek universities, the novel as a form quickly emerged for the student of Greek society as an important repository of information about the lives and attitudes of the urban Greek, in works of the imagination that are frequently compelling, exciting, and moving. It is no mean feat for a score or so of young men and women to create in slightly more than a decade a rich and complex literature where before there were – no matter how important – only scattered titles.

With the emergence of the individual in the foreground of a more and more carefully observed urban society came an interest in the presence of the outsider to that society. For the first time we are shown the foreigner (a category in which the Anatolian refugee is, of course, not included) not as a minor figure, but as an important character in the novel's action. Kosmas Politis has a special fondness for showing the attraction of his Greeks for the exotic foreign women who people his fiction, while M. Karagatsis in ambitious works like *Colonel Liapkin* (1933) and *Jungermann* (1940), a massive two-volume novel, studies the assimilation of a White Russian and a Finn, respectively, in Greece after the Russian Revolution, providing in the meantime thorough and convincing pictures of societies in Larissa and Athens.

Other "minorities" suddenly become important, not only the foreigner or the Anatolian refugee, but the child as an inhabitant of his own, very special world, assuming an importance previously unknown in Greek letters. Elli Alexiou's collection of fictional vignettes in *Hard Struggles for a Humble Life* (1931) and *The Third Christian Girls' School* (1934) exploits her knowledge and experiences as a teacher and provides us for the first time with touching, non-stereotyped views of the helplessness and vulnerability of the child. Adolescents, hardly ever seen clearly in Greek fiction (except possibly for Kondylakis's *Patouchas*, 1892) become a theme for important works like George Theotokas's *Leonis* (1940), Kosmas Politis's *Eroica* (1938), Terzakis's *Voyage with Hesperus* (1946), and even Venezis's *Aeolian Earth* (1943). The Greek abroad, another theme that had never been adequately exploited (even with the novels of Yiannis Psycharis) is given pre-eminent place in Pentzikis's *Andreas Dimakoudis* (1935), Petsalis's *The Human Adventure* (1937), Theotokas's *Euripides Pentozalis* (1937), Lilika Nakou's *The Lost* (1935), and the uneven fiction of Thrasos Kastanakis.

The greatest minority, however, previously almost silent in Greek letters, though certainly not in life, appeared for the first time in the works of the Generation of the 1930s: woman. Before the Generation began to publish, woman had only a minor role in literature. Without too great an exaggeration, and excepting Frangoyiannou in *The Murderess* and a few Xenopoulos heroines, she was only someone about whom one wrote poems, rarely someone whose interior life was interesting or important. This was, however, only a reflection of her actual place in society. As late as the Balkan Wars, women in Athens had no more personal freedom than they did in the asphyxiating village. They were oriented toward the home exclusively, devoid of freedom and initiative, limited — if they were of marriagable age — to looking through the grills of their windows at their lovers from afar, who composed poetry or sang *cantades* for them. "It was seldom one met women in the streets of Athens one or two hours after sundown," writes Adamantios Papadimas. "As late as 1911, a little before the Balkan Wars," he continues, "the chief of police at the time signed a decree forbidding the circulation of women without escort after ten at night," which in Greece, it must be realized, is dinner time.[26]

The Great War and the Asia Minor Disaster changed all that, of course; before this time, it was the very rare woman who could lead the sort of life she wanted. She had to be either of the upper class, like Penelope Delta, or in one of the arts, like Marika Kotopouli or Galateia Kazantzaki. Otherwise, freedom of expression and association were denied her. With the Generation of the 1930s, things began to change radically. Women like Tatiana Stavrou, Elli Alexiou, Melpo Axioti, and Lilika Nakou, every bit as talented and independent as men of their age group, began to express themselves with audacity, power, and eloquence. The middle-class origins of the Generation proved, with the women writers, to be an asset again, for they were products of homes that by and large supported and respected their ambitions.[27]

When, added to the exploitation of the themes of fictional "minorities," one considers the scores of novels that conscientiously chronicle modern Greek life, one comes to the inescapable conclusion that the Generation of the 1930s left as its heritage, within a very short time, a fictional achievement the like of which not many minor cultures can boast.

Born with the century, seared by the fires of Anatolia just as they entered adulthood, these writers viewed fiction not as a gentle and amusing pastime but as a means by which they would subdue and order the chaos they saw about, and felt within, themselves. They began to publish when the novel in Greek letters was indifferently cultivated, at the precise time, moreover,

26. Adamantios Papadimas, *Nea Elliniki Grammatologia* (Athens, 1948), p. 269.
27. Lilika Nakou seems to have had her share of troubles, though, about which I. M. Panayotopoulos is rather specific in *Ta Prosopa*, pp. 158-167.

when most of the important practicing prose writers had either died or ceased serious publication. They appeared, therefore, in a void and built up in the space of a decade or two an impressive body of fiction. If they had not appeared, the Greek novel might still be at its ethographic stage, and its development would have been greatly retarded because its natural audience would have preferred to read foreign novels, either in translation or in the original (the knowledge of foreign languages in Greece is unusually high), which would speak directly and eloquently about the issues of their time.

The achievement of the Generation of the 1930s is manifold. Having traveled, studied, and lived in Europe, the young men and women saw Greece, not as their fathers did, a land potentially large, powerful and glorious, but as it was after the Disaster of 1922 — a small, defeated, fiscally bankrupt Balkan nation with little future. "What position," Theotokas asked,

> does Greece hold in the creative ferment of contemporary Europe? What contribution do we make to the great attempts made around us? Nothing! Once we cross the borders we sense profoundly the fact that we represent nothing, that no one takes us seriously, that we cannot justify the position we hold in Europe, that we are in the eyes of foreigners only financial brokers, ship-owners, and small-time grocers and nothing more. So we wander a little through European civilization and return home with a heavy heart. Where, then, are the Greeks? We searched everywhere and could not find them.[28]

But the fact that they *knew* this was the most important step. From the beginning, the work they published was permeated with the sense of the new Greek reality, consciously aware of its time and place, without those great and unexamined certitudes of their well-meaning but now desperately confused fathers. The

28. Theotokas, *Elefthero Pnevma,* p. 16.

mood of a generation of Greek writers, for the first time in the literary history of the nation, corresponded with that of its European counterparts. Rather than inclining them to defeatism, as it had most of the younger poets, this mood acted as a challenge to them and was accepted creatively by the Generation. They seemed to sense that the time was ripe: a whole new world of the imagination was waiting to be created. They had become heirs to a rich, pliable language that had achieved almost universal literary recognition within their own young lives, and inheritors of a fairly large, complex, and variegated urban society that had emerged, almost literally, overnight. They were also intellectually restless and talented.

Their experiences in Europe showed them not only that they were "nothing," but that they had much to accomplish if they wanted to "justify" the "position" they held in a Europe to which no one could any longer deny that Greece belonged. Asiatic Greece had perished in the Disaster of 1922 and the future of the other Greek communities in the "diaspora" was problematic. Greece was now, for better or worse, a part of Europe. The issue of "Greekness" (ἑλληνικότητα) that was debated in the 1930s was only proof that the attitude toward Greece would need to be redefined in the light of the nation's new position in Europe.

The Generation of the 1930s, therefore, was the first to break away from the limitations of ethography, the first to consider themselves conscious literary craftsmen in the form of the novel, the first to tip the balance in a literature previously heavily weighted toward poetry, the first to represent the life of the urban dweller in fiction, primarily because they were the first generation in Greek letters to be almost exclusively of the urban middle class. Though the Asia Minor Disaster was "the shadow on their soul," the Generation of the 1930s did not fear its darkness.

In spite of it, they saw clearly enough to create a world that had not existed in Greek literature before.

Xenopoulos, too, sensed their power and felt that the younger writers, at last, would see in his efforts the beginnings of the urban novel in Greek and follow his lead. After an extremely careful historical analysis of the novel in Greek, given as a lecture on his election to the Academy of Athens, Xenopoulos concludes:

> I honor and praise my predecessors. But I expect more and greater achievements from my successors. Doesn't the future always belong to the young? And they, more fortunate than we, find a more perfect linguistic medium and a more worthy [novelistic] tradition. They have somewhere to base themselves so that they may ascend higher. They will prove the Greek novel to be equal in all respects to that of Europe. And later . . . who can say?[29]

29. Xenopoulos, "O Logos tou K^ou Gr. Xenopoulou eis tin Dexiosi tou eis tin Akadimia," *Nea Estia,* 2, No. 124, Feb. 15 (1932), pp. 176-185.

5 The Resurrection of the Asia Minor Theme

As we have seen, the Asia Minor Disaster had been a traumatic blow that the Greek mind was unable to forget through the interwar period. Besides the appalling losses to human life, property, and the historical-cultural integrity of the race, the disgraceful defeat brought with it a corrosive sense of unworthiness and inferiority, an exaggerated self-assessment as low as the previous one had been high.

For a people like the Greeks, however, this sense of unworthiness could not last long. The failure of one democratic government after another and the success of one military coup after another may have indicated that the Greeks had not discovered a way to impose order upon themselves; this dreadful and seemingly perpetual national problem, however, did not imply that they would be willing to have order imposed upon them by another nation. In October 1940 the world was treated to the spectacle of a large, highly mechanized Italian army being stopped and then pushed back by the Greek army. This army, nominally "fascist" itself, owed little to the Metaxas dictatorship except its initial refusal to accept the humiliating terms Mussolini had offered. It is true that after the Kondylis coup of 1935 and the imposition of the Metaxas regime in 1936, the army had become the domain of monarchists and fascists. Following the

Italian attack, however, the retired Venizelist officers were commissioned again and the armed forces became pan-Hellenic once more. Regardless of their considerable political and personal differences, and despite the lack of war matériel, the Greeks fought for their own vision of Greece. The series of victories on the Albanian Front, coming at a time when the Western democracies were confronting what seemed to be invincible enemies, was an inspiration to the Free World.

To the Greeks, of course, living for almost two decades with the taste of humiliation and defeat, the Albanian campaign was the assurance historical reality gave them that they were worthy of their past, and that the exalted ideas they nourished about their destiny were not delusions. October 28, 1940, is, consequently, the next historical watershed. As the Academician Dionysios Zakythinos stated in a lecture commemorating the Twenty-Fifth anniversary of the Albanian campaign, the Disaster of Asia Minor had created a new nation from the "miserable remains of overseas Hellenism." It was "of this State that the generation of October 28, 1940, belonged ... [which] had reached manhood in the midst of national trials and gained its maturity."[1] The men who fought heroically against the Axis were the products of the intermingling of Anatolian and native Greek stock that had come about after the Disaster and wiped the slate clean of the humiliation of 1922.

The effect on the intellectuals of the heroism of an entire people previously considered decadent was electrifying. Varnalis, as indicated earlier, seriously harmed the effect of *The Diary of Penelope* by changing his interpretation of *laos*, always used in the pejorative before then, to a favorable one. The full effect of this can be seen in his final chapter, "The Legend," in which

1. "Apo tis Ptoseos tou Mikrasiatikou Ellinismou eis tin 28[in] Oktovriou, 1940," Panygeric Conference of 27th October, 1966, *Records of the Academy of Athens,* 41 (1966).

Penelope, previously confident of the pliability of the *laos*, re-members with fondness "the four years . . . [of] the Third Ithacan Civilization," which were "the best of years, the world's most tidy (years)," all destroyed by an unprovoked attack that found the previously malleable *laos* hard and heroic.

> And the *laos* took up arms and fought like lions. Not for the land, which did not belong to them; not for the ancestors, which they did not have; not for the gods, who had disinher-ited them; not even for the freedom of others. That was the excuse they gave. They fought to rid themselves of the foreign and native bandits, thus achieving land and homeland and gods and ancestors — and their own freedom.
>
> How ungrateful![2]

Kazantzakis, as though he had totally forgotten his anguish at the "miserable" and "wretched" Greeks, behaved as though he had always known they were heroes. In *Report to Greco* (1961), the fictionalized autobiography that is more fiction than fact (he calls it a *mythistorima*), he relates an incident that occurred on a trip near Mount Psiloritis in Crete, at the time of the German attack on Norway. A giant of an old shepherd rushed down a hill and stopped him, asking "how is Norway doing?" Kazantzakis assured him that Norway was doing well, confident that the old man was not quite sure what or where Norway was, merely that human freedom was being threatened. Overjoyed, the old shep-herd made the sign of the cross and refused the offer of a cigarette. "Why do I need a cigarette? I don't need a thing. It's enough that Norway is well." He returned to his flock, leaving Kazantzakis behind to ponder:

> Truly, the air of Greece is holy, I thought, and certainly freedom was born here. I don't know if any other peasant or

2. Kostas Varnalis, "To Imerologio tis Pinelopis," *Pezos Logos* (Athens, 1957), pp. 183-184.

shepherd in the world would have lived with so much agony and so much selflessness as this shepherd the agony of a far-away, unknown land that fought for its freedom. The battle of Norway had become the battle of this Greek shepherd, because he considered freedom as his daughter.[3]

It is hard to believe that the Kazantzakis of the 1920s would have thought the remarks of a peasant or shepherd important enough to comment upon. Viewed after the historic victory on the Albanian Front, however, they are seen as noble expressions of a representative of a unique people. Although the incident takes place in Crete, the operative words here are "Greece" and "Greek," and there is no reference to the putative "corruption" the Cretans had undergone because of their union with a "decadent" Greece.

The Civil War in Greece destroyed the brief cohesion that the Albanian campaign had forged. This is not the place for a historical recapitulation of an era not crucial to the present study. Suffice it to say that the forces of the Greek establishment — liberal as well as monarchical — supported by the Allies, crushed the Greek partisan army of EAM-ELAS and were forced, given the explosive climate of the time, to impose martial law on the nation as a whole. The partisans, who were undeniably Communist-controlled and who dominated much of the countryside, counting for one reason or another on the loyalties of much of the Greek people, at least initially, were exiled, imprisoned, or otherwise suppressed.

3. Nikos Kazantzakis, *Anaphora ston Greko,* p. 545. Bien states it this way: "He [Kazantzakis] grew increasingly reconciled not only to the visible, palpable world, but to his own nation, for the Greek people's suffering and resistance during this period gave them a unity and dignity that had been lacking in the years following the Asia Minor catastrophe." See Bien, *Kazantzakis and the Linguistic Revolution in Greek Literature*, P. 224.

Whatever the merits and demerits of either side, the fact is that a whole wealth of issues and themes were declared taboo by this internecine struggle. The vanquished, given a romantic aura by their defeat, identified their cause with that of social justice and that of the victors with brutal subservience to the demands of foreign powers, specifically Great Britain and the United States. The government, on the other hand, controlling the full apparatus of the state machinery, saw any effort to criticize it, in literature or in public life, as a covert threat from the Slavic and Communist north to the security of the nation. The division was abyssmal, a dissension reminiscent of the one between the Monarchists and Liberals of 1916-1922.

Contrary to the past, however, this new national torment found its expression in works of fiction because of the development the novel had undergone in the intervening decades. The differences in the fiction that relates to the decades 1912-1922 and 1940-1950 are qualitative as well as quantitative. Once the rigidities of censorship were relaxed with the establishment of security and certain democratic liberties, the novel became the forum for the discussion of issues that had never been previously entertained in imaginative prose. Works of fiction, among them many trilogies, narrate the events of the 1940s from the point of view of the Left, the Right, and the Center. Depending on the classifier, writers who have dealt with this era are considered "Reds" or "Blacks." Whatever the categories, there should be no doubt that this novelistic output is the direct result of the Greek novel's establishment as an important and comprehensive literary form in the 1930s.

As far as the Asia Minor theme was concerned, the chronological as well as the emotional distance caused by the decade of war provided the writers with the esthetic distance they did not have before. This lack of immediacy enabled novelists, many of whom had no connection with the Asia Minor tragedy at all, to view the Disaster from unexpected perspectives.[4]

Categories are always basically arbitrary divisions of subject matter that could as easily, though perhaps with less logical justification, be divided otherwise. Bearing in mind, therefore, the many qualifications to which the simple act of categorization is perpetually vulnerable, the works that appeared after the conclusion of civil strife in Greece can be divided into two groups: first, those for which the historical uniqueness of the Asia Minor tragedy is ever-present, to be studied in this chapter under the heading "The Fiction of History"; and second, those for which this uniqueness is less insistent, those that select episodes, psychological states, tensions, and moral dramas from what is by now "the Legend of Asia Minor" for their own esthetic purposes. This second group will be studied under the heading "The Fiction of Myth" in order to show that, though they may not have broken away from the linear or sequential plot, they have nevertheless broken with the necessity to recapitulate history. I hasten to add that, although "The Fiction of Myth" may mark the final liberation of the artist from the tyranny of reproducing historical causality, a fictional work is not "better" because it belongs in this category rather than in the first. In fact, Dido Sotiriou's *Bloodied Earth*, for what it attempts to do, is equal as a novel to the best works studied under "The Fiction of Myth."

Despite their other and more complex ambitions, the works to be studied under "The Fiction of History" view the events of 1922 primarily as historical and social. *In Youthful Battle* (1953),

4. The interest in Asia Minor continued unabated, however, in those writers of discursive prose who had Anatolian roots. Michael Argyropoulos, the Vatidou sisters, Socrates Prokopiou, Christos Solomonidis, and others continued to publish through the 1940s and 1950s their memoirs and studies of folklore, the arts, and everyday life in Asia Minor.

by Alekos Doukas, and the trilogy *In the Shadow of History* (1961-1966), by Byron Kamberoglou, are novels that might have been more successful had they been autobiographies, for their concern is more the reproduction of history than the description of its effects on fictional characters. This is why *The Vine-Shoot* (1955) by Spyros Plaskovitis and *The Stone Lions* (1963) by Julia Iatridi, though chronicles of Greek life that employ the Asia Minor Disaster as a starting point, are greatly superior: they both use central characters who are clearly distinct from the authors and who, as refugees, witness the evolution of Greece through the interwar years to the Civil War and after. After studying Dido Sotiriou's qualified success, *The Dead Wait* (1959), but before analyzing her unqualified success, *Bloodied Earth* (1962), both of which attempt to achieve a synthesis of fiction and history, we shall discuss *Niobe* (1926), by Kostas Zoumboulidis, and *Like Lies and Like the Truth* (1928), by Socrates Prokopiou, novels that were doomed to failure, if not by their authors' lack of fictional competence, then by the very prematurity of their attempt to synthesize an historical experience not yet absorbed. Finally, we shall analyze the notable exception to this category, *The Mermaid Madonna* (1949) by Stratis Myrivilis, which aspires to a mythic dimension but which, for many reasons, besides its ultimate failure to achieve mythic resonance, is firmly rooted in its historical time.

In the second category, "The Fiction of Myth," we shall find works that, no matter how close they are to historical fact, are more interested in abstracting it for philosophical, moralistic, or psychological motives. If "The Fiction of History" viewed history as a linear process tied to logical causality, "The Fiction of Myth" follows its own causality, one in which non-historical considerations are paramount. Where we find acceptance of the linear plot – pre-eminently true in *Christ Recrucified* (1948) by Nikos

Kazantzakis and *The Sailing* (1964) by Menis Koumendareas —
the tendency is to elevate the action to the level of moral parable
in which the actual context of history is ignored for the moral
reality upon which the writer focuses. In works, moreover, like
The Garden of Princes (1966) by Nikos Bakolas, *The Dreams of
Angelika* (1958) by Eva Vlami, and *At Hadzifrangos's* (1962) by
Kosmas Politis, we find no concern at all for the reproduction of
historical causality. Here, the ambitions of fiction to rise to the
mythic level are inescapable, for all three novels — with varying
success, of course — though using the historical facts of the Asia
Minor tragedy, employ them for their own purposes. Abandoning
the sequential plot, these novels are more interested in replacing
historical causality with the psychological or mythological apprehension of reality.

The Fiction of History

What would in other literatures be unabashed
autobiographies, often fascinating and always instructive, with
candid references to the first person, his family, social environment, and the period of historical change through which he lived
become, in Greek literature, fiction of an inferior sort because the
authors are men and women who feel that they have something
to say but are not concerned about how they say it. The genre of
autobiography reserves itself in Greek letters to the "memoirs" of
those who have played important roles in military or political life,
while the others, whose witness through the course of history
may be just as interesting, feel that their literary efforts would be
met with scorn if they related the events of their own lives with
no attempt to fictionalize them somewhat. Thus, the major
problem with the two novels to be treated at this point is their
incorrect choice of genre.

Alekos Doukas's *In Youthful Battle*[5] tells the story of a man whom the author does not name but calls Little Brother (Mikros Adelfos, frequently just M.A.); it describes his life in Moschonisia, his role in the Greek Army in Asia Minor, his injury at the battle of Afion Karahissar, his life in Greece after the Disaster, his growing Marxist convictions, and, following his rebellion against Greek repression, his emigration to Australia. What is no more than an unconvincing novel might have been an invaluable auto-biography, with fine scenes of Ottoman-controlled Moschonisia and Aivalik, with informative views of the military campaign, and with the at-times important descriptions of post-Disaster Greek labor disputes, notably the lockout at the tobacco factories at Xanthe and Kavalla.

In Youthful Battle is important not for its style but for its content. For the first time, it presented the attitudes that the newer view of the Asia Minor theme would include. Doukas insists on the relatively good life the common Greeks and Turks lived during the "blessed" days before the Great War and Liman von Sanders's arrival in Turkey. We see this bond of friendship between the races in the persons of Little Brother, the central character, and Sueliman, an idealized version of the poet Nazim Hikmet. Besides this "myth of brotherhood" that crops up in the fiction of Dido Sotiriou and in a comment by Kosmas Politis, there is in Doukas's book a strong interest in Anatolian folklore, a subject that began to occupy a greater role in the attempt to reconstruct the world view of Asia Minor Hellenism. As a Marxist, again, Doukas would have his own views of Greek political life, but since he lived in Australia he could express freely his criticism of governmental bureaucracy, of individual chicanery, of turmoil in the state machinery, and of the social injustice shown the tobacco workers. Ultimately, however, none of the disparate

5. *Stin Pali, Sta Neiata* (Melbourne, Australia, 1953).

concerns, given equal importance to other, more fictionally pertinent events, is justified esthetically. A fact is mentioned merely
because it absorbs the author's attention at a particular time,
much as an annoyance may seduce the writer of a letter into the
discussion of a matter of less importance from his primary purpose of writing, and not because it is relevant to the artistic whole
of his work.

In the Shadow of History[6] by Byron Kamberoglou tells the
story of Lefteris, who had arrived in Chios as a child after the
Disaster in Smyrna, saw his family reunited, and then moved to
Thessaloniki, where his doctor father set up medical practice and
where the boy grew to manhood through the 1920s and 1930s.
The narrator learns the story from Lefteris during the Civil War
and relates it to his readers as a chronicle of the growth to
manhood of a young Greek during crucial times. We follow
Lefteris through a boyhood in Thessaloniki, a relatively sheltered
life as the son of a doctor, a gradual decline into shabby gentility
as his father struggles against the ravages of Parkinson's disease,
the turmoils of young love, the political disturbances of Greece in
the late 1930s, the coming of the War, the Occupation, the
famine in Athens, the choice of a career, university days, and life
as a dentist in a small town in the Peloponnesus, where the
Occupation is presented in a graphic manner.

Kamberoglou, like Alekos Doukas, is unable to remove himself
from reality and create fiction from the details of a life he renders
with autobiographical precision. It is in the convincing accuracy
of his description of life in Thessaloniki during the late 1920s and
the 1930s, of the famine in Athens of 1941, and the general
atmosphere of the Axis Occupation that Kamberoglou reveals
exactly how much damage had been done by his wrong choice of
genre. As the autobiography — for the reader is eventually told

6. *Ston Iskio tis Istorias,* in three volumes (Athens, 1961, 1962, 1966).

that "Lefteris" and "Byron" are one and the same – of a young man imprisoned by two major historical upheavals, *In the Shadow of History* would have been of great poignancy and value. Without the need to fictionalize, to dramatize, to manipulate reality, with only the demand that he be as truthful and as clear-sighted as possible, Kamberoglou might have given Greek letters a valuable witness of the interwar years, the perspective of one human being between the cataclysms of the Asia Minor Disaster and the World and Greek Civil Wars that dominated his life. In this way, he could have turned to practical and esthetic use the imprisonment within history that characterizes most of the writers in this category.

The Vine-Shoot (1955) by Spyros Plaskovitis chronicles, in a more symbolic way, the historical events that dominated Greek life from the Asia Minor Disaster until the end of the Civil War.[7] The central character, Asimis Tragoudas, known as "the refugee" by the peasant society of Volos where he settles after the Disaster, is a frugal, hard-working man whose attitudes betray a previous life destroyed and an entire family annihilated. All he has brought with him, aside from the memories no one around him shares, is a vine-shoot that itself looks dead, a mere piece of inert wood which, like the symbol of continuity it is, carries within its cells a potentiality for life.

After ten years of hard work, he marries a woman from a nearby village who gives him two sons before she dies during the German Occupation. These two boys are products of the new Greece, fusions of Anatolia and continental Greece. Asimis remains what he was, an industrious, capable, and thoughtful Anatolian, tied to his land, his productive vines, and his Bible, a symbol of the patriarchal life. His sons, however, see how dominated he tends to be by authority. The younger, Vlasis, falls

---

7. "I Klimatoverga," in *I Thyella kai to Fanari* (Athens, 1955).

under the influence of a pensioned solicitor who gives him booklets that preach revolution. Andreas, the older, who identifies his values with those of the state, finds himself increasingly in opposition to Vlasis, and the brothers begin their arguments and fights when the Germans, after killing off all the farm animals, withdraw from Greece.

The two brothers are, therefore, symbolic of the dissension that is to lead Greece to civil strife, while their father and the sturdy peasant girl both brothers love, Margaro, are more committed to the demands of life and have no interest in the ideologies that pit Andreas against Vlasis. Like the vine-shoot, Asimis and Margaro know that their loyalties lie with their kin and that their biological wisdom is more profound than the important but ultimately life-denying ideological orientations. Andreas, a lieutenant in the Royal Army, and Vlasis, a Partisan, kill each other in their father's vineyard, which is burned down and which, presumably, will provide Asimis another root with which to carry the past into the future.

Asimis Tragoudas is a "refugee" only in name and only because Plaskovitis wants to use him and his personal past as a symbol of Greek continuity through historical upheaval, much as the vine-shoot is a symbol of continuity in the non-rational world. The author makes no attempt to individualize Asimis or the other characters because his purpose is more general. To have brought to life Asimis's personal past and made it an active part of his present existence would have destroyed the esthetic distance Plaskovitis wanted to interpose between his characters and the reader.

The Vine-Shoot is an attempt to narrate in symbolic terms the role of Greece in recent history. That Plaskovitis, a Corfiot, would select a refugee and his family to stand for Greece reveals how much the post-1922 anti-refugee prejudices and tensions had diminished in the Greek community. Modern Greece was reborn in the Disaster, refashioned from what she had been before; it is this "new" Greece that Asimis and his sons symbolize. Andreas and Vlasis, fusions of Anatolia and Thessaly, are headstrong, uncompromising, and combative. Ultimately, it is these rigid attitudes that destroy them, while their mild-mannered and flexible father survives to see his shattered life.

Like much symbolic fiction, *The Vine-Shoot* confuses the reader in certain respects. To carry the symbolism to its logical conclusion, one would assume that with the death of his two sons, Asimis — or Greece — is once again destroyed. This time, however, he is beyond the age where he can start another family; the life span of individuals is infinitesimal compared to that of nations. The symbolic level of the novella is called into question by the factual reality at its most critical juncture.

The more closely the novella's chronology is studied, in fact, the less well it bears up, because the time span between the Asia Minor Disaster and the beginning of the Second World War is a precise eighteen years. It is upon this chronology that Plaskovitis and other writers whose fiction must reflect history falter, for they find themselves compelled to structure their stories by telescoping and blurring crucial, intermediate events. For example, Plaskovitis tells us that Asimis Tragoudas arrived in Volos after the Disaster, worked for a decade before he married, and had two sons. The reader, regardless of how much he wants to accept the symbolism of the novella, is nevertheless compelled to date the time of Asimis's marriage at no earlier than 1932. Assuming, therefore, that Andreas and Vlasis — who are not twins — are born in 1933 and 1934 respectively, they cannot be more than fifteen and sixteen years old by the end of the Civil War.

The technical problem faced by writers whose fiction is to chronicle Greece between the Disaster and the Second World War is that the Greek nation was not permitted a full generation of peace between the two upheavals. Plaskovitis could have avoided this problem easily by having Asimis marry earlier, two or three years after his migration. This would have made his sons too young for the Albanian campaign but old enough for the Civil War, which was his main symbolic concern.

A character less symbolic and much more individualized, whose personal involvement in the Asia Minor Disaster is an operative part of her personality, and thus of her everyday existence, is to be found in *The Stone Lions* (1963) by Julia Iatridi.[8]

Also a chronicle of Greece from 1922 until the end of civil strife in Greece, *The Stone Lions* tells the interesting story of an eight- to ten-year-old refugee orphan who becomes a maid and suffers the common fate of urban Greeks during those critical years. Unlike *The Vine-Shoot*, which employs a linear narrative, this novel experiments somewhat with technique by relating its story on two levels: the present, during which Panoria Fokianou oversees the construction of her house, and the past, which is told in alternating chapters that move the story forward from the horrors of the Fire at Smyrna to the fictional present.

The Stone Lions consciously employs the psychological and physical effects of the Disaster on Panoria as permanent marks on her personality and thus as functioning parts of her past. Her weaknesses, her gullibilities, her decency, and her fortitude make her a convincing character for the reader. The only memory she has of her prior life is of leaving her family's house, whose front door was flanked by stone lions, and of running through the burning streets of Smyrna, hands locked with members of her family, people who are faceless to her now. An explosion scatters them. She runs, alone, toward the Quay, finds herself in a rowboat, an orphan from that moment on, and partially deaf

8. *Ta Petrina Liontaria* (Athens, 1963).

from the explosion. In Piraeus she waits stolidly, for what she does not know, and is taken by a woman as a housemaid, a life she will lead for the thirty-two years until the fictional present. Because she is partially deaf, the information Panoria receives is limited; consequently, her role as the filter through which we learn of the historical events she lives through is lent an authenticity by its self-confessed inadequacy. She can mention her confusion at certain political events about which other characters — and the author — would have had to take a position. Occasionally, the very ignorance Panoria claims to have about politics permits her to question official history — notably that of the Decembrist battles in 1944 — in a way that would have been forbidden to any other character because of his own day-to-day involvement. Freed from the necessity of holding obtrusive ideas by her role in society, Panoria becomes for the reader a dependable witness to the small but significant events she sees daily in the various households she serves.

Writers of the Generation of the 1930s may have found Panoria a dull character, and other novelists of Mrs. Iatridi's own generation might have used her as a sounding board for their own ideologies. In either case, we would not have had the convincing portraiture of the daily, humble Athenian life we do have.

The events of the Disaster are used not merely as an exciting or lurid beginning to a novel not otherwise interested in them, but as ever-conscious memories in the psyche of Panoria. She, an attractive young woman, has been marked by 1922, not merely because she is partially deaf but because she has been declassed and orphaned, stripped of family as well as of personal past. She had a family — in comfortable circumstances, too, if one does not forget "the stone lions" that stood astride the front door — but now she has nothing of her own, not even the child she was to bear of the man she loved, for her mistress demanded that she miscarry. Then, after handing her on like a baton, her employers had fled to Switzerland at the outbreak of World War II, since they were implicated with the collapsing Metaxas regime. Passed from household to household, each with its own problems, political orientations, and life styles, Panoria owns nothing but the imaginative life she has been forced to cultivate because of her hearing disability and her dream of supporting the balcony of her new house with two stone lions. In the end, she does not even have the house, for it is to be given her by her new master under conditions she rejects. She will remain a housemaid all her life, but the symbols of her previous life will remain inviolate.

In *The Stone Lions* there is a more conscious effort to use the events of the Disaster not merely for the excitement they would lend a story but as facts that have changed personality and motivated character. The Disaster, tangible and searing, has been absorbed within the psyche of an individual who lives an interior life that is convincing to the reader. Like the problems of chronology faced by Spyros Plaskovitis in *The Vine-Shoot*, Panoria offers Mrs. Iatridi certain difficulties. The novelist tries to avoid these by making Panoria uncertain of her own age. Given the rough figure of ten years of age when she arrives, and knowing that she has lived in Athens for "thirty-two years and seven months," which dates the fictional present at March 1955, we know that Panoria can be no more than forty-two years old. But the impression she leaves on the reader is of a much older woman, particularly because she seems to have given up the battle for an independent and fulfilling life of her own. The reader is often told of her physical attractions and of her vitality, which makes it hard not to wonder if Panoria's acceptance of the bleakness of her life is reasonable, but he suspends his disbelief because he has been convinced of Panoria's reality.

Dido Sotiriou's *The Dead Wait* (1959) has esthetic intentions similar to those of the fictional works previously discussed, although its strong autobiographical elements are more fully

195

controlled and the writer's ability to create a distance between herself and her material is more clearly demonstrated.[9] If works like *In the Shadow of History*, *The Vine-Shoot*, and *The Stone Lions* used the Disaster as a starting point for their fictional interest, *The Dead Wait* is concerned with goals more general than the arrival and progress of one refugee. As we saw in *In Youthful Battle* and shall see in *Niobe* and *Like Lies and Like the Truth*, novels greatly inferior to hers, Mrs. Sotiriou's artistic intent is to recreate Greek life in Anatolia so that the reader will be made aware of precisely what had been lost in the Disaster. This is not the concern of the works of Kamberoglou, Plaskovitis, and Iatridi, for in their works the Disaster is accepted as an historical fact that is also the beginning of their fiction.

The considerable ambitions of Mrs. Sotiriou in her first novel proved too great for her technical abilities. Within the frame of one esthetic vision, she attempts to animate her characters over twenty-five years of Greek history, from the massacre of the Greeks in her native Aidin in 1918 to the events of the Nazi Occupation up to 1943. The technical problem Mrs. Sotiriou ran into was that *The Dead Wait* breaks into two main segments: the first part involves the massacre and looting of Aidin by Turks in 1918, the moving of the Magis family – the center of fictional interest – to the safety of Smyrna, the arrival of the Greek Army in 1919 as a peace-keeping force, the War, the Disaster, the migration to Greece, and the refugee life there; the second part, developing out of the family's refugee existence, becomes much more vivid in the descriptions of the Metaxas repression, as seen in the proletarian district of Kokkinia and in the treatment of World War II and the Resistance. As a consequence, *The Dead Wait* leaves the impression of being a "diptych," a long and interesting work that is really two novels, the first dealing with

9. *Oi Nekroi Perimenoun* (Athens, 1959).

the period 1918-1923 and the second with the period 1936-1943. The middle years, the refugee years, which lasted more than a decade, are slighted because they are less action-filled. *The Dead Wait* is clearly a novel that should have been a trilogy to have fulfilled the author's ambitions for it. This structural error, moreover, tends to lead to a misinterpretation of the political events of that time. Because the Germans were the controllers of vast capital resources in the Ottoman Empire (which meant vast areas in the Near and Middle East) before and during the Great War, as well as being the aggressors in World War II, they tend in *The Dead Wait* to emerge as the eternal opponents of the Greeks, a description that considerably distorts historical reality.

Despite the structural weakness, however, the fictional vision of Mrs. Sotiriou is impressive in the complex synthesis it attains. In a leisurely and convincing manner she narrates the story of the Magis family, which from the capitalist class in Asia Minor is gradually forced, because of the Disaster and Migration, into the proletarian class. Their acceptance of this decline and their moving to Kokkinia is seen as a liberation from the illusions of the past.

Vasilakis, the father, is an impractical man, unable to survive in an historical period where survival must be everyone's constant preoccupation. His relatives, more realistic than he, had quickly found a *modus vivendi* with the dominant German capital in Asia Minor and left hurriedly when its power was smashed in 1917, or had distrusted the officially expressed Greek determination to stay in Anatolia after the establishment of the Commission in 1919 and sent their fortunes out to Greece and elsewhere. Vasilakis, a blameless and naive patriot, did neither, and his only error was his unquenchable belief in the ideal of a Great Greece. His daughter, and the novel's narrator, Aliki Magi, is saved from the Fire at Smyrna when she and her aunt are sent by her uncle on what he calls an "insurance" trip to Athens that is to last until

197

the political situation has improved. When the two women arrive in Piraeus, they are mistaken for the first of the refugees and learn that only a day separated them from the horror and panic of the Disaster.

Viewed from the perspective of the late 1950s, when Mrs. Sotiriou wrote *The Dead Wait*, the second part of the novel is less concerned with the refugee as a type than with the proletarian who happens to be a refugee. The younger generation – Aliki, and her siblings Niobe and Stefos – are quickly assimilated into the everyday pattern of Greek life. Their involvement, as friends and lovers of native-born Greeks, creates a fusion of the refugees with the natives that is strengthened under the Metaxas dictatorship. There are no longer refugees and natives but the democratic and progressive Greek people who are pitted against their fascist rulers. Their struggle against fascism of the Metaxas and Mussolini variety and the Nazi Occupation is, in Mrs. Sotiriou's view, one and the same, a struggle which, according to *The Dead Wait*, finds the proletarians of Kokkinia in the forefront.

Because of her political orientation, Mrs. Sotiriou had to be careful in her treatment of the Resistance period lest she excite old animosities and risk legal action. Her portrait of Zisis Drogas, the patriot who is betrothed to Aliki's youngest sister, Niobe, is an idealized one. For obvious reasons, his political ideology is less explicitly Marxist than progressive, while her descriptions of the inner workings of the Greek upper class with fascism are accurate enough to convince but vague enough to discourage unwanted attention. The novel's action, moreover, ends in 1943 in order to avoid treating the conflicts that became obvious after that time between the different resistance organizations. Clearly, the fiction that takes political and historical reality as its province in a time as fraught with passion as this would expect to find its objectives and techniques distorted by extra-literary considerations.

Despite the vagueness of the middle years it covers, *The Dead Wait* is a compelling novel on the grand scale, a fictional synthesis that could only be produced years after an event has occurred. Its interests are the interests of a novelist who wants to recapture a world that has irrevocably disappeared, to record accurately the external aspects and the psychological texture of a way of life taken for granted while it lasted, a work of recreation that succeeds only because the passage of time and the intervening experiences have cleared the writer's vision of non-essentials and permitted her to focus on only those aspects of her story she needs.

A brief pause may perhaps be necessary at this point in order to discuss two fictional works that present a view similar to that of Mrs. Sotiriou, but with much less success. *Niobe* (1926), by Kostas Zoumboulidis, and *Like Lies and Like the Truth* (1928), by Socrates Prokopiou, appeared before Stratis Doukas's *Narrative of a Prisoner* and Ilias Venezis's *The Number 31,328*. Zoumboulidis, an Anatolian, has published frequently — scholarly efforts, primarily, and an extremely successful book on etiquette — while Prokopiou was a correspondent in Anatolia for a number of newspapers.

Both novels are thus works of memory and imagination, directly influenced by the events of the Disaster, and seen by men who had first-hand experiences of Anatolia but did not allow themselves the necessary time to absorb them. They attempted, in much less than a decade, to exorcise the horror and sorrow they felt because of the Disaster by recapitulating it historically, by expressing it in linear narratives in the hopes of freeing themselves of its horror.

Niobe, by Kostas Zoumboulidis, who is from Magnesia in Asia Minor, was published two years after having been given honorable mention in the novel contest of 1924 sponsored by the publishing firm of Zikakis.[10] As Ilias Voutieridis stated in his "Report of the Judges' Committee," *Niobe* was the first work of fiction to be directly inspired by the Disaster, and thus achieved "some sort of historical significance" for the study of the theme.

Niobe tells the story of Tonis Ioannidis, who returns to Smynra in 1921 after a Paris education that served also to save him from mobilization in the Ottoman Army in 1914. By using the technique of the return to scenes of youth, Zoumboulidis is able to describe the aspects of *Giaour Izmir* (infidel Smyrna) that would strike one so recently estranged from it. Descriptions of picturesque neighborhoods that are really inventories of a lost homeland, and a lurid plot full of incestuous longings, abductions, and trysts characterize this novel, which comes to a tragic close with the military defeat at Afion Karahissar, in which battle Tonis is killed. The Epilogue is a short but tough-minded description of the final, brutal days of Greek Smyrna. The title, of course, has mythological references to the daughter of Tantalos, who lost all but two of her score of beautiful children because of her pride and who was turned to stone by Zeus in Lydia of Asia Minor.

The tragic fate of Anatolian Hellenism is thus summed up in fictional form and given mythological reverberations within two years of the holocaust. The outlines of the plot, a sequential one beginning with descriptions of the sophisticated and cosmopolitan life of Smyrna, up to and including the Greek Army's occupation (1919-1922), the disastrous battles, and, finally, the fiery termination, are those that most subsequent novels will follow. If a novelist accepts the tragic sequence of events as the logic of his plot, there does not seem to be any way of breaking out of the confines that emerged with *Niobe*. All the later novels

10. *Niovi, Smyrnaiiko Aisthimatiko Mythistorima* (Athens, 1926).

seem to do differently is to supplement the linear plot with political, military, and social interpretations that deepen the particular writer's vision. The end, however, is ordained, and only a great imaginative break from the historical sequence can liberate the writer.

Like Lies and Like the Truth by Socrates Prokopiou[11] is no more than a barely fictionalized view of the time when the writer, a Smyrniot, was a war correspondent for newspapers that ranged from the *Amaltheia*, the *Telegraphos*, and the *Kosmos* of Smyrna, the *Akropolis* of Athens, and *The National Herald* of New York. Invaluable as a source of undigested factual material and as an archive of numerous and excellent photographs, the novel itself is of negligible value, consisting of war reportage that finds its significance reduced the more its fiction intrudes. Even General Leonidas Paraskevopoulos, a copy of whose letter from Paris is bound in the text between pages 164 and 165, recommends the reader of his friend's book to take it more as an *istorima* than as a *mythistorima*.

The passage of time — and consequently the psychological perspective — was lacking in works like *Niobe* and *Like Lies and Like the Truth*. Published so soon after the events they described, they lacked, among other things, the proper selection of detail that esthetic distance would, as a matter of course, have given them. As it is, they are unable to convince a reader not already emotionally committed to the world they describe. Since the everyday life of Anatolian Hellenism was still vivid in the imaginations of Zoumboulidis, of Prokopiou, and of their readers, each description, no matter how neutral it may have appeared to an outsider, was charged for them, the refugees, with countless

11. *San Psemmata kai san Alitheia, Mikrasiatikon Istorikon Mythistorima me Eikones* (Athens, 1928).

powerful connotations. This was clearly not art, in the sense of an imaginative recreation, but a short-hand used to unlock emotional reserves, a language understood and experienced only by those who shared a common culture.

The fact of the matter is that novels of this kind were no longer written after the 1920s. As we saw earlier, fiction followed another course, ignoring the Disaster per se and concentrating on its consequences: the captivity, the refugee experience, and the longing for the homeland that manifested itself before World War II. Like victims of, or witnesses to, a horrible accident or crime who are often psychologically unable to review it in their mind's eye and free themselves of its nightmarish hold, the Greeks – with only two premature exceptions – avoided for decades considering in their fiction the tragic events in Smyrna.

Even after the Second World War there is an almost insistent effort to subordinate the events of the Disaster and to see it in a "perspective" that neutralizes its awful power and reduces its unbearable intensity. One is reminded of Nikos Kazantzakis's insistence to Galateia during the worst horrors of the Disaster that these experiences will prove "instructive," a "rebirth," a "flowering" for the Greeks, as though he was unwilling and unprepared to *see* the death of Asia Minor Hellenism, wanting to ignore it in his hopes for an eventual "resurrection." It is not, in fact, until 1962, on the fortieth anniversary of the Disaster, that a novel appears that fearlessly gazes at Smyrna during the holocaust. But even *Bloodied Earth* by Dido Sotiriou had to be preceded by *The Dead Wait*, which acted for her as a preparation for the catharsis she experienced.

Instead of novels, therefore, that directly used the events of the Asia Minor Disaster, we find the disguised "chronicle," the autobiographical or totally fictional work that shows its central character living through or being operated upon by historical forces. In effect, and with few exceptions, all of these works are more concerned with documenting the post-Disaster era than they are with concentrating on the Disaster, and they use the events of 1922 as mere starting points for their fictional interest.

The perspective time had provided her liberated Mrs. Sotiriou from the illusion of complete communication. In *The Dead Wait* she knew that she needed to assume an ignorance of Anatolia on the part of her readers. Consequently, she was compelled to recreate convincingly the everyday existence of her fictional characters. Freed by time from the misunderstanding that her emotions were shared by her readers, she saw more clearly the effort she needed to invest in bringing to life her characters and their world. Her error, one of overall design rather than execution, in *The Dead Wait* was one she did not commit in her second novel, *Bloodied Earth* (1962).[12]

Manolis Axiotis, the point-of-view character in this novel, is a vivid, believable Anatolian peasant. As a humble, alert, and uncompromisingly honest man, Manolis acts as the moral guide of the reader from the turn of the century to the upheaval of the Disaster. Mrs. Sotiriou's objective, as in *The Dead Wait*, is not merely to document events but to interpret them in the light of an ideology. The lack of a broader political philosophy in *Niobe* and *Like Lies and Like the Truth* is what rendered earlier attempts at fictional synthesis inadequate, for they merely duplicated the efforts and insights of journalism without being able to claim factual authenticity as novels. *Bloodied Earth*, on the contrary, though it cleverly employs the factual and emotional substratum carefully built up by previous writers of Anatolia,

12. *Matomena Homata* (Athens, 1962).

focuses on those incidents and ideas that fulfill the writer's vision and are not merely inert facts.[13]

Modeled on an actual character, Manolis Axiotis is the novel's narrator and — by what may be either a coincidence or an effort on the novelist's part to connect her work with a "tradition" — he is from Kirkinze, the same village as Nicholas Kazakoglou, the narrator of Stratis Doukas's *Narrative of a Prisoner*. Manolis and his people, Anatolian villagers for whom Greece was a distant idea, follow their patriarchal patterns of life, gradually developing a consciousness of Greek nationality at the prodding of the schoolmaster, the priest, and the occasional tourist who comes to ask them about Old Ephesus, which neighbors Kirkinze. Not part of Greece, yet preeminently Greek, their region, Manolis informs the reader, is characterized by "sevens": it can claim the Temple of Artemis, one of the Seven Wonders of the World; the Church of St. John the Theologian, one of the Seven Stars of the Apocalypse; and the cave where the Seven Sleeping Children slumbered. It was only a matter of time, everyone agreed, until Asia Minor would be united with Greece.

In other novels, this irony would sound clear, unmuffled by reality's confused noises. But *Bloodied Earth* is the narration of Manolis Axiotis, who carefully disguises his artistry. In telling the story of his eventful life, he treats himself more as an object of interest than as the competent manipulator of fictional techniques. His mathematical abilities save him from a life of agricultural toil, and he is given the job of keeping an estate's books. He gives up his position, more out of unwillingness to be involved than out of disapproval, when he sees his Turkish employer and a

13. In a letter to me, dated September 13, 1971 from Vasilika, Mrs. Sotiriou states that "before and during the time I wrote [my books] I visited many eye-witnesses [of the Asia Minor events], elderly Anatolians, primarily of the working class. I read old books, even memoirs of generals, old archives, newspapers, periodicals from public and private libraries.

beautiful Greek village girl openly breaking the taboo on fraterni-
zation. Manolis goes to Smyrna and works for various merchants,
but he cannot accept the necessary cheating of the Moslem
peasants. He becomes a day-laborer, later finds work with a
smuggler, whom he admires, then leaves for another job where he
learns from a fellow-worker, Barba-Yiakoumis, of the political
conflicts in store for Anatolia, where Greeks are pitted, as he
says, not against the Turks, but against the Levantines, who act as
agents for the Western powers. Barba-Yiakoumis is the first appearance of the well-versed progressive worker who interprets the
historical developments from the point of view of Marxism. This
device frees the author from intruding into the novel's action in
order to establish and emphasize the political context as she views
it, as well as keeping Manolis himself, a clever but uneducated
man, in the character already established for him.

Part II, "Amele Ambourou," ("Labor Battalions," in Turkish)
details the forced "repatriation" and labor camps that the Turks,
instructed by Liman von Sanders, had used as devices to rid
themselves of minorities at the beginning of the Great War. After
carefully describing what it was like to be a helpless pawn in the
power games of states, Manolis is taken into the labor battalions
and undergoes the brutalization extensively treated in "Narratives
of Captivity" in Chapter Two and carefully documented in
sources which seem to have fulfilled their role as historic memory
only in the case of Mrs. Sotiriou. Manolis escapes from central
Turkey, travels westward to the Greek provinces, and is saved by
the Armistice. With the arrival of the Greek army, he comes into
conflict with the authorities — village elders, the priest, the
schoolmaster, and landowners — who demand that all Anatolian
Greek males allow themselves to be drafted into the Greek army
despite the fact that they are Ottoman subjects and formally, at
least, owe allegiance to the Sultan.

In embryo form we find here a conflict between a clear-sighted but not "progressive" man — Manolis — and what stands for official or semi-official Greek thinking. There were probably very few Greeks of Asia Minor who tried to refuse service in the Royal Hellenic Army out of a regard for their legal position as subjects of the Sultan. If they had resisted enlistment, they would have done so more out of personal than out of legal or ideological misgivings. In having Manolis resist service, however, Mrs. Sotiriou poses for the first time in fictional form the issue of treason that the triumphant Turks later used to execute any Anatolian Greeks suspected of having served in the defeated Greek forces. Certainly, the persecutions instituted throughout the centuries of the Ottoman Empire, which were merely continued in a more rational manner and for more strategic objectives in 1914-1917 under Liman von Sanders, had made the legal and moral commitments the Greeks and Armenians may have been subject to under the Sultan no more than pathetic formalities, but it was these that distinguished the Anatolians from the native Greeks in service in Asia Minor. In employing this incident, Mrs. Sotiriou attempts to provide a more complex political background to the Anatolian events than hitherto seen in Greek historical fiction.

Manolis finds himself an enlisted man in the Greek army, which seems to him completely officered by men from Old Greece. At the front with a company of Cretans, deliberately posted there on orders of the Populist government so that they can take the brunt of the fighting, Manolis meets Nikitas Drosakis, who is like Barba-Yiakoumis a man who knows the background of greed and corruption to the Asia Minor Expedition, but who, unlike the first "tutor," is an intellectual who has surpassed the arid disputes between Venizelists and Monarchists and who instructs Manolis, the intelligent "common man," convincing him of ideas that challenge his — and presumably, the reader's — previous attitudes toward the history of the time. Drosakis's opponent in an unequal ideological battle is Lefteris Kanakis, the son of a rich

Cretan and a young man known to Venizelos, who is without political ideas or beliefs other than those of a Greater Greece. He stands for nothing besides personal gain and he knows it. Even if he tried to, Lefteris Kanakis could not convince Manolis of the validity of his ideas.

The ideological battle, therefore, is not between Liberalism and Monarchy, since the two political parties have roughly the same ideologies. The Monarchists had proved, as a result of the 1920 elections, to have only negative ideas when they were in opposition, ideas they immediately rejected once they became the government, whereupon they assumed the expansionist ideas they had previously attacked. The only difference between them, therefore, is in the degrees of competence and efficiency they reveal. The battle is rather between the Venizelists and "history," whose best interpreters are Marxist intellectuals just as badly overwhelmed by historical forces as anyone else. Lefteris Kanakis, proving his lack of political beliefs, quickly manages to locate a soft and safe post back in Smyrna, but he fails to convince Nikitas Drosakis to go with him, much to Manolis's secret satisfaction: he has found one man, at last, who acts out of personal belief. The decision of Drosakis to die at the front is totally unconvincing, however, since it is a fulfillment of a duty he himself cannot possibly respect.

The front breaks and Manolis arrives in Smyrna after a wild retreat. There is a particularly fine scene in which Manolis tries but fails to convince a patriotic barber of the front's collapse, a conversation terminated by the Greek fleet's weighing anchor and sailing out of the harbor of Smyrna. Manolis finds his family confidently viewing a future he has difficulty persuading them will be harsh indeed. His brother, in fact, has just invested most of their money in an estate being offered at a price too good to ignore. After Manolis has put on civilian clothes, they go to the Quay and, with thousands of Smyrniots, are herded onto barges before the Turkish cavalry rides into Smyrna. They ignore the Turkish request that they return to their homes and see, from the Armenian Quarter, the beginning of the fire that will end *Giaour Izmir*. The barges are towed back to the Quay by the Turks – the ships of the Allies stand by without intervening – and men are chosen for execution and women for rape. When the troops go elsewhere, the Greeks rush to the cemetery, already crowded with families living in mausoleums, their daughters literally buried under marble slabs to save them from the attention of Turks. Manolis's family leaves, searching for a protected place, but his brother is seized and taken along with forty thousand others to death in Magnesia, while he and a friend go back to Kirkinze, like Nicholas Kazakoglou before them, find it deserted, then head toward the shores of the Aegean and safety.

Purged by reliving the horror of the Disaster, Mrs. Sotiriou repeats with more success the theme of a peaceful, pleasant time in Greco-Turkish relations first introduced by Alekos Doukas. "Why are you looking at me so wildly, partisan of Kior Memet?" Manolis asks the spirit of his enemy.

> I killed you and weep for that. Think about what you cost me. Brothers, sisters, friends, countrymen, the labor battalions, an entire generation slaughtered!
>
> So much poison, so much misfortune, and my mind still wants to return to the past. Why couldn't all we suffered be lies so that we could return to our homeland now, to our gardens . . . our forests . . . our orchards . . . our feast-days. . . .
>
> Partisan of Kior Memet, greet for me the land that bore us both. . . . Let it not bear hatred for our drenching it with blood. . . . A curse on those responsible![14]

14. *Ibid.,* p. 306. Because I was doing the research for this book in Greece during the Junta years, I was unable to secure a copy of the Kedros publication, and as a result I refer to the only text I was able to consult, published by "Political and Literary Publications," n.p., 1963.

All the novels discussed so far in this category have concentrated on the historical aspect of the Disaster and its aftermath. Regardless of their success or failure as works of literary art, the objectives were to place fictional characters in an actual era and to observe their interactions with other characters and the political events of the time. Depending upon the writer's ability, of course, some works were more convincing than others; but all, without question, accepted as their primary goal the accurate portrayal of the period in which their action took place. A number of them tried, in fictional terms, to reinterpret chapters of national history thought to be misinterpreted or misunderstood in the past; others ignored the political context of the Disaster and tried to present an overall view of Greek life throughout the interwar period to the Civil War and after; still others, notably *Niobe* and *Like Lies and Like the Truth*, merely repeated the attitudes found in the journalism of their time, the last 1920s.

The Mermaid Madonna (1949) by Stratis Myrivilis[15] is the only novel in this category, set squarely in its historical time, that nevertheless attempts to break free of the era in which it is placed and to aspire to the level of myth. It fails to do this for a number of reasons, but formally this is because it is the final novel of what Myrivilis called "the trilogy of the war." As the conclusion of a sequence of novels, it is fixed irrevocably in an historical development against which its subject matter clearly strains. Yet it is not a "trilogy" in the way the term is usually understood, because the characters, the themes, and the moods of the three books differ radically. Though ostensibly about the establishment of Anatolian refugees in the Skala of Mytilene, *The Mermaid Madonna* is actually about the growth into great beauty of Smaragdi, a foundling raised by a refugee couple, whose physical

15. *I Panaghia I Gorgona* (Athens, 1955).

and spiritual differences from those of her human environment lead her fellow villagers to believe that she is of a supernatural order, the daughter of a mermaid.

The novel's title comes from a religious painting in the Skala done by a half-mythical person named Captain Ilias, from Aivalik, who had conceived of the Virgin Mary as a mermaid and who disappeared from the Skala in the midsummer of 1914, the day before the refugees arrived from Anatolia following the first mass persecutions by the Turks. The initial stages of the novel's action, after the leisurely beginning, concern the arrival of the refugees of the 1922 Disaster. With the perspective of the late 1940s, Myrivilis details the difficulties the Anatolians encountered in establishing themselves in Mytilene; their arguments among themselves and with the native inhabitants; their gradually diminishing desire to return to their homes on the opposite shore, despite the efforts of the schoolmaster, Avghoustis, to keep their minds fixed on their eventual return; and the efforts of the Greek state (with which Myrivilis by the late 1940s identified almost completely) to house them in their own living quarters.

Despite the importance of these issues, the distance of time and emotion has enabled Myrivilis to subordinate the refugee theme of *The Mermaid Madonna* and to make something else of the novel — a study of the children of refugee parents who grow up as citizens of a new, unified Greece and have little interest in the dreams of their elders. It is the tragedy of Avghoustis that he has no success in keeping alive the desire for return to the lost homelands, which are now clearly identified in Old Testament terms. He refuses a house offered him by the government and takes to drink, but he keeps alive the dream of return until the unscrupulous political leader upon whom he has invested all his hopes, a man called "the Thunderbolt," capitulates and accepts a portfolio with a coalition government committed to "friendship" with Turkey. This destroys Avghoustis. He knows now that he has lost everything – wife, daughters, home, property and "two thousand years of history."

It is out of this environment that Smaragdi emerges. Found by Varouchos, the president of the refugee community in the Skala, she is adopted by him and his wife, Nerantzi, who believes that the Mermaid Madonna, to whom she had prayed, has given them a daughter to make up for the sickly girl-child they had lost earlier. Blonde, with eyes the color of the sea, Smaragdi grows like a child of nature, accepting the quiet but confident interpretations of her supernatural origins that are offered by Aunt Permachoula, a woman of great age and spiritual awareness. Smaragdi has certain "proofs" of her difference from others, ranging from the inexplicable hatred of an otherwise docile dog, who attacks her furiously, to her impatience with the domestic life of women, to the disquieting beauty that destroys the men who love her. It is, finally, less because of her guilt at the suicide of Lambis, the young man who loved her desperately, and more because of her repugnance at and rejection of the role of subservience to man and object of his sexual needs that she becomes a devotee of the Mermaid Madonna, abandoning her individuality for the black uniform of the Greek peasant woman.

The character of Smaragdi, the keystone of *The Mermaid Madonna*, is ultimately the weak point of this ambitious and fascinating novel. She does not convince the reader with the reality of her torment, and he tends to agree with an interpretation by a character within the novel that Smaragdi is an intellectually and emotionally immature girl, retarded in every respect but the physical. Myrivilis provides a strong reason for why this should be so: her rape, in her early teens, by her adoptive father, Varouchos, subsequently driven away from the village. Her fear of sexuality after this can be understood, and her rejection of the suitors available to her in the Skala need not be considered an irrevocable rejection of sexuality. In fact, it is just as she is becoming interested in a young sponge diver from another island that Lambis commits suicide because Smaragdi happened to witness a disgraceful episode in his life. The guilt she feels because of this, according to Myrivilis, makes her refuse to continue her life as a free woman. (She can, by the way, be no more than fifteen, since she was probably not born before 1924 and since the Second World War is not mentioned in the course of the novel.) Her wearing of black and her nun-like devotion to the Mermaid Madonna are thus explicable in psychological terms.

The crucial problem, however, was that Myrivilis did not take a stand on Smaragdi's supernatural origins. Though he had consciously created a social and cultural milieu that would not have found her supernatural birth impossible to accept — one which would, in fact, have found it a convenient way to explain her disquieting beauty, her ability, and her unavailability — he himself could not accept the plausibility of mermaids. Too much the rationalist, too much a part of the Generation of the 1930s, he found himself initially attracted by the idea of supernatural beings in direct and unbroken descent from the Greek pagan tradition, but he ultimately denied them as possible. Rejecting the Greek folk tradition, which would have given him all the support he needed and which he had recreated in such a masterly way, Myrivilis ignored the archetype of the Mermaid Madonna, felt unable to insist on the authenticity of his vision, and ended his novel by having Smaragdi accept a role totally out of keeping with her character. Unable to endure the logic of his own conception, Myrivilis might still have persisted if the literary convention of the Mermaid had existed in the modern Greek literary tradition, as distinct from the folk tale. He might even have done so if Greek letters had cultivated the realm of fantasy, as other national literatures have done with children's stories, with tales of horror and mystery, and with science fiction. Nikos Kazantzakis, on the contrary, was able to harness his personal torments and to narrate the events of the life of Jesus, Who was both Man and God, in *The Last Temptation of Christ*, because the literary and pictorial conventions of the entire Christian tradition supported him in this.

Even denying it its mythic dimension, *The Mermaid Madonna* is not a "refugee novel" in the way Tatiana Stavrou's *The First Roots* and Ilias Venezis's *Serenity* are. Despite the life-denying conclusion, there is little in the esthetic vision of Myrivilis of the hopelessness and the asphyxiating concentration on the here and now of the novels written in the second half of the 1930s. Something had occurred in the interval that had given to Greek life a new outlook, a new vista. Nature, and the Aegean at that, had helped considerably, certainly, but a new attitude toward the Greek himself had changed the defeatism prevalent in the inter-war period.

We see this quite clearly with the episode of the arrival at the Skala of a Turk, Ahmet Reiz, from the Anatolian mainland. At first treated with reserve, he is later accepted by the Greeks at Fortis's cafe in a friendly manner. In the course of his conversation, during which he dissociates the activities of the Turkish Tsetes, the brutal irregulars, from the warmth and respect the average Turk had for the Greek subjects of the Ottoman Empire, Ahmet Reiz clears up a mystery that had existed from the beginning of the novel.

No one knew what had happened to the wealthy Genatos, a bearded, withdrawn man who summered on the island every year. According to Ahmet Reiz, when the Tsetes were in the area and Genatos knew that his end and the violation of his daughters was near, he called in his Turkish workers, divided his property among them, destroyed his factory, and invited Kara Ali, the leader of the Tsetes, to see the daughters he would doubtless want to carry off as booty. They were all lying on sofas, dead, killed by their own father, who then shot down the Turk, set fire to his own house, and killed himself.

Avghoustis, listening to this narrative, appears convinced of its authenticity and seems to approve of Genatos's actions, even though the reader knows that he has, for the entire interwar period, mourned the loss of his own family. "That's how it is with us," Avghoustis generalizes, "We are usually gnawed at by our vices and our dissensions. Our interests make us behave terribly at times. Occasionally, we go too far. Suddenly we are seized by the "Greek" in us, as Captain Ilias once said. Then the sky opens and we see the face of God. The God of old pagan times, who never died and is always near us at the important moments."[16]

The present writer believes that an incident like this would have been considered both inconceivable and offensive in fiction written before World War II. Myrivilis, himself, would have been the first to deny its realism. Though evidence exists of incidents like this occurring throughout Asia Minor at the time of the Disaster, the material could not be employed by writers of fiction while memories of horror were still vivid. In all of the fiction read by the present writer after the Disaster and before the Albanian campaign, there is no example of this sort. Nor would the reason given for this – being seized by the "Greek" in one's psyche (τούς ἐπιασε τό ἐλληνικό τους) and compelled to act in an heroic way that refutes petty rationality – have been credited as feasible. This wild but grand gesture can appear possible and attractive to Myrivilis only after the refutation of petty reason, which was how the Greeks viewed their behavior during the Albanian campaign, and only after the brutal facts had been digested.

16. *Ibid.*, pp. 421-422.

Begun during the years of Occupation[17] and worked on throughout the Civil War, *The Mermaid Madonna* fails because Myrivilis was unable to decide what ultimately to do with Smaragdi. Without a religious belief in Christianity (which is attested to by most of his fiction), without even the willingness to tolerate the Church and its representatives, who are always viewed with a fairly conventional anticlerical hostility, Myrivilis was also unable to insist on the divinity of the Nature which he believed, doggedly, was the only supernatural fact. The concluding motto of all his novels, "The End, and to God the Glory" reveals only his desperate theological confusion.

The Mermaid Madonna is thus suspended midway between history and myth, aspiring to myth by the inherent demands of the novel's tensions, but held down by history, by the inability of Myrivilis to free his imagination from the novel's specific historical context.

In most of the fiction set in Anatolia and published after World War II, there is the clearly stated assumption of a harmony existing between Greeks and Turks before 1914 and the execution of Liman von Sanders's policies. This arises in a number of incidents whose total effect is to exonerate the common Greeks and Turks from the crimes of the past. The blame, perhaps conveniently, falls on others, men who bore the responsibility for decisions that had been proved disastrously wrong, men who were in positions of power when the forces of history appeared to favor Greek irredentism, when "the ripe fruit" of Anatolia was ready to fall into Greek laps. In those novels set in Asia Minor and written by Anatolians, who would be presumed to know their culture well, this attitude appears as a result of the perspective of time and is totally at variance with what the careful reader

17. Venezis mentions this in *Prosfygikos Kosmos* (Jan. 24, 1943). See Chapter Six.

had been led to expect by most of the literature published before the Second World War.

Perhaps out of a mature reflection of a reality previously ignored; perhaps because of the idealization of "the lost paradise" that Asia Minor had become in the memories of Anatolians, or those with Anatolian connections; perhaps even out of the desire to focus the blame more precisely for the loss of this paradise; whatever the reasons, writers as diverse as Alekos Doukas, Dido Sotiriou, Stratis Myrivilis, and Kosmas Politis, whose *At Hadzifrangos's* will conclude this chapter, insist that life in the Ottoman Empire, before 1914 at any rate, was relatively free and pleasant, a view diametrically opposed to that which dominated Greek thought in the early decades of the twentieth century. "Even in the interior of Asia Minor," Kosmas Politis says, "there was, on the whole, a feeling of harmony between the Turks and the Greeks."[18]

The very diversity of these writers leads one to the conclusion that there is some truth in this belief. Alekos Doukas, Mrs. Sotiriou, and Kosmas Politis share an orientation that finds them in opposition to what they consider the reactionary nature of the Greek state. Myrivilis, on the other hand, had found himself by the late 1940s in almost complete agreement with it. In believing that the harmony purported to have existed between Greek and Turk was destroyed first in 1914 by Liman von Sanders, then in 1919 by the establishment of the Greek Commission in Smyrna, the first three writers, one might say, used the recently asserted "harmony" to criticize, overtly or covertly, the Greek state, which would include recent governments as well as those responsible for the Disaster. But the witness of Stratis Myrivilis, the most powerful and outspoken foe of the "opposition" and a man

18. *Stou Hadzifrangou, Ta Sarantachrona mias Hamenis Politeias* (Athens, 1963), p. xi.

whose authority on Anatolian matters cannot be questioned, seems to support the contention that there was indeed a harmony between Greeks and Turks in the Ottoman Empire.

The final word, historically, was had by Politis in *At Hadzifrangos's*, but it is a curious fact that the image of the Turk in Greek fiction is at once so contradictory and so vague. Docile yet violent, noble yet base, pliable yet cunning, upright yet devious, he is all of these things, but more often he is absent, in a void somewhere, unseen in fiction, faceless, a partner of the Greek in a harmonious world that emerges only after more than a generation has passed, a world whose harmony, now irrevocably destroyed, is created to stand in condemnation of "those responsible."

"As far as Smyrna is concerned," Politis says,

> I can say we lived in ignorance of the Turkish element. When the Greek Commission was established in Smyrna, on the contrary, there were moments when we, the local people, felt that we lived under a foreign — I don't mean "enemy" — occupation. As far as the feeling of the *rayah* that I say I've been made to feel in my own country [the motto of the novel], I don't know how many other refugees share in this — what I do know for certain is that it is felt by many of the native Greeks.[19]

Though he would probably agree neither with the general tenor of Politis's statement nor his conclusion, Myrivilis seems to have accepted the general Anatolian contention that there was harmony between the Turks and the Greeks before 1914, a harmony that is, nevertheless, neither mentioned nor described in pre-World War II fiction. By the irony of history and man's capacity to forget, however, this "harmony" would emerge almost half a century later as an important issue in fiction.

19. *Ibid.*, p. xi.

The Fiction of Myth

There is a kind of fiction that, no matter how specific and detailed it may claim to be, succeeds in avoiding the direct representation of historical reality. No one can deny that all fiction selects carefully the facts it needs to use, but "the fiction of myth" is much more exploitative than that which claims a basis in history. The writer of the latter tries to reflect, as accurately as possible, the historical period in which his fiction is set, while the writer of "the fiction of myth" makes no claim to historical authenticity, willfully exaggerating character, distorting incidents, and changing perspective. Of the works discussed under "The Fiction of History," only *The Mermaid Madonna* tried to break into another dimension; the other works were rooted deeply in their time, viewing history as an unrepeatable sequential thrust from past to present to future. The fictions of myth, on the contrary, even those works whose linear austerity might lead one to suspect that they belong in the other category, come closer to the moral parable than to social realism. Spyros Plaskovitis's *The Vine-Shoot*, certainly, has this parable effect, but nothing leads a reader to infer that its philosophical meaning can be abstracted from its time and place, so deeply rooted is it in the history it represents. Whereas the fiction of history can often be described in pictorial terms as "representational," the fiction of myth would more accurately be termed "expressionist." In its extreme — *The Dreams of Angelika*, for example — it becomes almost *grand guignol*.

The works in this category are more easily studied in two groups, those that employ the linear plot and tend, despite all their realistic appearances, to be moral parables, and those whose complexity can not be fully expressed by the sequential plot but must employ various levels of time and action. In the first category we shall study Nikos Kazantzakis's *Christ Recrucified*

218

(1950) and a "chronicle" — actually a short novella — by Menis Koumendareas, entitled *The Sailing* (1964). In the second category, we shall discuss Nikos Bakolas's *The Garden of Princes* (1966), Eva Vlami's *The Dreams of Angelika* (1958), and Kosmas Politis's *At Hadzifrangos's* (1962).

The Linear Plot — The events of the German Occupation and the Civil War were centripetal, forcing Greek writers, regardless of their political and ideological orientations, back to Greece. We have traced the career of Nikos Kazantzakis immediately after the Asia Minor Disaster. Though the effect of the events of 1922 may have been crucial to his development as a thinker and creator, little artistic evidence can be found for this in prose fiction until the appearance of *Zorba* (1946) and *Christ Recrucified* (1950), an intricate and powerful novel set in Asia Minor.

The Life and Times of Alexis Zorbas — to give it its full Greek title — concerns us here only because in it the Professor and Zorba, polar opposites in character, join briefly in a friendship that reveals Kazantzakis's ideas, as expressed in *The Saviors of God* and as articulated by the Professor, to be challenged by the world view of Zorba. As is usual in autobiographical novels of this sort, the narrator is a mere blur, while Zorba is clearly focused upon; this should not and does not obscure the fact that the ideas previously held by Kazantzakis, though never formally repudiated, prove to be incapable of explaining the complexity of man's multiple needs, desires, weaknesses, and strengths, besides being dull, sterile, and even life-denying compared to the alternative expressed by Zorba. Under the older man's influence, the intellectual begins purging himself, in a quest for personal freedom, from the abstractions he names: Buddhas, Gods, Motherlands, and Ideas. There is no certainty, however, that the effects of this purgation last any longer than the relationship of the two men.

Zorba is a novel that Kazantzakis could have written only after the Greco-Italian War, for the character of Alexis Zorba, though it may have a firm basis in reality, is also a justification of the "miserable" and "wretched" Greeks upon whom the writer lavished such abuse in his letters to Galateia. Zorba is a hero who is heroic without being inhuman – a characteristic from which Kazantzakis's early heroes were never free – a man who accepts his weaknesses as unavoidable aspects of his humanity, a vividly real being in a Kazantzakian portrait gallery that had previously housed only heroic shades. *Zorba* did more than bring Nikos Kazantzakis back to the novel form; it brought him back to the novel written in Greek and set in a Greek world.[20] Seemingly without plot, it is most concentrated, for its plot is a dialogue between matter and spirit.

A few years later, *Christ Recrucified*, a novel without any precedent in Greek fiction, appeared.[21] It breaks tradition in a number of ways. Technically, there is no example in previous Greek novels for such an intricate, architectonic plot that had been executed so well. The elegance of the novel's structure, an abrupt break from the looser, less intensely guided fiction of the

20. Peter Bien expresses it in this manner: "It seems obvious to us, who know Kazantzakis almost exclusively through the late novels, that the modern Greeks were his proper, inevitable subject-matter, and thus it is difficult for us to realize that in the thirty-three-year period between *The Masterbuilder* (1908) and *Zorba* (begun 1941), there was not a single page of his published imaginative writing – that is, of completed, published fiction or poetry or drama – that treated modern Greece directly or in which an actual modern Greek was allowed to speak the demotic tongue that Kazantzakis had worshipped so continuously. His heroes and settings had been either non-Greek, or drawn exclusively from ancient Greek mythology or from Byzantium, though he insisted that he always wrote about contemporary problems, symbolically. Kazantzakis's acceptances in later life were thus twofold: a new prosaic genre involving prose, and a new prosaic subject matter, the Greek people." *Kazantzakis and the Linguistic Revolution in Greek Literature,* pp. 243-244.

21. *O Christos Xanastavronetai* (Athens, 1950). In the United States the book is entitled *The Greek Passion.*

Greek past, was also a rejection of the experimentation that the novel in Western literatures had been going through since the first decades of the twentieth century. But since the break from ethography had occurred only a few decades before, and since great examples of experimentation had yet to appear in Greek fiction (although the Generation of the 1930s had begun to experiment), *Christ Recrucified* was in the unlikely position of being considered a "traditional novel" in a fictional tradition that had no precedent for it. The linear plot was here stretched to its maximum point, with characters quickly but believably sketched into an elaborate mechanism whose only outcome was tragic. *Christ Recrucified* was, then, a tragic novel whose technique had to reflect the tensions and strains its meaning demanded of it. Because the novel's issues were, at the time of its publication, explosive ones for the Greek reader, the choice of locale enabled Kazantzakis to approach his subject matter as indirectly as possible: he set his portrayal of a Passion Play in Asia Minor during a historically vague period of time.

Predictably, Greek critics have commented that the tradition of the Passion Play is not observed in the Greek world and that the'depiction of historical forces in the choice of an Anatolian setting is not convincing. Both attacks are justified but neither is particularly relevant, for a novel as symbolic as *Christ Recrucified* needs to be persuasive more within its internal tensions than in its accurate reflection of everyday reality. A symbolic novel has other objectives, and the reality that *Christ Recrucified* was designed to reflect was in the late 1940s and early 1950s much too explosive to be straightforwardly depicted. It would have demanded, furthermore, a specific political commitment, and this Kazantzakis was rarely willing to make.

The village of Lykovrisi, in a vaguely described Anatolia, is the locale of this tragic novel. The time is uncertain, sometime after the Russian Revolution but before the Asia Minor Disaster.

221

Kazantzakis makes no effort to place the action in any particular province, nor are any Turks present except for those who represent authority. It is Easter time and the elders and the priest, Grigoris, gather the villagers to choose the actors for a Passion Play given every seven years. The persons chosen to act out the Divine Tragedy have one year to purify and otherwise prepare themselves for the roles they are to portray. Yiannakos, a charming but roguish peddler, is to be Peter; Michalis, the Archon's son, is John; Konstandis, the owner of the village coffeehouse and Yiannakos's brother-in-law, is James; the violent Panayotaros is Judas; Katerina, the village prostitute, is the Magdalene; and Manolios, the quiet, serious shepherd, is given the sacred role of Christ. The villagers take their roles seriously and decide to change their ways of life. Like the finger of God, however, a band of Greek refugees escaping from Turkish persecutions arrive in Lykovrisi and beg for food and help in reestablishing themselves. Despite the commitment to Christianity implied by their tradition of the Passion Play, the villagers turn against the refugees, while those chosen to portray the Apostles, Magdalene, and Christ, accepting the responsibilities their roles demand, try to help them.

The conflict is, therefore, one between personal selfishness and justice, human and divine. The Agha, a complacent Turk, representative of the Ottoman Empire in the village and thus cast unwittingly in the role of Pontius Pilate, becomes involved in the maelstrom of the novel's action when his beloved Youssoufaki is killed, out of homosexual jealousy, by Hussein, one of the Agha's guards. The blame falls on someone in the village and the Agha threatens to hang all the Christians unless the murderer steps forward. Manolios, proving that he takes seriously his role as Messiah, accepts the guilt for the salvation of his fellows and is about to be hanged when the identity of the murderer is revealed.

On the day of the prophet Elijah, when the Lykovrisiotes go

to the chapel on the hill for their annual service and feast, Priest Fotis, the leader of the refugees, arrives with his people and asks again for Christian charity. He is repulsed. "Judas" tells Priest Grigoris and the Archon that Fotis and Manolios are "Bolsheviks" who are plotting the overthrow of Church, state, family, and private property. The last matter strikes home to the priest because Mariori, his daughter, is betrothed to Michalis, and if the "Apostle John" continues in his folly of associating with the "Muscovites," the priest's property (the Archon's wealth) will be given to the refugees. He complains to the Agha, who by now has found another boy, though not as pliable to his wishes as Youssoufaki, and the Turk promises to do something about the refugees if the priest will get a young girl for Youssoufaki's successor. Priest Grigoris, adding procurement to his religious duties, promptly recruits Pelageia, the daughter of "Judas."

The Archon dies after a serious illness and his property passes to his son, the "Apostle John" who, in anguish over the deplorable condition of the refugees, grants them his lands in Lykovrisi. Priest Grigoris is furious when he hears of this and tells the Agha that the young man is not of sound mind. Persuaded, the Turk seals the Archon's house and property against the refugees.

Obviously, the tensions inherent in the novel have nothing to do with those of the Great War or the Asia Minor Disaster. The novelist has chosen his story not to mirror with historical accuracy the time in which his work is theoretically set, but to reflect, in an emotionally accurate way, the time in which he was writing the book: the novel was completed in 1948. Despite its uncompromisingly linear structure, *Christ Recrucified* is concerned more with the *myth* of a Passion Play whose tensions revolve around social justice than with clearly describing any particular historical event. In fact, the novel's sequential structure aids its mythic objectives because the Passion Play's performance every seven years assures us of its mythic recurrence. Still troubled by his

223

"meta-communistic" credo, Kazantzakis finds that the problem of rich and poor — which he sees in fairly simplistic terms — had not yet been solved by mankind.

The novel ends with a battle outside the village. The two priests, rather than allow a general melee, agree to a fight between themselves. Fotis, the refugee priest, defeats the softer Grigoris. "Judas," jealous because of "Christ's" hold on the "Magdalene" he loved, attacks Manolios, and the battle begins in all earnestness. The Agha, in order to protect the peace, calls out his troops and stops the fighting. Grigoris has already excommunicated Manolios and, on Christmas Eve, helped by Judas, kills "Christ" in the village church. The novel concludes with the refugees leaving the village and continuing "their interminable journey to the East."

Certainly the values Kazantzakis pits against each other in this novel are eternal ones, but their conflict was exaggerated during and immediately after the Greek Civil War. Though his views of Church, state, family, and private property can be identified without any hesitation as representing those of the Greek establishment, Kazantzakis — for reasons that are political and ideological as well as psychological — was unable to make a clear identification between the cause of the refugees and the cause of the defeated EAM-ELAS. *Christ Recrucified*, as a symbolic novel, enables Nikos Kazantzakis to say what he wants to say about social justice without committing himself to a one-to-one political identification because the novel's setting, Asia Minor, was neutral enough by the late 1940s and early 1950s not to interfere by raising emotional and ideological obstacles to the symbolic action he wants to express.

By the late 1940s the Disaster had become "historical" and did not cause the dissension and the sorrow it had brought two decades before. World War II and the Civil War had brought new dissensions and sorrows which colored the thinking of everyone.

Despite his use of the neutral locale of Asia Minor, Kazantzakis came under fire for *Christ Recrucified*, as well as for other works, from the Greek Church, various representatives of the government, and important individuals for his "espousal" of "antinational" causes. Though controversy seems to be a permanent feature of life in Greece, a new conflict usually renders an old one neutral by taking its place. The Disaster, the culmination of the Liberal-Monarchist dissension, was unique in that it made more than two millennia of Greek history a dead issue, neutral to all appearances, but actually capable of bearing a wealth of contemporary social, moral, political, and ideological problems.

That is why critics who attack the use of the Passion Play and the historical inaccuracy of the Asia Minor setting miss Kazantzakis's intention. In creating his own, non-historical elaboration upon the Asia Minor theme, Kazantzakis is using to its utmost the wealth of fictional possibilities that the Disaster of 1922 had provided the Greek writer. For here was a forever-lost civilization, by now almost emotionally neutral, capable of providing the subject matter and of reflecting any values the novelist cared to treat. That Kazantzakis was one of the few to see this does not mean that he will be one of the last. Anatolia, in the years to come, will be a rich granary of plots, characters, tensions, and moods for the Greek writer who, for one reason or another, would prefer not to treat his subject matter directly.

This was certainly the case when Menis Koumendareas wrote his story "A Day in 1638" which, set in Constantinople, tells the story of one day in the life of a young Greek boy, Simos, who is a chance witness to the assassination by Janissaries of the Grand Vizier. Simos is tracked down by the Janissaries for fear that he will tell what he knows; he is to die at the story's end. This subject — the assassination of an important political figure, planned and executed by official representatives of law and order, – would be one that a Greek writer would avoid in 1965, after the murder of Lambrakis, if he was at all concerned with preserving an undisturbed routine of living.

Less directly involved with issues narrowly Greek is the powerful title story of the same collection, *The Sailing* (1966),[22] a "chronicle" held by its author to a strict linear narrative, with action so taut that the conception itself might easily have been treated at novella or even novel length.

Captain Thanasis, the central character, is a "sea-monk" who has devoted his life to the merchant navy. His family, from one of the Islands, are all comfortably established in Athens, living the ordinary life of society with its convenient superficialities and its perpetual involvement with formality. The character of Captain Thanasis, as much a product of his profession as the reason for its initial choice, is withdrawn, serious, "self-taught, as every child of his land," demanding independence in all those areas where he is not circumscribed by duty. It is precisely in his duty that this "sea-monk" will be challenged by another, less common demand that he declare his position as a human being.

His vessel, the "King Constantine," loads up with a human "cargo" of five thousand Armenian refugees from Turkish oppression. The time is October 1921 and the place Myrsene of Cilicia. Initially, his orders to transport them to Larnaca, Cyprus, do not seem difficult to carry out. A case of smallpox is discovered on board, however, and the refugees are not permitted to land by the British authorities in Cyprus. This is the beginning of their aimless travel from port to port, seeking refuge, and it is made clear by Koumendareas that the presence of smallpox is merely the excuse used to get rid of the unwelcome refugees. In this respect, *The Sailing* resembles *Christ Recrucified*.

22. *To Armenisma: Tria Chronika* (Athens, 1966). The title story was completed in 1964.

226

Captain Thanasis finds himself in moral isolation. None of his messages to the shipping firm's offices for support, information, or orders seems to have been received, and the requests he makes to other authorities are answered negatively. Faced with societies that deny them entry, and – in Cyprus and Constantinople – impose impossible financial qualifications for disembarking, the "King Constantine" is physically and morally cut off from the world, forced into an isolation that compels the captain, crew, and passengers to create a society of their own, a harsh but essentially just and democratic one.

Those refugees with smallpox are segregated. The crew and the more enlightened of the passengers are given inoculations first, to provide an example for the others, who follow suit. The dead are not thrown overboard but are burned in the furnace. When the danger of epidemic is clearly over, the British authorities are prepared to accept fifty families with enough money to pay for landing and setting up households in Cyprus. The remainder are doomed to return to Smyrna, where they are not allowed to land, then to Constantinople, where fifty more families are to be accepted, then back to Smyrna again.

At this point Captain Thanasis, informed that he has fuel only for the return to Piraeus, decides to gamble with his career. He sets sail for Greece, where the Armenians are allowed to enter like lost children coming home at last. Thanasis has risen above his official duty and has fulfilled his task as a human being in spite of bureaucracy and official coldness.

The conflict Captain Thanasis faces is between the two interpretations of his duty. The fact that he is a "sea-monk," separated by his personality and his career from the formalities of land-society, means that he is left essentially unsupported by the landsman's everyday code of conduct, which in the terms of Koumendareas's story would demand that he think only of his career and abandon the refugees to their own fate. But their fate is his fate, again in the story's terms, because there is literally nothing he can do with the refugees but sail to Piraeus and bull his way past any legal formalities thrown up against him. He cuts through the bureaucratic entanglements of officialdom by ignoring them, and discovers on presenting himself at his firm's offices that none of his requests for aid, information, or orders had even been read — while he had considered himself bound inflexibly by bureaucratic rules and regulations, he had been free all along to act as his conscience demanded.

The events in *The Sailing* clearly refer not to the suffering of the Greeks in Anatolia, but to that of a persecuted minority within the "minorities" of Asia Minor. They are, in fact, the most persecuted of minorities in the Ottoman Empire. "We've accepted it, my lad," Old Toumbekian tells Captain Thanasis, "Just ask me how often and from how many places I've been chased . . . and by everyone, too. . . . They say that the Jews are tormented . . . because they crucified Christ. I ask you, then, how many Christs must we have crucified?"[23]

Had they been Greek refugees they would have had no difficulty being accepted once the authorities were assured that the smallpox danger had passed. As long as they were in Aegean and Mediterranean waters, however, the Armenians, despite the existence of Soviet Armenia, were essentially state-less, at least for the purposes of the story's moral tensions. Without bureaucratic machinery of their own to protect them like a carapace, they are naked, defenseless. Their only protection is the "sea-monk" and his sense of duty. In their misery and worry they do not know how much they depend upon him, but it is through them that he learns which of his duties he must fulfill — the one he owes this company as an employee, or the one he owes the refugees as a human being. It is through their despair that Captain

23. *Ibid.*, p. 14.

Thanasis sees the effects of the conflicts of nations and political personalities on "a people who are marionettes in the hands of the powerful." [24] He hears "the moan of the refugees" coming to him from the deck.

> The mountain of human protest rose threateningly, at times with anger, at times with pleas, seeking to attach responsibilities [for their lot].... Next to them were the French [soldiers] exuding wine and dirty thoughts, further away [were] the English opportunists; in the center, the primitive, savage, and idiotic Turk.
>
> What was this world he was born into? Without protection, without a guide, left to his fortune. The bureaucrats held the reins and he, a pawn in their hands, counted the hours and the lives of people. [25]

Koumendareas, by using Armenians rather than Greeks, is able to ignore issues that would otherwise be ever-present. Greeks would have had no difficulty in entering most ports, for once the threat of plague had passed they would have been welcome in Smyrna or Greece, if not Cyprus or Constantinople. The point of the story, however, is Captain Thanasis's fulfillment of his duty, not of his ordinary one but of the unique, moral duty he was confronted with by the five thousand Armenians. If the refugees were Greeks there would have been no crisis, and the tensions of the story would either have been concluded when the ship left Asia Minor or would have begun when it docked in Greece; in the first case, it would have been a study of persecution, and in the second, one of refugee establishment. The dilemma of Captain Thanasis, in either case, would have been nonexistent. The point of *The Sailing*, however, is the mass displacement of people whom no one, for a number of reasons, wants.

24. *Ibid.*, p. 38.
25. *Ibid.*, p. 39.

The fact that the Armenians were, in effect, state-less freed Menis Koumendareas from the extraneous issues and enabled him to concentrate on the moral tensions that were his primary concern. The suffering of these displaced people in "1921" is clearly a reflection of tensions that became important after World War II in the light of the German extermination of the Jews, and the attempts, in many cases doomed to failure, of shiploads of refugees to find a haven that was refused them. Although cases like this may have occurred between 1914 and 1922, they were not seen as noteworthy or as possible subjects for fiction at that time. This was probably because they were not considered to have any moral relevance to their era. Koumendareas took an incident — whether real or imagined is not indicated — and used it as a moral parable of a man forced to create or express his own values when he finds the values for which his society stands inadequate. In the midst of the commercialization of human values and the pharisaical insistence of nations on official proprieties, Captain Thanasis asserts that his primary duty as a man is to other human beings.

Both Kazantzakis and Koumendareas, revealing no interest in the narrowly interpreted Disaster theme, nevertheless use the subject matter of Asia Minor in a way no writer rooted in the actual context of the Anatolia he lost could have done before World War II. Confining themselves to the linear plot, they place the stories that interest them in an Anatolia they need not describe, confident that their audience will share the meanings their narratives demand, thus freed from the chore of nondramatic description to create a world of heightened and somber tensions. As a result, there is no sense in these two narratives that the authors felt any compulsion to recapitulate history, as was the case in the linear narratives of the first category.

Perhaps because neither Kazantzakis nor Koumendareas has Anatolian roots (Kazantzakis, of course, is a Cretan, and

Koumendareas was born in Athens of Spartan parents), each was more free to pick out what was relevant to the story he wanted to narrate from the complex social background of Asia Minor. Writers from Anatolia, in fact, have tended to be overwhelmed by the actual experience of the Disaster, and to feel that they have treated it sufficiently after simply recapitulating it. Of the nine novels in our first category, "The Fiction of History," six were written by Anatolians, one — *The Mermaid Madonna* — was written by a novelist with strong Anatolian identifications, and only two were written by non-Anatolians with no Asia Minor past at all. In "The Fiction of Myth," on the other hand, of the five works treated, only one — *At Hadzifrangos's* — was written by someone with an Anatolian past.

The Multi-Level Plot — Man in linear time and direct historical causality has been, up to this point in our study, the major concern of writers. Fixed in a stable world that gradually became distorted by horror and the Disaster, the characters of the previous works and the world they inhabited looked forward to a "future" which they, like all men, could not know until it occurred; rooted in time, they needed to wait for its fullness to see their fate. When they recalled it as the "past," they needed to review it in strict chronological order, unable for some reason to break into its sequential flow. Even those fictional works that resemble parables subscribe rigidly to the impression of time's inviolability and uniqueness.

Yet there were works of fiction whose execution demanded a rejection of the demands of realism. The effects they strove for and which, once achieved, became their unique characteristics, were gained by the deliberate destruction of linear time and the unitary plot. Realism was viewed not merely as inadequate for the writers' purposes, but as inhibiting, if not imprisoning. The effects the novelists aimed at would have been muffled and

231

obscured without the varying chronological perspectives and the conflicting psychological states represented in *The Garden of Princes* (1966) by Nikos Bakolas, *The Dreams of Angelika* (1958) by Eva Vlami, and *At Hadzifrangos's* (1962) by Kosmas Politis.

Far from employing a clear, direct, and rational view for the events they wanted to narrate, these three novelists seem deliberately to have placed obstacles in the way of the reader's comprehension of the events, to have distorted the precision of the focus, and to have insisted, therefore, on the irrationality that underlies much of human life. These techniques are not used with full success in the three novels in question, but it is clear that all are attempts to undermine the belief in the ultimate rationality of things implicit in realism. By plunging into the irrational, they hoped to treat the Asia Minor theme in a way that realism could never have done.

The events of the Asia Minor expedition and personages from the Legend of Troy are combined in a fascinating but unsuccessful attempt to modernize the Oresteia plot in Nikos Bakolas's *The Garden of Princes* (1966).[26] As an artistic whole the novel fails because of its overriding ambition, for Bakolas wanted not only to unify two exciting historical events whose conclusions were totally divergent — the Trojan War and the Greek Expedition in Anatolia — but also to experiment with fictional form by employing the techniques of interior monologue and stream-of-consciousness. But the experimentation, as we shall see in this section, is not obtrusive, nor is the difference in Greek fortunes in the Trojan and Greco-Turkish Wars at fault. The core problem in *The Garden of Princes* is the writer's inability to employ, in a clearer and more universal way, the psychological insight that pervades the characters of his novel.

Cassandra, a girl from Asia Minor, with a brother in the

26. *O Kipos ton Prinkipon* (Thessaloniki, 1966).

Evangelical School of Smyrna, begins to relate, in 1922, her love affair with a Greek staff officer, Agamemnon Iatridis; it is a complex and interlocking story that is continued and elaborated on by others. In a madhouse, Orestes Iatridis adds to the narration in 1933 and 1935; Aegisthus, awaiting trial in 1924, shows his contempt for the reporters who badger him for information, but is unable to disguise his plan to use Clytemnestra's sexual attraction to him to revenge himself on Agamemnon for what he had done to Theano, his sister, in 1919. It is through Clytemnestra that we see her lover kill the returning Agamemnon, who is described as "a ragman from Asia Minor, without boots or garrison cap."[27]

The character upon whom the action of *The Garden of Princes* revolves is Agamemnon — not the triumphant King of Mycenae, of course, but an aging artillery colonel whose unchecked libidinal drives destroy what little domestic happiness his strange family might have been able to provide him. "At that time," Aegisthus says,

> Agamemnon threshed through Asia Minor a victor and triumphant, sending home countless snapshots of himself on a white horse, much before it was possible for him or me or Clytemnestra, or his general or even the staff back in Athens to know that a day was coming when he Agamemnon would have lost pride horse and maps lost battalion and machine gun, would have been left with ten men with weapons and sergeant abandoned to wander through burned villages and past blown-up bridges and slaughtered horses steers, in dug up fields, searching for the sea in despair, without time or the mood to take the honor of girls, cowering during the day, preferring the light of the stars, trying to save his skin.[28]

27. *Ibid.*, p. 97.
28. *Ibid.*, pp. 35-36. Punctuation as in the original.

The attention of the reader is transferred from one character to another, each speaking as he thinks, confusedly, pursuing his own obsessions, without attempting to clarify story-line or motivation. Bakolas should have been aided in his uncompromising attitude toward technical purity because the basic outlines of his story are well known. The motivations of Cassandra, Agamemnon, Aegisthus, and Clytemnestra, however, are contemporary, permeated with overpowering sexual drives and jealousies. But this is a psychological world so indebted to Freud that the unexpected occurs: the Homeric framework emerges more as an obstacle to understanding than as a guide to fictional action.

The reader finds himself unable to forget the Legend of Troy in order to accept Bakolas's reinterpretation of it, unwilling to allow the characters handed down by tradition to be manipulated so freely. The central obstacle Bakolas faces and cannot surmount is that the writer's license to adapt mythological personages to his own purposes is not an unrestricted one. He can reinterpret, he can change motivation, he can substitute the heroic world view for another, but he is limited in the number of changes he can make in the actual plot of his story.

More familiar with American literature than most Greeks, Bakolas is clearly operating in the world of Eugene O'Neill's *Mourning Becomes Electra,* and he consciously uses the fictional techniques of William Faulkner, whose *The Sound and the Fury* he has translated into Greek. But these do not help him overcome the major weakness of his conception: a re-use of the Trojan legend forces upon him a series of events whose integrity must not be violated, no matter how much they can be reinterpreted according to modern tastes. By deliberately juxtaposing the legend of Troy to the Asia Minor Disaster but allowing himself to be drawn into a world of private symbols, Bakolas confuses the reader about his intentions while at the same time proving his competence as a creator of mood.

The Greek defeat in Asia Minor, as we have seen in Kostas Varnalis's *The Diary of Penelope,* precludes the extended use of the legend of Troy as a fictional point of reference. Parallels may be found to exist, but they prove valid only when not insisted upon by writers and only when they concern the anonymous, never the famed. Agamemnon, Orestes, Electra, Aegisthus, and Clytemnestra are names forever linked with horror and victory, never with horror and defeat.

It is clear that Bakolas, unlike the writers whose novels were studied in the previous category, wanted to break free of the hold realism might have exercised on him. He wanted a mythical framework in which to set the concerns he gave to his characters and freedom from the necessity to narrate his story in a chronological manner. The technique he used permitted him to experiment with time and allowed him to enter the thoughts of his characters at various junctures in their lives. This, roughly, is the freedom from the sequential plot we shall find in *The Dreams of Angelika* and *At Hadzifrangos's,* the other novels in this category.

It is only after he had achieved esthetic distance that the Greek writer was able to break the hold that the historical reality of the Disaster had exercised on him and to experiment with new techniques for relating the stories he needed to narrate. We have seen this in *The Garden of Princes.* In no novel up to this point, however, has the attempt to liberate one's preoccupations in order to discover the ideal vehicle for an esthetic vision found a more extreme, yet still successful, realization than in Eva Vlami's extraordinary *The Dreams of Angelika* (1958).[29] It is only in symbolic terms, by using interior monologue, by violating the sequential conception of plot and chronology, and by not compromising with her readers' historical ignorance of the period that she could possibly hope to do all she did in this novel.

29. *Ta Oneira tis Angelikas* (Athens, 1958).

One important problem that Eva Vlami faced in *The Dreams of Angelika* was that those readers who had a detailed, personal knowledge of her subject matter would tend to reject, or not understand, the techniques she felt compelled to use to narrate the novel's events, while those readers who would understand the technical problems she faced and might have been interested in her solution to them would tend to be ignorant of the historical events that formed the basis of her novel. In other words, those who would be old enough to remember the period about which she wrote would be unwilling to read an experimental novel, while those interested in literary experimentation would not be willing to do the background reading necessary to a full understanding of the achievement that is *The Dreams of Angelika.* We are dealing, clearly, with a highly complex and personal novel in a literature not rich in idiosyncratic works and with a readership not inclined to close reading or the "skeleton key" approach to writing, or educated for it. Eva Vlami faced this problem by ignoring it; if she had tried to cope with it she would only have succeeded in diluting the content and weakening the form of her novel.

Eva Vlami could not have written *The Dreams of Angelika* if she had forced her thematic content into the confines of the realistic novel of society. But neither could she have written it if the realistic social novel had not been established in the 1930s, for she needed a foundation upon which to experiment, a convention through which she could elaborate her own vision, and a tradition from which to rebel. This was the tradition she had mastered with her fine sea novel, *Skeletovrachos* (1949). [30] In *The Dreams of Angelika,* however, she had to deal, not with a

30. For a general view of the work of Eva Vlami, see my essay, "Eva Vlami and the Imprisonment of the Past," *Balkan Studies,* 10 (1) 1969.

realistic conflict between progress, symbolized by steam power, and tradition, as symbolized by clipper ships, but with a dream state that is never rational and that verges on the surreal and the *grand guignol*. *The Dreams of Angelika* is a psychological novel, told frequently in interior monologue, in a timeless present that we discover is a dream while the dreamer is dying.[31] "Those who are about to die have very confused dreams" is a refrain that weaves its way through the novel almost as counterpoint. As a novel that reflects the mind of its society, *The Dreams of Angelika* is probably the most searing document of the psychological effect of the Asia Minor Disaster, and it shows that, despite its range of fictional possibilities and esthetic power, the realistic novel — even for those who consider it the index of a nation's literary maturity — has severe limitations.

The novel is set in the years between 1913 and 1923 (or perhaps 1924), but there is no attempt to reflect actual conditions in a realistic manner, or to order time or actions in any linear, chronological sense, at least not after the first chapter, which details in the form of letters from the front the victories of the Greek army in the First Balkan War. *The Dreams of Angelika* gives the impression, therefore, of being a hallucination on the part of Angelika who, for much of the novel, is the only point of reference the reader has. Without an awareness of the historical events of that decade, the reader is certain to be confused, unable to determine what is true and what is delusion, what has a factual

31. Since *The Dreams of Angelika* is a symbolic novel and since the narration makes no effort to explain events to the reader, there would conceivably be a number of interpretations. In this study, I accept Angelika as a woman who dies despite the fact that she symbolizes Greece. In strict terms, if she were the symbol of Greece she could not die as long as Greece still existed. For the purposes of this study, therefore, Angelika is symbolic of the Greece that was "betrothed" to the Megale Idea and she dies when it perishes in 1922.

basis and what is so exaggerated as to be surreal. The dilemma the writer confronted was pitiless, for if she succumbed to the demand to clarify what a reader ignorant of the history of the time would consider obscure, she would have destroyed the necessary hallucinatory character of the novel.

Angelika is betrothed to Asimis Pallaskas, a young man who has seen his share of the nation's struggles, having gone through the battles the Greeks had fought from 1912 to the fictional "present" of the early 1920s. Their wedding has been delayed because of the Greek expedition to Asia Minor that was to be the fulfillment of the ancient Greek aspiration to reconquer Anatolia, to restore the Byzantine Empire, and to make Saint Sophia once more a Greek Orthodox shrine. Angelika is never married because Asimis and thousands of young men like him perish in that disastrous war. With him, and them, dies the Megale Idea, never to be resurrected. From its death and the inevitable flux of history comes a new Greece, one smaller and more humble than the dreams of the Greeks.

The dreams of Angelika, the dreams of the Greeks, are really ideals now seen to be vain, almost delusory, and the nation cannot bear their loss. Angelika was bound to Asimis as Greece was bound to the Megale Idea in a betrothal so profound that one member took on the identity of the other. When the partner died, when the mate perished, the other could not survive. They were one, despite their apparent separateness. Angelika does not allow herself to accept Asimis's death until the very end. Throughout the novel she hears reports of his return from the front; people tell her they have seen him in the city, that he has deserted the colors and is somewhere in Athens. If he is in Athens, she knows he must be there on a secret mission. As a matter of "fact," she sees him many times, but when she approaches to study his likeness, she discovers he is someone else, a sinister man by the name of Stylianos Soudaras, exactly like Asimis in appearance (except for totally white hair), but a polar opposite in character, a negation of everything Asimis Pallaskas stood for, a negative image of the triumphant hero. The certitude that Asimis is no more seizes her whenever she is unprepared, evading the obstacles her mind places before it, forcing upon her images of her own death, which she sees in vivid terms; she lies in her coffin, wearing the wedding gown she has saved all these years. "Those who are about to die have very confused dreams."

But hallucination is not an exceptional state in *The Dreams of Angelika;* everyone is slightly mad. General Markou, Angelika's uncle, is a fantast, a believer in tradition to an irrational extreme. "I am certainly not one of those who believe that Constantine Paleologos died and needs a memorial service," he tells her. "These are stories that the Turks and Turk-corrupted historians tell, ... fairy tales." [32] In the General's rooms there is a wild assortment of deadly weapons, heavy Byzantine brocades, and patriotic souvenirs. He is a believer in spiritualism and participates in a number of seances with other retired generals and admirals.

But how better to describe a state of mind that seemed to characterize all the Greeks? Living the "myth" of the Megale Idea, permeated by the legends that appeared to be on the verge of realization and the occult belief in the numerology that promised the key to the future of the Greek race, General Markou and his companions were representative of their society, not a fringe element distinct from it. When Angelika, as a young woman, in 1912-1913, received triumphant letters from her betrothed, telling her of the great military advances in the north, she knew she was living in times where actuality was straining to achieve the grandeur of myth. This was how she and all of Greece accepted the shocking news of the beloved King George I's assassination in

32. *Ibid.,* p. 33.

Thessaloniki in 1913: he died to make way for the heir whom legend had anointed for the Byzantine throne.

> Everyone felt like an orphan; the entire orphaned people had lost its dear father. Still, they were not without consolation, a golden ray of sunlight reflecting off the claws of the Two-Headed Eagle. Was it not the Will of God that a King by the name of Constantine would retake the City? At one point the people cried for the hard loss of their King, then they cocked their ears to hear the quiet words of Fate. Here was Constantine passing before them, pale, but heroic and sun-splashed; thus, he would stretch out his hand and seize the gigantic fortresses of Constantine and Theodosios. You could even say he already held, intact, within his palm, the City of the Seven Hills. There are the City's scattered towers, there the domes of Saint Sophia, shimmering in the tear-filled eyes. As the dead King's life slowly extinguished, the place flooded with waves of blue and white flags. . . .[33]

Soudaras, with his uncanny likeness to the dead Asimis, is a baffling, obsessive political figure, in some way responsible for the Disaster in Anatolia who, in the perplexing time-scheme of the novel, goes about buying up all the land he can in order to create a vast graveyard for the dead soldiers — not those killed during the Asia Minor campaign, for whom it is too late, but for those of future wars. He has a stewardess, a strange, wraith-like woman named Kyria Zoë, who speaks in a language so archaic it approaches liturgical Greek. It is she whom Angelika finds in the house of Asimis when she goes to see if her fiancé has really returned, as she has heard, and Kyria Zoë tells her that a "new master has taken over the house of your betrothed." In truth, Soudaras — or is it a transformed, sepulchral Asimis? — has pur-

33. *Ibid.,* p. 24.

chased the Pallaskas home for his *own* great dream, the vast graveyard.

During this time, also, there is a curious series of thefts in the cemeteries of Athens and Piraeus: crosses disappear overnight from graves and no one, not even the military guards who are commanded to watch over them and apprehend, even kill, the cross-robbers, is able to put an end to this. The incidents eventually are given a political interpretation and charges are exchanged in Parliament. It is clear, however, that the cross-thefts, though initially real, perhaps, have seized the entire people as a craze and become surrealistic reminders of the cost in human lives for which the disastrous policies of the government in power — the Populists — is responsible. The issue of the stolen crosses comes to represent the issue no one can talk about — the frightful hatred of Venizelists and Royalists for each other. Papa-Mathios gives a sermon, at which Angelika is present, in which he asks anyone with knowledge of the cross-stealing to save his soul by revealing the information to the authorities. One night, as troops are guarding a graveyard, the spotlights trained on the area are extinguished by a power failure. The soldiers, convinced that "dark forces" are at work, rush in to do battle and fight among themselves with bayonets. Before withdrawing "grave by grave," they leave thirty-two dead and sixty or so wounded. The result of all this wartime hysteria is that "everyone is a 'suspect' in the eyes of the others, and people begin to accuse others to the police with anonymous letters."[34] Five suspects are arrested who have nothing in common but their Venizelism. "Light Shed on Satanic Plot," read the headlines of pro-Government newspapers, and angry mobs, incited by the clergy and the authorities, go on a

34. *Ibid.,* p. 141.

rampage against Venizelist newspapers, demoticists, opponents, business competitors, and anyone they find unpleasant.

Parliament all this time has been preoccupied with an important debate on whether or not the state religion should be disestablished, a matter that must be preceded by a series of educational lectures on other faiths. Angelika attends one evening to listen to a long lecture, in a mandarin-like *katharevousa,* on the Birth of Buddha, his life, and his passage through the various stages of consciousness to Nirvana; the recitation, a masterpiece of surrealistic prose, is constantly interrupted by shouts from the Opposition demanding a return to political debate, particularly since the Disaster is imminent in Asia Minor.

Asimis is dead. But is he? He and Soudaras have too much in common: are they the same man, two faces of the same ideal? Whatever the truth is, Angelika cannot know, for she is trying to hold on to her sanity in a world that seems to have gone mad itself. The only possible representative of rationality in her life is Stratis, a journalist and friend of Asimis, who tries to answer the riddle of the stolen crosses, is jailed as the man responsible for their loss, then released. But he is shot dead in a theater crowded with people who have gone to see a famous spiritualist portray, before their very eyes, the long hoped-for fall of Constantinople to the Greeks.

Soudaras is the dominating character in the novel, for it is his obsession with death that impresses itself indelibly on the dreams of Angelika and makes them nightmares. She cannot escape this "gothic" figure set by some strange quirk in a wintry, sepulchral Athens. In Soudaras's mansion, the Six are present in a dining room whose every surface is covered with a black cloth, where instead of food they see a large thermometer on an oval platter, and where, while waiting for the "seventh" guest — whose importance is intimidating — they discuss their trial, feign confidence of their acquital, and express their desire to learn of Soudaras's plans for their safety in case the impossible happens and they are condemned. Kyria Zoë, walking around the table to refill their glasses, sees the decanters floating along by themselves, "filling the glasses again, one after the other, in front of the six empty chairs."[35] The "seventh" guest arrives at the end, however, knocking on the door three times, causing the Commander of the Armed Forces to faint, for the guest is none other than Constantine XI Paleologos, the last Emperor of Byzantium.

In fact, Paleologos can be considered the great absent hero of *The Dreams of Angelika,* for it is he who is mourned throughout the novel and he whose resurrection is not effected by history. The conflict in the novel — unseen and unmentioned — is between the myth-permeated certitudes of the Greek mind and history's cold brutality, between a covenant the Greeks believed they had had with God, sealed and sanctified by the torments they had undergone during the past centuries, and the God Who seemed to be prepared to fulfill His part of the bargain but Who refused at the last minute to recognize their claims.

Angelika accompanies her uncle to Saint Constantine's Church for a memorial service commemorating the 469th anniversary of the City's fall (which dates the event at May 29, 1922). During the services, Angelika — who acts in the novel not only as a character in her own right but as the summation of all the characters and their aspirations, as well as the filter by which all these are made known to the reader — reflects the mystical and supra-logical way in which the members of the congregation in the church are swept up into the myth, slowly losing consciousness of the reality around them, forgetting where they are, dreaming themselves to be in Constantinople, at the precise moment of King Constantine's entry into the City of the Byzantines, dreaming that they are in Saint Sophia, when the

35. *Ibid.,* p. 185.

half-completed liturgy is about to resume; dreaming that the Patriarch is about to crown the King of the Hellenes as Emperor of Byzantium, Emperor of the newly reconstituted Rome. The fantasy ends as the exalted populace leaves the church of their imagined "Saint Sophia" to enter again the streets of the Athens of 1922, three months before the Deluge.

Crushed by life and bereft of illusions, Angelika returns to her house, now condemned for the death-enamored Soudaras's goal, his vast graveyard, a woman betrothed without the possibility of being married, a woman who remembers the warmth and light of family memories in a home now darkened and cold. There is nothing left for her. She is alone. Like most of Eva Vlami's heroines, Angelika must die unwed, dressed in her bridal finery, placed in her coffin, married to death.

The novel is clearly symbolic: Asimis and Soudaras *are* two faces of the same ideal, each "betrothed" – at different times of the national fortunes – to the reality Angelika represents. Because Greece had expected glory but witnessed Disaster, Angelika, the bride, goes in her wedding gown to meet her "new master." A major problem in *The Dreams of Angelika,* however, is that the reader is dependent upon Angelika for information about much of the story's events, and Angelika's mind has lost the ability to order them chronologically or logically. Besides this, the reader has a further obstacle: he may be willing to accept the confusion of chronological time, the *grand guignol* atmosphere, the surrealism, and the great demands on his historical knowledge, but he lives in a time that, though it finds symbolism acceptable, does not tolerate allegory. He may find himself resisting figures who represent fairly specific ideas. For example, Kyria Zoë, like all of the characters, is more symbolic than real and represents the Church in an arbitrary but esthetically valid way: reactionary, a handmaiden to some governments, a fierce enemy to other, more progressive ones, possessing a value system more alien than other-wordly, more death-obsessed, despite her name, than life-enhancing.

But realism could not have succeeded in creating the phantasmagoric world that Eva Vlami had erected, a distorted world where obsessions, following their own "logic," puncture the rigid confines of sequential time and drift backward and forward, much as characters in modern drama walk through nonexistent walls in theatrical sets to suggest the passage of time or the assumption of other psychological states.

Ultimately, it is doubtful whether realism could ever communicate the magnitude and profundity of the Asia Minor Disaster. Realistic fiction, in its best example, *Bloodied Earth,* would by its very accuracy be limited to the definable, the assessable, and consequently the surface, while the loss of Anatolia and the rout of the Asia Minor Expedition destroyed certitudes deeper than the rational mind could ever sound. No matter how affected the reader may be by Mrs. Sotiriou's powerful book, he is still focused on Manolis Axiotis as a character; the racial Disaster blurs into the background while the personal anguish of Manolis remains the focus of the reader's attention.

As we have seen earlier, these racial myths were genuinely believed; the Greeks — educated ones as well as the folk — accepted them as parts of a credo throughout the centuries of slavery, as a covenant with the Byzantine God for the liberation of their own "Jerusalem." In some respects, these myths constituted the only valid and universally accepted national ideas. Their destruction, even in the most gradual and bloodless of circumstances, let alone after a trauma of the magnitude of the Disaster of 1922, would have caused a psychological and national crisis of identity.

Angelika had to be the reader's sole witness, and her madness had to be the vehicle for his awareness of the novel's events, in order to distort his sense of perspective and block the feeling of rational superiority sanity would have given him. The reader had to be whirled about in the maelstrom of the dreams of Angelika in order to be part of the phantasmagoric world the writer wanted to create. The realistic novel could not do this. *The Dreams of Angelika* is the success it is because Eva Vlami did not weaken in her resolve.

Like all Greeks, Kosmas Politis felt powerfully the events of World War II, the Occupation, and civil strife. As a novelist, he had created a Greece unlike the one documented by the other writers of the interwar years, a Greece in which a sophisticated class of cosmopolitan men and women pursued their vision of wholeness and ideal love regardless of the consequences. In *The Ghyri* (1944), however, a new and broader view of society entered his fiction. In this novel and in *The Plum Tree* (1959), a collection of shorter works, he revealed an important change in his attitudes toward social classes, a view quite different from that which had previously characterized his fiction. Alienated from the sophisticated class that had been his milieu before, from 1944 on he began to identify with the Greek people, the peasants and the working class. This identification brought him clearly to the point where he wrote in conscious opposition to the established values of Greek society, values to which he had never subscribed wholeheartedly. In general, his work after *The Ghyri* possesses a substantial social texture that was absent in his earlier fiction, and his well-researched but unconvincing drama *Constantine the Great* (1957) reveals a questioning attitude toward history. His final novel, *At Hadzifrangos's* (1962) would not have been the masterpiece it is if it had not been invested with the political and social commitment he revealed with the publication of *The Ghyri* in 1944.

Carrying the subtitle "The Fortieth Anniversary of a Lost City," *At Hadzifrangos's* appeared first in installments in the periodical *Tachydromos* in 1962, and then in book form the following year; it was immediately and correctly recognized as a major work. And it is not merely Politis's greatest work; this novel of a never-forgotten Smyrna is the summation, the fruition, of the preoccupations evident in the entire body of his work until its appearance. But Smyrna had never provided the setting for any of Politis's previous novels during his four-decade sojourn among the "alien corn" of Greece. The locale of his works had been the Island of Poros, Athens, Patras, the Heptanese, and the Island of Paros, but these settings had usually left the reader with the impression that they were composite landscapes, compromises with reality rather than descriptions of it. Somehow, *Eroica* was not really set in Patras, despite the internal evidence that this was so. In order to create a cosmopolitan setting, Politis superimposed another world on the ordinary Greek one he was describing. Yet Smyrna, this other world, is never mentioned in his earlier fiction. "One often talks about his beloved dead without naming them," he explained in an interview, "feeling that it would be something like disrespect to their memory to speak their names."[36]

At Hadzifrangos's, the novel of the "lost city," is the synthesis of all of Politis's preoccupations, the locus of all his tensions, explaining their existence in retrospect and giving them a depth they would not otherwise have had. The time-scheme of the novel is of the utmost importance. The major action takes place between 1902 and 1903, a happy era for the Greeks in Anatolia. All reckoning must be by the Old, or Julian, Calendar, since the Greeks of Asia Minor were still using it while the Catholics and other Westerners in Anatolia had adopted the Gregorian Calendar. The novel begins on Ascension Thursday, forty days after Easter, and concludes on Clean Monday, the Monday that marks the

36. Politis, *Stou Hadzifrangou (At Hadzifrangos's)* (Athens: Karavias, 1963), p. xi. Interview with George Savidis.

beginning of the Great Lent. Since all of these feast days are dependent on the phases of the moon, Ascension Thursday is a movable feast, which means that the action of the novel begins in mid-May of 1902 and concludes the following February. When it is considered that Politis makes it a point to note, immediately after the "Telos" of the novel, the time it took to write the first draft — an astonishing five months — and that this working time lasted from May to September 1962 (exactly four decades after the final act of the tragedy at Smyrna), the reader should begin to see the multi-layered intricacy of *At Hadzifrangos's*.[37]

The three levels of chronology encompass sixty years. The novelist, between May and September of 1962, is writing a novel about life in the "lost city" of Smyrna of 1902-1903, and the awful and irrevocable date — 1922, between May and September — which removes that land from Greek civilization with a disastrous finality is perpetually on the minds of both the writer and the reader.

The function of the three time phases is never forgotten by the reader, who finds himself constantly referring to a "fictional present" that is always tentative. By selecting the happy, prosperous, but inconsequential era of 1902-1903, Politis has found an effective artistic device for lending a majesty and a sanctity to the daily and otherwise insignificant details of life in a small, proletarian quarter of Smyrna. Without the knowledge of the future cataclysm, the lives of his characters would appear to be no more than scattered and fragmented vignettes without an overriding scheme. Because we know that Politis is writing *At Hadzifrangos's* exactly four decades after the Disaster, however, we are compelled by him to see Smyrna from an omniscient, God-like point

37. The working time may be found on p. 318. The assertion that he had written the first draft in a certain time — not clarifying how much added work was needed to polish the novel — may be found on p. ix.

of view. The great fire, we know, will purge it all. Despite its insignificance, however, daily life has a majesty precisely because it is transient.

It is this transience of life that becomes sanctified by Politis's technique. The greatness of *At Hadzifrangos's* is not that the fiction convinces with its verisimilitude, but that the verisimilitude is never convincing enough to permit the reader to forget the terrible end of *Giaour Izmir.* The reader willingly suspends his disbelief in order to relive the past, but finds that he can forget neither the "present" nor the Disaster that has intervened. There is an oneiric quality to even the most precisely observed scenes, a resonance to the most commonplace phrases, a constant sense of the eternal in the ephemeral. Yet there is nothing pretentious, or portentous, about the novel, which for all its anguish and sorrow communicates a glorious sense of freedom and simultaneity.

Politis employs four major story lines to tell the story that reconstructs the lost, cosmopolitan city.

Though he is not an important character type in the fiction of Politis, Papa-Nicholas − as a representative of the clergy − is not unknown in the early work. In *The Ghyri,* the type was represented by Father Iakovos, a modernist priest "exiled" to the poor Ghyri parish in Patras. Papa-Nicholas is a man whose brilliance and education would have qualified him for the hierarchy if he had not married the woman he still loves. As the "proto-papas" of the Hadzifrangos quarter, he finds himself alienated from the Church as an administrative body, and in open conflict with the hierarchy of Smyrna. Besides the free rein he gives to speculation, Papa-Nicholas's only other "sin" comes from his love of listening to Zacharias Simonas, an Ionian Jew, play his *oud.*

The appearance of the erudite priest, whose conflict with the ecclesiastical administration grows into a more general criticism of the Church as a defender of the status quo, seems to be a direct outgrowth of Politis's postwar attitudes. Father Iakovos in *The*

Ghyri is the first indication of this. Politis's developing interest in social issues — or at least the manifestation of this interest in his work — compelled him to try to place the Church as an institution in Greek life, and his loyalties led him to the character type with whom he could identify in criticizing the position of the Church in social matters.[38]

The priest is important, among other reasons, because he provides the reader with an overview of the Quarter, since his position as an official of his community demands his awareness of and participation in local events, significant or otherwise.

Pandelis, another important character in the novel, marks a change for Politis, whose previous male protagonists were, by and large, free of workaday concerns. The death of his father compels Pandelis to withdraw from the Gymnasion and to begin manual work. He is, thus, the only proletarian hero of Politis's fiction. A clever boy, he is responsible — as coxswain — for the victory of the Greek rowboat in the annual races, won every previous year by another nationality, the Lazoi, and held on the Ascension Thursday that begins the novel. Sharing a scientific interest with the other Politis male characters, moreover, Pandelis is preoccupied by the project of devising acetylene lamps for lighting the streets of Smyrna. It is love that motivates him, however, a love so perplexing he is not quite sure at first who the object of his passion is, Siora Fiora, the lovely wife of Zacharias Simonas, or Perla, her sixteen-year-old daughter.

The story of Aristos and Stavrakis introduces what is, perhaps, the strongest interest of Politis: the theme of adolescence. *Eroica* had shown the profundity with which Politis viewed the tensions of adolescence, and this was certainly because the erotic instinct,

38. Compare Father Iakovos and Papa-Nicholas, for example, with the hero-priests of Kazantzakis's fiction, notably Fotis in *Christ Recrucified* and Yiannaros in *The Fraticides.*

which was the tension he had used as the motivating force in his earlier fiction, was expressed more powerfully and despairingly at this age. Aristos and Stavrakis bring to *At Hadzifrangos's* the fascination in and terror of the erotic seen, more or less, in all of Politis's work. Not quite in their teens, Aristos and Stavrakis provide the reader — as does Papa-Nicholas — with an overview of Smyrna and its environs, acting in a broader geographical radius as catalogues of *Giaour Izmir.* They listen to Kyra Ntountou's stories and absorb folk knowledge from her, a wisdom stored in the racial unconscious throughout the unbroken millennia of the Greek existence in Asia Minor.

From their teacher, Kourmentios, however, they gain a conscious knowledge of their Hellenism and of the Greekness of Smyrna and its hinterland. On a tour of their city, during which he insists that they learn the Greek names of the surrounding mountains, since they know them only by their Turkish names, Kormentios informs them of the Greeks' hopes for the fulfillment of the Megale Idea.

> Stand up while we have a moment's silence in honor of the glory of Ancient Greece. In this theater the tragedies of Aeschylus and Sophocles still reverberate. Here ... Homer sang his immortal epics. ... All these places were Greek. All these places (his voice suddenly trembled, his eyes shone from the tears he tried to restrain) were, are, and shall be Greek. ... He turned to hide his emotion, and he concluded with a sob — as though it was not his sob, but that of the dreams and hopes that listened to his words and mourned: "From Ages unto Ages."[39]

In fact, Kyra Ntountou and Kourmentios are convincing, not as individuals, but as types. In the terms of Myrivilis's *The Mermaid Madonna,* they are Aunt Permachoula and Avghoustis

39. Politis, *At Hadzifrangos's* pp. 59-60.

before the Disaster, repositories of millennia of Hellenic wisdom, both supra-rational and rational, deeply rooted in an Anatolia that exists no more.

It is boys in the age group of Aristos and Stavrakis who, twenty years later, would witness the Disaster in the prime of their manhood. Sixty years later, one of their number, Yiakoumis, would recite, for the person who interviews him for a "book" he is writing on the Disaster, the moving narration of the destruction of Smyrna.

Stavrakis, death-obsessed and unhappy in his home life, maintains a strange, semi-hostile relationship with the intelligent and affectionate Aristos, whose family is stable and loving. One day, having been told by Kyra Ntountou of the existence of a water nymph — a nereid — at the Lake of Artemis, Stavrakis and Aristos decide to go to find her. But they mistake the road and go instead to the sea where Aristos, while swimming, encounters a dead girl floating nude in the water. The beauty of the "nereid" awakens the dormant sexuality of Aristos. It is the fascination with her that brings the boys back again, and it is Aristos's exhaustion while diving for her that weakens him to the point where, due to a misunderstanding, he can be drowned by Stavrakis. The fact that Aristos's clothes are gone when Stavrakis returns with the frantic father, leads to a belief that "the Jews took him". But there were no Jews about, only a gypsy, and Politis leads us to believe that it is he who took Aristos's clothes.

But the presence of Jews and gypsies leads the reader who knows Politis's earlier work to the theme of exoticism, an unavoidable one in the fiction of Politis, since these two races hold the promise of a wisdom or knowledge not easily available to his other characters. Removed from the social structure of the Greeks, outsiders to the Hellenic community, the Jews and gypsies appear in Politis's fiction as carriers of their own ancient wisdom. Music and the occult sciences are their province, and their presence is a challenge to the rationalistic basis of society.

Foreign women in the fiction of Politis always offer a promise of freedom from the rigid conventions of Greek society. In *At Hadzifrangos's,* with the appearance of Siora Fiora, that brilliant creation of femininity, the fascination of Politis with the exotic is brought one stage further. Like the unnamed daughter of Ezra in "Eleonora" of *Three Women* (1943), Siora Fiora, the wife of Zacharias Simonas, is Jewish; but neither she nor her husband knows Hebrew or Spanish.

> They were neither, they claimed, Spanish Jews, Sephardim, nor Polish Jews, Ashkenazi. His family came from Corinth. His ancestors, as far as he knew, had migrated to Greece two thousand years ago, even before the Destruction of Jerusalem and the Diaspora. But about eighty years ago, his great-grandfather left Corinth and established himself in Corfu. . . .
>
> "All our lives we've lived with Christians and Greeks. We'd feel strange in the Jewish Quarter. Besides, we don't understand their language."[40]

They are Jews, therefore, but also Greeks. They are different from the Greeks, but also similar. The two races live in that "pre-exilian" condition where they attract each other because they are opposites, but their opposition seems negligible, though their attraction is not. The music of Zacharias Simonas attracts the rationalist priest, Papa-Nicholas, but the beauty of Siora Fiora attracts young Pandelis, who sees her as both mother and sexual goal, who would even be willing to become a Jew for her, and who succeeds in making love to her only to lose her immediately afterward. She is the eternal Politis heroine, in other words, attracting the protagonist with an exoticism that is by now

40. *Ibid.,* p. 45.

virtually commonplace. Fifteen years her husband's junior, she has given him two children, but despite this a great part of her life seems blank. She is unaware of what others might call her unhappiness or her lack of communication with her husband. There is something unconscious and unoccupied about Siora Fiora, an abstraction that reminds one more of an adolescent girl than a mature woman. Perhaps that is the reason Pandelis ignores Perla, the sixteen-year-old daughter, and loves the mother.

The theme has been encountered before in Politis's fiction. What is unexpected is the depth and significance that he gives the theme of exoticism, for it is central to his strategy in *At Hadzifrangos's* and adds another dimension to his previous fiction. The Jews are exotic because they are not like the Greeks, though they seem to be. Though they have lived in the Greek world for two millennia, they are homeless, wanderers since "before the Destruction of Jerusalem and the Diaspora." The appearance in Politis's fiction of the Jew or gypsy who embodied the attraction of the exotic becomes in *At Hadzifrangos's* the foreshadowing of the destruction of Smyrna and the dispersion and homelessness of the Ionian Greeks.

(Siora Fiora's) mind went to her son who lived abroad. He, too, had scattered. Unconsciously, Jacob personified the scattering and eternal wandering of Israel. Within her, like the sediment raised by the pain of her son's [loss], the nostalgia for the – now forbidden – promised, ancestral land of hers was silent. [But] her Jewish spirit began to stir in this hour of loneliness. . . . When she happened to hear, there, in her homeland [the Ionian Islands] the erudite men of the Synagogue endlessly discussing a certain passage in the Talmud and sifting for its meaning, she shrugged her shoulders. What was the use? She was an uneducated woman and may Jehovah, Holy be His Name, give her rest in the bosom of Abraham and Isaac, but all of these discussions did not help Israel to stop at some time, to reach its goal and to rest. Yet, in this hour of her great loneliness, she was not sure if she mourned a distant and unknown land, or if she languished in nostalgia for a land of whose location she was ignorant, that might even have been an age-old fairy tale, recited from mouth to mouth and from generation to generation.[41]

Siora Fiora does not understand the Talmud, nor can she be sure that the fields of Boaz or the River Jordan are as they have been described. "Nor do the stars say anything that Siora Fiora might understand."[42] She is thus barred from any understanding of the exoticism she personifies and she bears, embodied in her character, the vestigial sorrows of Israel, compelling the reader to identify her sorrows with those of the Anatolian Greeks whose loss of homeland she foreshadows. The Anatolian feels he is in "exile" — in ξενητιά — despite the fact that he is in Greece, among his own countrymen, who for one reason or another had "succeeded in giving" him, the refugee, "the feeling of being a *rayah* in [his] own country." But Siora Fiora had been lost *before* the Loss of Smyrna; she had been uprooted *before* the Uprooting of 1922. Her presence in *At Hadzifrangos's* adds another dimension to the three-layered time-scheme, a dimension that contributes to the mythic resonance of the work.

Zacharias and Siora Fiora are at the core of the novel, for it is they who fuse the other three story-lines: that of Papa-Nicholas, of Pandelis, and of Aristos and Stavrakis. The disappearance of Aristos is attributed to ritual murder on the part of the Jews. This excites a violent reaction in Smyrna, a conflict Politis is at pains to dismiss as uncharacteristic, for he makes a strong case for the ability of the two ancient races to live together harmoniously. But it is this uncharacteristic reaction, this threat of violence, that

41. *Ibid.,* p. 210.
42. *Ibid.,* p. 210

forces Zacharias and Siora Fiora to withdraw Perla from the Greek school, to leave the Hadzifrangos Quarter, and a life indistinguishable from that of the other Greeks, and to move to the Jewish Quarter. It is this separation, after one night of love, that embitters and alienates Pandelis. From now on, sexual intimacy is merely a physical act, one he can share with prostitutes. The death of Aristos is also connected with the decision of Papa-Nicholas to leave the priesthood and open a private school. *At Hadzifrangos's,* a novel that at first sight appears deceptively episodic, reveals itself as a masterpiece of architectonic unity.

It is the story of the fall of a city, the end of things, and the perspective is *ξενητιά,* a Greece that is both Diaspora and Babylonian Exile for the Smyrniots. This is clearly seen in "Parodos," a section revealing its "tragic" ambitions between Chapters Seven and Eight, a monologue by "Yiakoumis the Gardener" told in the "fictional present" of 1962 to a man who wants to write a book about Smyrna. The monologue acts as the funnel of the whirlpool that is *At Hadzifrangos's* because Yiakoumis, a friend and contemporary of Aristos and Stavrakis in 1902, tells about his love for Katerina, a girl of the Quarter, his marriage to her, and her death by miscarriage during the fire in 1922. Before we learn who he is, however, he establishes the celestial significance of the City's loss.

> Have you ever seen a city raised high? Tied by thousands of cords and hoisted to the heavens? Well, you never saw nor will you ever see such a miracle again. That would begin on Clean Monday ... and continue every Sunday and holiday until Palm Sunday. From Hadzifrangos's Quarter and from every terrace ... of every quarter in the City, they'd fly barrel kites. The sky was crowded with them, so full that there was no room for the birds. Because of this the cranes would lead the doves in [on their migration] only on Holy Week, so they

could celebrate Easter with us. All during the Great Lent, every Sunday and holiday, the city traveled in the sky. It would climb to the heavens and be blessed by God. It was impossible to understand how she could remain rooted down on the earth after such a wrenching to the heights. And because we were always looking upwards, our eyes were filled with sky, we breathed sky, our chests would broaden and we'd have angels for company. . . . There, everything was planned with intelligence and knowledge, every street was tied to heaven. . . .[43]

Fastened to God by a thousand cords, Smyrna was Eden, the Homeland. The fire, however, had ended it all, the promised land was irrevocably gone, and the earth and heavens were severed in 1922, exactly forty years before Yiakoumis's narration.

The Megale Idea had perished, bringing with its collapse the millennia-old Hellenism of Asia Minor. It is Yiakoumis who condemns the behavior of the Helladic Greeks in Smyrna. He recalls the editorial of a Smyrna newspaper: "It wrote about how the Greeks betrayed us, how the Turks were good people, how we must recover [from the illusions] that sucked our brains for three years [during the Commission] with ideas about freedom and glory, about the chosen people, about Constantinople and Saint Sophia, and about sending the Turk back to the Red Apple Tree."[44]

As the narration continues, the fear of the approaching Turkish armies throws the Greek government commission into panic, a panic they try to keep from the Smyrniots. "Don't leave, they told us, we'll come back. Long live Greece."[45] Yiakoumis repeats the sentiments of a barber with whom he spoke before going

43. *Ibid.,* pp. 170-171.
44. *Ibid.,* p. 175
45. *Ibid.,* p. 177.

home, before the fire: "The Motherland isn't an idea up in the air, it isn't past glories and graves and marble ruins. The Motherland is the soil, the place, the fields and the seas and the mountains. Motherland is the current people, and love of the Motherland is the desire for their happiness. I say that because I am a good Greek. . . ."[46]

Yiakoumis returns home to his pregnant wife, in whom he tries to instill a confidence he does not feel himself. They speak about everyday matters, unable to suppress, however, the bitter sorrow at the wreckage of national dreams to which they were witness. He goes outside to discuss the events briefly with his neighbors and sees the woman next door bringing in her wash, still dripping. There was smoke about, but she did not know where it was coming from. Rather than have them covered with soot, she would hang her clothes up again tomorrow. He and Katerina have dinner and go to bed early, but something wakes them both at eleven. "The heat? The shouts? Dogs were barking." He goes out to his garden, sees the great flames, and hears the birds, deceived by the brilliant glare, beginning to chirp. Then, a horde of silent people runs through the Quarter's narrow streets, "bent, breathless, with bundles on their shoulders or a child in arms," carrying irrelevant objects like a kettle or a coffee-mill. "The women were not screaming, nor the old men moaning, nor the children whining." All one could hear was "the sound of feet tramping on the earth."[47]

There is not much Yiakoumis can do as the end approaches. A bell begins to toll; like the one in the folksong that signaled the Fall of Constantinople and Saint Sophia, this one tolls for the eternal death of Hellenism in Asia Minor. The bellfry collapses, but the bell continues to ring, while every other sound is blurred

46. *Ibid.,* p. 180.
47. *Ibid.,* p. 185.

out in the roar of the fire soon to engulf them. A shaggy rug here, a mattress there, a blanket, a large basket, objects brought out by neighbors and set in the square burst into flames from the intense heat. "Then the pine tree in our garden ignited like a torch, throwing out its pine cones like flaming balls." He and Katerina run, but she is stopped by pain and miscarries. The child would have been a boy, Yiakoumis sees in the light of the flames of his own house.

At Hadzifrangos's is a great work, for which Politis had to devise a form to contain the complexity of meanings he wanted it to hold. He was no longer able to employ the linear plot, as he had in his earlier novels, to narrate the events of the novel. Without the "Parodos," which gives the perspective of 1922 and of the "present" on the events of 1902-1903, the major story would be inconsequential, though not pointless. The greatness of *At Hadzifrangos's* stems from the fact that it is a discovery of a "lost city," a resurrection of the spirit of everyday life forever gone, a "dig" into the emotional past of a civilization that is restored on the verge of its being forgotten. None of this could have been accomplished if Politis had seen his work in terms of the social novel, as the Generation of which he was such an important member had established it in Greek letters. *At Hadzifrangos's*, the apex of Politis's *oeuvre*, breaks away, like the other fiction in this category, from the form of the conventional novel and exists as proof – if any more were necessary – that the Generation of the 1930s was marked indelibly by the Asia Minor Disaster of 1922.

Unlike those who employed the linear scheme, the writers of *The Garden of Princes, The Dreams of Angelika,* and *At Hadzifrangos's* felt clearly the need to break out of the restraints of time. Demanding freedom from the bonds of chronology, they followed a psychological rather than a chronological order, moving backwards and forwards in time in order to treat or to focus upon incidents that could not otherwise be used. Regardless of their varying success, these three novels reveal a maturation of the Asia Minor theme not encountered before and a willingness – if not a need – to experiment with the form of the novel that is rare in Greek fiction. It seems fairly clear in these three novels that the complexity of the subject matter of the Asia Minor Disaster, as well as the distance from the events, liberated or perhaps compelled the novelist to experiment with a corresponding complexity in form, a complexity he was able to express because fiction, as a genre, had developed and matured since the 1930s.

6 Critics of the Fiction of Disaster

The central thesis of this study had been that the Asia Minor Disaster has had two sorts of impact on modern Greek fiction. The *first* has been expressed in two distinct historical phases by the "theme." The *second*, caused by changed social, moral, and political (ideological) conditions, has resulted in an artistic escape from the previously inhibiting ethographic confines to the freedom offered by modern fiction to describe a complex, usually urban society, initially in terms of realism, and later — after the establishment of the social novel — in terms of experimentation.

Most Greek critics, addressing themselves exclusively to what in this study has been called the Asia Minor "theme," have concluded that its effect has been slight. The representation in fiction of the Greco-Turkish War, the Greek military rout, the massacre and persecution of the Christian minorities, their migration, their life as refugees in Greece; and their eventual assimilation into the mainstream of Greek society has not had, the Greek critics almost unanimously claim, the abundant witness that a series of events of such magnitude should have had.

To be fair, however, the critics should have added that not only had Greek fiction never previously been able to mirror its society or the historical events the Greek people had undergone, but that previous writers never even made the attempt to do so. They had made no effort to document the society around them, moreover, because very few writers thought in novelistic terms. The fact that critics after the Disaster began demanding that fiction reflect history bespeaks the delayed recognition that literature is directly related to society and that the novel, more than any other literary form, bears the major weight of this social role.

Yet, despite the criticism leveled at the novelists by the Greek critics for not reflecting the events of the Disaster adequately, there have been no systematic critical studies of either the theme or of the great development prose fiction had undergone during the interwar period. In this chapter, which is concerned with the way criticism, primarily Greek criticism, has viewed the impact of the Asia Minor Disaster on Greek fiction, we shall find ourselves limited to using texts no more extensive than book reviews, fewer than five literary essays, and one pamphlet-length study.

Perhaps in order to get a fuller picture of the literary problems involved in the issue of the two-fold impact, we should view briefly the situation as it appears in poetry. The first thing one notices is that the immediate feelings the Disaster excited were expressed in poetry of a fairly low quality, in verse that is explicit, descriptive, emotional and that has, in effect, the same relation to serious poetry that journalistic prose has to serious fiction. George Seferis, a Smyrniot and by any informed critic's standards a major poet, had never written directly about the Disaster, although the entire body of his work, at least beginning with "The Cistern" (1932) and *Mythistorima* (1935) and up to the "Cyprus" poems is suffused with the theme of the loss of homeland. The poets who dominated the expression of the loss of Anatolia in the Disaster, or the hard life of the refugees, were either established poets like Palamas, Skipis, Malakasis, or Athanasiadis-Novas, whose verse in this respect, though it shows strongly felt emotion, appears esthetically unsuccessful, or versifiers like Michael Argyropoulos, Stergios Skiadas, and others.[1]

Yet limiting oneself to the versifiers and excluding the poetic climate would make for a narrow and superficial view of the development of Greek poetry; the *direct* reaction of poets to the Disaster was infinitesimal compared to the revolution in the attitudes toward poetry brought about by the events of 1922. Greece and Greek culture, it must not be forgotten, were still dominated by the national optimism of the dynamic Venizelist era, when Europe began to experience in 1918 the postwar frenzy. The intellectual climate of Greece in 1919 had not fundamentally differed from what it had been in 1913. We saw this in Varnalis and Kazantzakis, both of whom, despite their interest in Marxism, were more personally affected by the elections of 1920 than they had been by the Great War or by the Russian Revolution. Aimilios Hourmouzios states in no uncertain terms that the First World War had left "unmoved the entire Greek intellectual world from Kostis Palamas to the least poetaster and from the most firmly established writers of prose down to the mere beginners."[2]

The Greeks, who had been fighting from 1912 rather than from 1914, had experienced, in the years during and immediately after the Great War, not the shattering of their ideas of moral and cultural progress and man's rationality, but the virtual realization of the promise that history had made to them, the fulfillment of the Megale Idea. For them, the greatest poet of their nation from 1880 to the first two decades of the twentieth century was Kostis

1. Romos Philyras, Stelios Sperantzas, Angelos Simioritis, Sylvios Papadopoulos, Nikos Toutounzakis, Elli Papadimitriou, Olga Vatidou, Lily Vatidou, Michalis Petridis, Yiannis Damvergis, Apostolos Mamelis, K. Misailidis, and others.

2. Aimilios Hourmouzios, *Ilios Enkyklopaidia,* Tomos Ellas, 7, p. 1113, n.d.

Palamas, the artist who summed up the most advanced ideas of their culture. His epics, *The Dodecalogue of the Gypsy* (1907) and *The King's Flute* (1910) were considered the visions of a poet whose mission it was "to inspire and lead his people out of the deadly slumber of defeat." [3] Palamas was the bard of his people, a familiar figure, whose greatness was agreed upon and who was firmly committed to the struggle for the demotic, a commitment that certified his proper orientation toward progress and parliamentary government.

In our time, the victory of Constantine Cavafy over Palamas is indisputable, but in those days the Alexandrian poet was little known and less respected. Like that of most non-Helladic Greeks, Cavafy's view of Hellenism was a racial one, not limited to the national boundaries of the modern state, which until 1922 could not presume to reflect the breadth and complexity of the Greek people. Cavafy was unimportant, known only to a few; his "mixed language" seemed to question his dedication to the genuinely progressive Demotic movement; his method of publication, which consisted of handing out broadsheets to his friends, was not calculated to win him a large following; and, finally, his homosexuality tended to isolate him from the bourgeois society of Alexandria.

The Generation of the 1930s, represented by men like George Seferis and George Theotokas, might have hurried the ascendancy of Cavafy and the decline of Palamas, but non-esthetic considerations intruded here, for the politico-linguistic position of Palamas made them his loyalists. He had become for them a symbol of the Greek artist as a public man, and too much emotion and admiration were invested in him to be jettisoned for what they wanted to be liberated from — the sense of dissolution and despair that

3. Thanasis Maskaleris, *Kostis Palamas* (Twayne World Authors Series 197), (New York: 1972), Twayne Publishers, p. 71. See his Chapters Three and Four for an extended treatment of both epic poems.

they experienced as a generation as a result of the Asia Minor Disaster. For them, Cavafy may have been a far better poet than Constantine Karyotakis, who committed suicide in 1928, but he was certainly no better as a symbol. In their work they were going to wipe out the disgrace of 1922; the sad voices, no matter how great, that spoke of death and historical decline were their enemies.

Cavafy, under these circumstances, did not have a chance. The young recognized his greatness but were ambivalent about him. "What was this strange game of metered prose," Theotokas writes, "these taunting rhymes, this unexpected mixing of journalism, history, the ecclesiastical style, and an improbable lyricism, which made us wonder if he took himself seriously?" But the reason went even deeper, Theotokas sensed, for Cavafy's sarcasm undermined the very ideals that, as a young man who had just seen his nation suffer a profound humiliation, he needed to nourish. "I believed passionately in my land, in my generation, in our future, and I worshipped life." He wanted his people "to do great things," while Cavafy, he felt, was "mercilessly sarcastic . . . within the cloudy figures of his exhausted sensitivity and his bitter wisdom."[4]

The Greek youth had a choice to make and they chose the most important poet of their time and nation, Kostis Palamas, and rejected Constantine Cavafy, the greatest Greek poet of their era. The funeral of Palamas in 1943 during the Nazi Occupation was a patriotic gathering, a gesture of defiance; Cavafy had died in 1933, in peripheral Alexandria, and there was certainly no sense among the Metropolitan Greeks that a great force had left Greek letters.

The impact of the Asia Minor Disaster was thus also reflected

4. George Theotokas, "K. P. Kavafis," in *Pnevmatiki Poreia* (Athens, 1961), p. 237.

in poetry, not necessarily in its subject matter, where its effects tended to be immediate and superficial, but in the more profound, though temporarily repressed, questioning of the optimism and the patriotism that had previously characterized Greek verse. As far as the certitude of national greatness was concerned, however, there was no hope of rekindling that until the excitement and the glory of the Albanian campaign.

Greece "had her own 1914," Michael Meraklis writes, trying to explain the change in poetry as well as in the psychology of the poets themselves.

> It is 1922. . . . A deep scar in our recent history. Nineteen Twenty-Two can be considered . . . as a watershed in our contemporary epoch, national as well as poetic. . . . [After this] there is a loss of equilibrium everywhere and the poets, in order to save themselves, begin to move, to emigrate. But even this emigration is divided, some go inwards, others outwards. . . . Some are introspective and others outward-looking. . . . They are divided as though by a vacuum, like a wide river whose bridges have been blown up and which is now divided clearly in two.[5]

If one may pursue the insight of Mr. Meraklis, those poets who went "inwards," like George Seferis and Odysseus Elytis, experimented with many of the techniques of the post-World War I literary movements of Western Europe and America, while those who looked outwards, like Yiannis Ritsos and Nikiphoros Vrettakos, accepted a political role for poetry.

Few critics doubt that the effect of the Disaster of 1922 was vast. For those who consider fiction as a mirror of its society, however, the relative lack of representation of the Asia Minor theme is a problem that disturbs them. Given the fact that the

5. Michalis Meraklis, *I Poiisi mas, O Dichasmos, To Metaichmio* (Kalamata, 1959), pp. 9-10.

novel before the Generation of the 1930s had never been considered an important genre, and that no period in modern Greek history had been adequately represented in fiction, why — they insist on asking — had so few writers shown an interest in the possibilities of the Asia Minor theme?

A number of explanations have been offered, ranging from the ingenious but unverifiable to the convincing, for why this should be so. Some critics, characterizing the Greeks as people who easily forget, or who want to forget, unfortunate events, make no attempt to support this generalization with proofs or with comparisons to other cultures. Besides this "national trait," there was the "anti-refugee climate" of the interwar period, a climate which, according to Pavlos Floros, was cultivated for "political or economic reasons" and which tended to repress an interest in the subject matter of Asia Minor.[6] One wishes that he would have been more specific, because antipathy to the refugee, which certainly existed, need not have dampened interest in the events of Asia Minor. Serious fiction, at any rate, would not have been influenced by the economic rivalries between Anatolians and natives, nor by the desire to minimize the blunders of one party or another during the period in question. Only the sort of writing whose natural outlet would be the newspaper — always a party organ in Greece — would be affected by the torturous career of Greek politics between the wars.

Floros's allegation that the cause lies in the censorship imposed on Greek culture by the Metaxas dictatorship is more probable. "In the period 1936-1940," he says, "every expression that would have annoyed 'friendly' foreign lands was forbidden. The application of this principle to Art was unwise [and] completely unjustifiable. The fact was ignored that whatever has

6. Pavlos Floros, "I Mikra Asia stin Elliniki Logotechnia meta to 1923" *Mikrasiatiki Estia,* No. 1, July-Sept. (1946), pp. 74-85.

artistic form transcends the political sphere and becomes a higher truth, independent of place and time ... [the] property of a nation's culture."[7]

Historically, censorship has been a constant in Greek life, taking a variety of forms, from the attempts to seize and sequester the manuscripts of Makriyannis under King Othon; to the more legally supported efforts throughout the nineteenth and twentieth centuries to stop the publication of newspapers and to imprison, for a number of reasons, the publishers and editors; to the formalized process in recent years of compelling writers to submit their works to a committee (which under most civilian governments is composed of writers or under most military regimes is composed of military officers) that would allow or disallow the publication of a work, using political or moral criteria.[8] Censorship per se, though a hated device in Greek culture, is frequently accepted as a necessary formality when it is exercised by a regime with which a particular writer, or intellectual generally, finds himself in sympathy. Then again, even if one does not accept censorship at all, one would tend to avoid discussions of this sort and rarely speak out against it, since Greece's rather turbulent political history must always be kept in

7. *Ibid.,* p. 78.
8. Censorship existed from the very beginning of the Greek state, as attested to by these lines of Alexandros Soutsos, attacking the government of John Capodistrias.

Εἶν' ἐλεύθερος ὁ τύπος, φθάνει μόνο νά μη βλάψῃς
τῆς 'Αρχῆς τούς ὑπαλλήλους,
τούς κριτάς, τούς 'Υπουργούς μας, και τῶν 'Υπουργῶν τούς φίλους,
Εἶν' ἐλεύθερος ὁ τύπος, φθάνει μόνο να μη' γράψῃς.

Quoted by Yianis Kordatos in *Istoria tis Neoellinikis Logotechnias, apo to 1453 os to 1961,* Vol. I, p. 170. This is all formal censorship. There is, moreover, as in most other cultures, a great deal of informal censorship, even more difficult to prove, that is the result of the strong pressures exercised on the Greek writer by his friends, his relatives, his political connections, or his class orientation.

mind. It is only rarely that writers like Floros mention the fact of censorship in writing, and a rare occasion indeed when someone dares to offer documentary proof of it.

Christos Spanomanolis, in his "Introduction" to *Prisoners of The Turks* (1956) provides just such proof when he states that the newspaper *Ethnos* was asked in 1932 "to stop the publication" of the first, serial version of his book "at the instigation of the Turkish Embassy, as a gesture to Greco-Turkish Friendship, which was just beginning." The government was Liberal at the time, and Venizelos and Kemal Ataturk had signed the Friendship Treaty two years before. In this case, a newspaper — liberal, as it turns out — with a large circulation, was stopped from publishing a chronicle, which made no claim to be fiction, of the actual brutalization of Greeks at the hands of their Turkish captors. Its continuation would obviously have aggravated old and deeply rooted hatreds at the time when the Greek government was attempting to work out a pact with Turkey and to forge a federation of the Balkans that would have included the ancient enemy. The decision was clearly a political one, and Spanomanolis's words lead us to believe that there was no outright prohibition — no threat to close the newspaper down and to jail its publisher and editor — but merely that *Ethnos,* "as a gesture" (χάριν τῆς ἑλληνοτουρκικῆς φιλίας) decided to respect the government's wishes and cease publication.[9]

There is, however, a great difference between this and the censorship of works of fiction. The Metaxas regime (1936-1940) clearly interfered with the republication of *The Number 31,328* by Ilias Venezis, a fact mentioned by Dimitris Liatsos in "The Asia Minor Disaster in Modern Greek Literature" (1962), and of

9. It promptly began the series again, twenty-three years later, after the anti-Greek riots in Constantinople of September 6, 1955. See Spanomanolis, *Aichmalotoi ton Tourkon,* p. 18.

Argo by George Theotokas.[10] This censorship was imposed upon the writers at the very time writers of the Generation of the 1930s were reaching the age of artistic maturity and when the Greek novel had clearly shown itself to be capable of bearing the weight of ideas; coming at this time, it removed from the writer the greatest store of subject matter recent history could offer him. The Metaxas censorship was crass, certainly, but it also had a timidity about it that seems to characterize Greek military governments, for during the four years of intellectual suppression, nothing was allowed to be published that could conceivably have elicited a protest from any foreign government.

Besides Pavlos Floros's unverifiable and doubtful allegation of the Greeks' ability to forget, the no more convincing effects of the "anti-refugee" spirit,[11] and the more probable assertions about censorship, there is the factor of the refugees' rapid assimilation into the mainstream of Greek life, which according to Aimilios Hourmouzios tended to dissipate the intensity of interest in the uniqueness of the refugees. "Refugee literature" as a category itself could never really exist in Greece, he writes, "because within four or five years the power of adjustment, helped by the common language, by roughly the same manners and morals, and the identical struggle for life within a Greek

10. The ban on *Argo* forced the author, as he states in a note, to circulate the novel in 1939 using the pre-Metaxas publishing date, 1936. The phrase κατ' ἀπαίτηση is confusing since it could mean that Theotokas, wanting to avoid difficulty with the authorities, had printed and released the second edition in 1939 with the previous date – presenting, in other words, the newly printed copies as having just been released from a three-year storage; or it could possibly mean that the censorship board "compelled" him to use the earlier date in order to extricate themselves from any responsibility. This second possibility seems unlikely to me.
11. Unless Mr. Floros means by this that the Greek state, sensing a corporate blame for the Disaster, deliberately tried to suppress or discourage any interest in the events of 1922. This, however, is not what he says.

environment reduced the possibilities of a self-existent intellectual career." [12]

The effort to establish themselves in their new, Helladic environment was so insistent, so consuming of time and effort for the refugees, that they could not in any numbers set about to express themselves in art. By the time the mass of Anatolians had succeeded in rooting themselves in the Greek soil, they were so fully absorbed in the Greek reality that they had no interest in maintaining a way of life and in reading a literature that would speak only to themselves. "The refugee was no longer a refugee. . . . The fact that the refugee situation has, in its many facets, remained a dead issue for the refugee writers and the natives who have come into direct contact with the refugee drama does not controvert a reality that was a major landmark for the development of postwar Greek life." [13]

Hourmouzios seems to feel that the reason the "vast subject of the establishment of the refugee" was virtually ignored by Greek writers was that the Disaster and the migration formed a "new race," a mixture of native and Anatolian Greeks. It is not clear, however, why this "new Greek" would not, as an artist, be vitally interested in the elements that had gone into his creation.

The most important and most convincing reason offered by Greek critics for the relative infrequency of the Asia Minor theme's treatment, however, is the lack of chronological distance. Pavlos Floros gives this priority, claiming quite correctly that an artist cannot be expected to absorb an experience and turn it into art so rapidly. Hourmouzios agrees. The most compelling witness of this, though, is to be found in an article by Ilias Venezis,

12. Aimilios Hourmouzios, "Prosfygiki Logotechnia," *Nea Estia,* 27 No. 314, Jan. 15 (1940), p. 106.
13. *Ibid.,* p. 107.

because it comes from an established novelist who at that very time, 1943, was struggling with the implications of esthetic distance on the Anatolian subject matter. Writing in the newspaper *Refugee World*, Venezis states that time is the all-important factor, that a mere two decades have passed since the Disaster and that, though only Tatiana Stavrou's *The First Roots*, his own *Serenity*, and, he hears, a novel in progress by Stratis Myrivilis (obviously *The Mermaid Madonna*) have been attempted, he is sure that shortly "an entire cycle of works in the form of the novel, drama, poetry, painting, and music will be inspired by the drama of Anatolia."[14]

Unstated, of course, is the certitude that this "entire cycle of works" will require the peace and tranquility necessary for artistic creation. The frightful experiences awaiting the Greek people after the horrors of Occupation were over were certainly instrumental in denying the Asia Minor theme a primacy that was, quite understandably, taken by the drama of the Resistance and the Civil War.

The subject of Asia Minor itself, according to I. M. Panayotopoulos in 1962, may have been too vast for complete documentation. The tragedy that the race had undergone had nevertheless made the present Greeks "men who live *after* the Asia Minor Disaster," which he calls "that terrible watershed that divides our history in two." As his criticism of 1943 had indicated, Panayotopoulos saw clearly the double impact of the Disaster. Though its direct representation in fictional works may have been less complete than it should have been, its presence "as a stable, underlying factor in artistic creation" had not ceased to exist. The Asia Minor Disaster "has created, either directly or

14. Ilias Venezis, "I Prosfygia tou 1922 stin Elliniki Logotechnia," *Prosfygikos Kosmos,* January 24, 1943, pp. 1-2.

indirectly, a special area in our literary production, a special climate and a special mood."[15]

It is this very "mood" that comes under the special fire of certain literary critics. Chrysos Esperas claims that "refugee fiction" was unable to avoid "the dirge of refugee pain" and mentions Tatiana Stavrou's *The First Roots*, which certainly is vulnerable to this stricture, as well as Stratis Doukas's *Narrative of a Prisoner*, which most certainly is not.[16]

Alekos Doukas, too, in the introduction to his novel *In Youthful Battle* (1953), finds the poetry and fiction of Anatolian writers about Asia Minor unsatisfactory because of their "lamentations of Jeremiah." He adds a note not heard before, however, when he accuses Greek writers of being unable to see the sufferings that the Turkish people had undergone during that time and of concentrating, instead, exclusively on the eradication of Hellenism from Anatolia. This was a sentiment only someone gifted with a great psychological distance could make, and only after the end of the Civil War, when writers who considered themselves "progressives" would have the emotional freedom to reinterpret the history of their youth.

Dimitris Yiaghos, one of the few Greek critics to devote an entire essay to "The National Disaster and our Literature," finds the interwar writers gloomy, unable because of the magnitude of the blow to "raise new symbols of direction and struggle, as had occurred in 1897," impotent to produce men like Palamas, Karkavitsas, and Psycharis. Instead, the Disaster produced men like Karyotakis, who preferred to write about private rather than universal experiences. The Disaster, he concludes, agreeing with

15. I. M. Panayotopoulos, "Istoria kai Logotechnia," *Eleftheria*, Oct. 7, 1962, pp. 1-8.
16. Chrysos Esperas, *To Mythistorima* (Athens, 1940) p. 82.

Michael Meraklis, brought with it subjectivity rather than objectivity. But Yiaghos's thesis – despite his perceptiveness – is vitiated by his short-sightedness. The interwar period did not end in 1928 with the suicide of Constantine Karyotakis, but continued for another twelve years and, before ending in a moment of national heroism, saw the emergence of a gifted and productive generation, in prose and poetry, whose work placed Greek literature for the first time on an unchallengably European footing. We have limited ourselves to prose in this study, but to pick Karyotakis as typical of the "interwar generation" one must ignore other poets like George Seferis, Odysseus Elytis, Andreas Embirikos, Nikiphoros Vrettakos, or Yiannis Ritsos, all of whom first published between the wars. Like most Greek critics except I. M. Panayotopoulos, Yiaghos focuses exclusively on fiction that represents the events of 1922, ignoring other works in which the actual events of the Disaster have secondary importance. Accordingly, Theotokas is mentioned only for "Narrative of 1922," a slight sketch, but not for *Argo* or *Leonis*, novels permeated with the *fact* of the Disaster.

With the exception, again, of I. M. Panayotopoulos, only foreign critics seem to give the Asia Minor Disaster its due, perhaps because they come from another culture and cultivate by necessity the comparative approach, or perhaps – as Renos Apostolidis accuses – because they do not know the literature well enough and misread the literary tradition by emphasizing only that era – the modern – about which they are authoritative.

The targets of Apostolidis's scorn are Filippo Maria Pontani and Mario Vitti, both of whom consider the Disaster an important watershed for Greek literature. Pontani claims, in 1950, that the events of 1922 opened a "tragic chasm of intellectual as well as practical problems whose consequences are felt even today." Concentrating on poetry, he finds that the crisis following the

Asia Minor Disaster was met by the Greek poets with "revolutionary radicalism." Influenced by "Futurist, Dadaist, and Surrealist ideas," Greek verse quickly absorbed these European movements.[17]

Vitti, discussing prose fiction after 1922, concentrates on the work of writers from Anatolia. Adding, he says, to the "immeasurable love they had for the country that had nourished the traditions of Ancient Greece, these writers also brought the trauma of separation from the land of their birth, where they had lived the unforgettable years of their adolescence, and drew from this spiritual drama the experience of a world in which they had lived and the sense of debt to express [their feelings in their art]."[18]

Possibly out of a desire to clarify by reinterpreting, possibly because of misreading the sometimes awkward translation from the Italian, possibly even because of a deliberate attempt to assign other words to Pontani and Vitti, Apostolidis claims that the Italian critics, and Vitti in particular, believe it was the Anatolian writers who changed the course of Greek literature and that the conditions existing in Greece at the time had no hand in it. By interpreting their statements to be either-or ones, Apostolidis finds room to attack them. What annoys him, in particular, is Vitti's remark that the Disaster acted as an "unexpected awakening" to Greek intellectual life. "How many prose writers came from Asia Minor?" he demands. "Two or three." It was not the writers but the problems of the time, the one and a half million refugees, that "awakened" Greece, he states, ignoring the fact

17. Filippo Maria Pontani, "I Synchroni Elliniki Poiisi," *O Aionas Mas,* 5, No. 6, June (1951), p. 118. The article was translated from the Nov.-Dec. 1950 issue of *Rivista di Critica* of Rome.

18. Mario Vitti, "I Neoelliniki Pezographia apo ti Genia tou '20 os Simera," *O Aionas Mas,* 5, No. 7, July (1951), p. 166.

that neither Pontani nor Vitti had said otherwise. Chaotic conditions, he reminds us, have existed in Greece since time immemorial. It was the international postwar crisis, not the consequences of the Asia Minor Disaster; it was the general – social, economic, and political – impact on the organization of national life, not the appearance of two or three individual writers, that caused Greek literature to be renewed. "I repeat: there were one and a half million uprooted people . . . who inundated a small, poor land. . . . If we waited for someone to 'wake us unexpectedly,' we had had noises and upheavals and shakings stronger than the voice and power of the melancholy, soft and sweet Mr. Venezis, the naturally isolated Kontoglou, or the necessarily marginal Mr. Seferis. . . ." [19]

Apostolidis's occasionally brilliant comments, directed against the inaccuracies that he, as much as Vitti, had a hand in creating, are not enough to dispel the obfuscations that his feverish prose creates. Ultimately, however, he seems to accept the fact that Greek literature, despite its frequent "awakenings" in the past, *was* "renewed" after the Great War. For Greece, as we have seen, this necessarily meant after 1922, not after 1918.

Although the permeation of the Megale Idea in Greek life is accepted as being overwhelming, and although many critics accept 1922 as its date of termination (others choose 1923 with the Lausanne Treaty, others 1930 with the Friendship Pact), none specifically identifies this ideological collapse with its reflection in Greek literature, though as we have seen, notably in Chapters Three and Four, the impact was undeniable.

No critic, moreover, Greek or foreign, seems to discuss the nature of Greek publishing and of the audience to which works of literary art are directed.

19. Renos Apostolidis, "Apantisi stous k. k. F. M. Pontani kai M. Vitti: I Neoelliniki Logotechnia kai oi Xenoi Meletites tis," *O Aionas Mas,* 5, No. 7, July (1951), p. 176.

Those who would have been expected to write about the events of the Disaster immediately — that is, within the first decade — would be those with the moral authority to do so; those, in other words, who had actually undergone the experiences they wrote about. But the publishing industry of Greece in the 1920s, as distinct from the daily press, was still in a rudimentary stage. Aside from *Noumas* and one or two short-lived periodicals, there were no outlets for serious fiction. Even by the 1930s Greece — because of limited population, lack of purchasing power, the expensiveness of paper and high printing costs — was unable to maintain a publishing industry that could produce important works of fiction, or even non-fiction, at a profit. It is questionable if Greece today can do so. Since a market for non-subsidized books did not exist, the publication costs of most (if not all) of the works relating to the Asia Minor Disaster were paid for by the writers themselves, except when they could get a newspaper to publish their books in serial form.

There is little place in the Greek publishing scheme for the author who chooses a subject to write about because he knows that it will arouse interest within the "industry." There are few if any commissions for books, and it is still only the established writer who can get his books printed and distributed without paying for the process himself. This means that the author who writes a book does so because he cannot do otherwise; he *must* write it. The next stage, publication, is also up to him and his resources alone. If he has the money and is willing to spend it, he has the book printed and distributed. If not, it remains in manuscript. It is not unusual for writers to wait for a decade or more before they are able to publish a book of theirs. The critic of Greek letters must never forget this vital difference in publishing practices.

Besides this, the Greek state or institutions like the Church, the educational establishments, and the cultural foundations, even assuming that they had not been overwhelmed by the crushing burdens of physically absorbing and caring for the million and a half refugees, had for a number of reasons never previously revealed themselves able to fulfill the taxing demands placed upon them to safeguard, catalogue, and maintain for posterity the vast and complex cultural heritage of the modern Greek. Much is demanded of the Greek state which, given its meager resources, it will never be able to fulfill. Yet it behaved with great flexibility in giving Greek citizenship at once to the million and more refugees and in accepting into professional practice the thousands of lawyers, doctors, nurses, and teachers who found themselves in a country most of them had never seen before they arrived on its shores as penniless refugees. It is also difficult to expect the Greek state, which bore corporate blame for the events of 1922 (events which, in the eyes of the refugees, no number of executions could efface), to accept as a duty the documentation and commemoration of a Disaster of such magnitude.

Under these circumstances, private publishing efforts are clearly the most productive. One commendable foundation, The Center for Asia Minor Studies, instituted by Madame Melpo Merlier, is a veritable treasure house of information about the Hellenism of Anatolia. Under the aegis of the French Institute, moreover, Madame Merlier, an Anatolian Greek herself, has brought out a series of monographs on the linguistic character of the Greek-speaking people of Asia Minor and maintains an Archive of the Popular Music and Folklore of Asia Minor. The Pontian Society, the Union of Smyrniots, and other organizations keep the interest in the material of Asia Minor current. Besides this, there is *Refugee World*, a weekly newspaper, and *Mikrasiatika Chronika*, which, however, ceased publication after the military coup of 1967.

The only official (or semi-official) attempt to record the

narratives of victims of the Asia Minor Disaster for posterity was made by the International Women's Convention in Athens in 1926, which published the heart-breaking *Autobiographies of Refugee Girls* (subtitled "Descriptions by Children of the Asia Minor Persecutions") in the hopes of gaining financial support for an orphanage in Glyfada. Despite the occasionally annoying mandarin-purist language, quite out of character for the ten- to sixteen-year-olds who are supposed to be relating their personal experiences, *Autobiographies* is an invaluable source of information for a study of the Disaster. Although the organization was headquartered in the House of Parliament in Constitution Square, one wonders how much official backing it had.

The only other attempt to record narratives of people actually involved in the Disaster occurred on its fortieth anniversary, in the September 1962 issue of *Epitheorisi Technis*, which includes five "folk narratives" edited by Elli Padadimitriou. Unless there are resources unlisted in all the bibliographies, these and the narratives embedded in individual works in Greek, or those few memoirs published by foreigners, will be the only first-hand sources future historians will have about one of the most important events in Greek history. As Gerasimos Grigoris says in "A Folk Chronicler," "even the slightest fragment of that great adventure of the Race, which forever defined its future fate, is a precious thing." [20]

Given, then, the difficulties of the publishing industry, the inadequacies of the cultural institutions, and the politicization of the Asia Minor issue, it remained up to the refugee organizations — with their limited financial resources — and to the writers themselves, to keep alive the interest in the Disaster theme.

The subject matter, of course, was tragically unpleasant and

20. Gerasimos Grigoris, *Epitheorisi Technis,* 9, No. 93, September (1962), p. 302.

thus of limited interest, and those in its primary market, the refugees themselves, were too busy adjusting to life in Greece, financially limited, and desperately waiting for the return of loved ones. As most of the critics implied, literature requires leisure and a measure of tranquility, and time for imaginative fiction was not available. The strong emotions that had to be expressed were more easily expressed in the arenas of politics and journalism. The prose and poetry that was published in newspapers is notable only for its direct and explicit nature.

If one may be permitted to criticize the critics, what Greek critics have seemed to demand, and to demand much too early, is a creative synthesis of the Asia Minor experience. I. M. Panayotopoulos implied that this was lost effort when he said that the theme itself may be too vast for treatment. Besides, he asked, what representation did the other important historical events like the Revolution of 1821 and the Macedonian Struggle have in Greek fiction? Even less. The present writer would tend to agree with this evaluation, particularly since the Greek novel had only recently come of age at the time a grand historical synthesis was demanded of it.

Ilias Venezis, surprisingly, was the first to sound this demand when, during the Occupation, he found that the attitude toward fiction held by contemporary interwar writers inhibited the full development of the Asia Minor theme. Interestingly enough, he seemed to ignore the rather thin novelistic tradition in Greece. Considering that the overwhelming interest of a whole epoch of modern Greek literature had been ethography, "the picturesque and totally external aspect of the life of our people," Venezis did not think it unrealistic to expect that the refugees flooding into Greece after the Disaster would have provided a vast body of fiction describing the life of the uprooted and their conflicts with the natives. "The exact opposite, however, has occurred."

This is an interesting and valid point. The ethographic bias of previous Greek fiction should have been expected to serve as an impetus to record the lives and struggles of the Anatolian refugees. Instead, with the exception of the works studied in Chapter Two, there is little in the way of conscious observation of this major event in Greek history. The Generation of the 1930s, vowing to break with the Greek literary past, broke also with the "photographic realism" implicit in ethography.

Venezis blames this "lack of record" on the interest in and glorification of "the individual and his psychological make-up," an interest that "went even further by searching beyond the conscious mind into the unconscious for the authentic in our lives." He ignores the crucial fact, however, that ethography possessed a patriotic bias that could no longer exist as it had before 1922, and that it was dedicated to the description, and celebration, of the stability and manners and morals hallowed by time – not to the portrayal of upheaval, dissolution, urban poverty, and despair.

The writers of the Generation of the 1930s were not interested in the surface apprehension of reality, Venezis implies, but in something more profound, a psychography of modern men and women and an esthetic orientation that would enable them to approach more closely the demands that the novel met in the Western bourgeois tradition. This search for modernity, however, tended to block the Greek writer from expressing another kind of reality. The modern temperament – introverted, sensitive to social tensions, ironic – was unable to handle adequately the "cycle of epic events" that the Asia Minor theme clearly is:

> To translate these into art we would have had to adjust ourselves to [the epic] atmosphere and confront life in the manner of the epic poet. Instead of studying individuals and analyzing them psychologically, we should have studied the mass [and] group movements. Instead of studying cases of

average people and ingrown lives, we should have seen heroes in the manner of epic poetry, figures above the ordinary.[21]

This is as clear an expression of the modern novelist's plight as any critic has the right to expect. It is made even more confessional when one recalls that Venezis had succeeded in conveying a sense of mass movements in *The Number 31,328,* where his primary interest was in illustrating the helplessness of the weak to resist the brutalization of the strong, while he failed to provide a proper balance between individual psychology and mass movements in *Serenity*, although this was obviously one of his esthetic goals.

It is clear that within the Occupation period, the longing to describe mass movements and "epic heroes" would present itself as a necessity. The time was heroic in that it forced men and women beyond the limitations they assumed they had and caused them to see their interwar attitudes in the perspective of man's long and bloody past – in the perspective, certainly, of the Albanian campaign. Perhaps the sense of anguish Venezis expresses has something to do with an esthetic conflict between what his critical intellect demanded he write about – "the cycle of epic events" that was the Asia Minor experience – and what his instincts as an artist demanded he write, a tale of a young boy's growing up on his grandfather's Anatolian estate, which is in fact what he wrote in *Aeolian Earth*, published in the same year as his article.

That Venezis followed his instincts, usually accepted as the better course for an artist, rather than his critical intellect, is the major critique Basil Laourdas makes in a negative review of *Aeolian Earth.*

The writers of Asia Minor have a supreme duty: to grasp within their work the meaning of the land and to pass it on to

21. Venezis, "I Prosfygia tou 1922," pp. 1-2.

later generations as an eternal lesson from that land, which was fertilized by the . . . Greeks for three thousand years. In the hands of a worthy writer, the Evangelical School [of Smyrna], the crypto-Christians, the crypto-Hellenophones, the bishops of Asia, and the memories of Byzantium — more broadly — the never-ending struggle of the "cultivated" Greek spirit with Eastern irrationality, could have provided material for a very substantial work. This work need not have appeared as an "example" for us because our spirit [ultimately] shaped and triumphed over the formlessness of the East; but we would have loved it very much, nevertheless, because it would have spoken to us about our people, about our own powers that had fused with another world [to form] new ways of life, or were defeated in an unequal but heroic struggle. Asia Minor Hellenism was and will remain for us, for the children of Greece proper, a world of Greek moral values; this is how we would have wanted it to live in the art of the Greeks of Asia Minor.[22]

As this extensive quotation indicates, the critics after the Greco-Italian War of 1940 demanded a radically different attitude toward the Asia Minor experience. The passive, introspective, ironic, sensitive — and ultimately defeatist — temperament the Greeks had had toward themselves as a result of the 1922 Disaster was inadequate to show the contradictions and complexities of the Greek spirit, which had just recently shown itself, again, to be heroic.

The novel most critics seemed to be looking for and not finding was one that would express the epic nature of the Asia Minor tragedy in a large-scale, panoramic manner. As has already been pointed out, all of them ignore the fact that within the national literary tradition there existed very few novels that could

22. Basil Laourdas, "I Aioliki Ghi," *Philologika Chronika,* I, No. 2 (1944), p. 73.

convince writers of this possibility. Aimilios Hourmouzios in 1953 urged the younger writers, particularly those "who have been moved by the 'collective myth'... and wanted to express certain moments in our national life" to study the way Nikos Kazantzakis orchestrated the characters and their complex story-lines in *Captain Michael* (*Freedom or Death*). Recalling his prewar essay "Refugee Literature," he repeats the statement that

> the uprooting of Asia Minor Hellenism and its grafting onto the other national trunk has not yet found its narrator, and it is never too late to exploit an event with so many national consequences. I noted with joy the most significant payment of his debt by Stratis Myrivilis with *The Mermaid Madonna*. Wherever we had attempts to exploit the collective myth, however, the plot was fragmented and left the impression of looseness and awkwardly joined episodes, while at other times, in trying to create ... mass movement from a specific case, it left the reader with an asphyxiated feeling [of having focused down too narrowly].[23]

But *The Dreams of Angelika* by Eva Vlami went virtually unnoticed by Greek criticism in 1958. It is ironic that the same critics who faulted Greek fiction for having ignored the Asia Minor theme should have failed to see the significance of this major work. Michael Meraklis, one of the few to appreciate Vlami's novel, felt he must defend the writer's continued interest in the Disaster. "Let no one rush to say that the theme is no longer important in our time," he cautions. "The spirits of many Greeks have not forgotten the Asia Minor tragedy. There are people," he reminds us, "who still wait [for loved ones], inquiring at ministries, listening to the pertinent radio announcements

23. Hourmouzios, "Diavazontas ena Mythistorima," *Kathimerini,* Nov. 12, 1953, p. 1.

of the Red Cross, hoping. The Asia Minor tragedy," he concludes, "still continues, exists."[24]

Aside from the overlooked novel by Eva Vlami, it is not until 1962, the fortieth anniversary of the Disaster, that the Asia Minor theme in Greek fiction appears in works that satisfy the critics. The passage of time, certainly, made most Greeks, now that their personal interests and emotions were no longer involved, aware of this chapter in their national history. Given the inability or unwillingness of the Greek state to commemorate such an unpleasant occasion, however, it was left, again, to the refugee organizations and to individuals to make their own, unofficial commemorations. The more conservative journals tended to avoid the topic, and it was left to the "critical opposition" which, intimidated from discussing issues of the more recent past, the Occupation, and the Civil War, saw in the Asia Minor theme further proof of the inability of the Greek state, as led by the political Center and Right, to represent what they considered the true interests of the Greek nation, being too concerned to serve the interests of their powerful allies. This is the major point of Nikos Psyroukis's fascinating study, partially excerpted in the September 1962 issue of *Epitheorisi Technis.*

To return to criticism of imaginative works, both Vasos Varikas, himself a refugee from Aidin, and Dimitris Raftopoulos, reviewing Dido Sotiriou's *Bloodied Earth* in the year of its publication (1962), restated their belief that the theme of the Disaster has been unexploited by Greek fiction. They even agree that Doukas's *Narrative of a Prisoner* and Venezis's *The Number 31,328* are imposing works. Varikas, including the fictions of Myrivilis as important contributions to the theme, finds, never-

24. Meraklis, "I Elliniki Pezographia tis Teleftaias Dekaetias," *Nea Poreia,* 10, Nos. 119-123, Jan.-May (1965), p. 30.

theless, that "one of the most significant events of our recent history, the fate of Ionian Hellenism, has left our writers unmoved."[25] Raftopoulos goes so far as to doubt that "the Asia Minor tragedy has had the slightest probability" of leaving any more of a trace on Greek literature than the works of Venezis and Doukas, though he makes no effort to explain such a sweeping statement. He admits, however, that he had not taken into consideration "the terrible power of childhood memory and the slow, retarded maturing of talent in the Greek cultural reality."[26] By far the greatest praise is reserved for *At Hadzifrangos's*, a novel considered by most critics as the apex of Kosmas Politis's career, an unexpected contribution to the Disaster theme by the greatest prose writer of Smyrna who previously, and perhaps deliberately, ignored the Asia Minor locale and set his fiction elsewhere, "feeling that it would be something like disrespect to the [ir] memory [of the beloved dead] to speak their names."[27]

Most Greek critics seem to agree, therefore, that before 1962 the theme of the Asia Minor Disaster had not been as well represented in Greek literature as it should have been. The reasons given for this were usually "the tendency of the Greek people to forget unpleasant things," the "anti-refugee spirit," the imposition of censorship under Metaxas, and the lack of chronological and thus emotional distance. The last two are verifiable and convincing reasons. It is beyond question, moreover, that the works appearing after World War II, whose subject matter is exclusively about the Disaster, are much more ambitious, elegant,

25. Varikas, "To Chroniko mias Epochis," *Vima,* July 1, 1962, p. 2.

26. Dimitris Raftopoulos, "Mikrasiatiki Anadromi," in *Oi Idees kai ta Erga* (Athens, 1965), p. 226.

27. Kosmas Politis, *Stou Hadzifrangou*, p. xi. "*Mia Synomilia me to Syngraphea,*" interview with George Savidis.

and powerful. Arbitrary or not, 1962, the "fortieth anniversary of the Lost City" and a forever-lost civilization, was seen by Greeks generally as the date when the Asia Minor theme could emerge from the impurities of life's pain and sorrow with the crystalline purity of esthetic truth.

Conclusion

It has been the thesis of this study that the Asia Minor Disaster of 1922 has had a double impact on Greek fiction. The "theme" of the events of 1922 and their aftermath has been considered by most Greek critics to be the only expression the Asia Minor Disaster has had in fiction, and the quantitative dearth of works describing the Disaster and its aftermath has been cited by them to prove that the literature has not adequately reflected the magnitude of the historic events.

On the other hand, most of these critics agree that the writers who have entered modern Greek literary history as The Generation of the 1930s have had an enormous influence on the Greek novel by cultivating a genre previously considered inferior to poetry and by establishing it unquestionably in Greek letters as the most comprehensive literary form with which to reflect the complexity of modern Greek society.

Although writers have on occasion pointed out the logical, as well as chronological, relationships between the Asia Minor Disaster of 1922 and the emergence of the Generation of the 1930s, no major study has proved that the event gave birth to the group. Viewing the "double impact" of the Disaster on Greek fiction, the present writer has had to study the ideological and historical background to the crucial date of 1922 in order to assess precisely what had happened in Anatolia. The trauma of the Disaster was a profound one, even for those writers not influenced in any obvious way, for it defined and limited the modern Greek future as did few other events in the long history of the nation. An exclusive interest in the "Asia Minor theme" would have ignored, therefore, the major part of the Disaster's ideological impact and would have rendered incomprehensible the emergence of Greek fiction from ethography into its modern phase. The Greek novel can be said to exist today in a way that it did not exist half a century ago because a new way of confronting the national history came about after the ideological collapse of 1922.

The Greek writer was, like most of his countrymen, patriotic to a high degree, confident of his nation's eventual greatness, and unaccustomed to considering literature as a vehicle for criticism. There are examples, of course, of nineteenth-century writers, like Emmanuel Royidis and Andreas Laskaratos, who used their society as a target for their criticism, but they are rare; by and large, most writers — whether they wrote in *katharevousa* or in the demotic — celebrate their people rather than point out their foibles. If they do criticize, they do so like George Souris, playfully and without violating the conventions of the society.

The Disaster of 1922, however, severed the bond that held the writers fast to the Greek people, changed the conditions under which Greek society functioned, and allowed for the emergence of the individual, primarily the urban man, tied to the group only by his family. For this individual, moral and ideological values were not inherited but had to be achieved through action, and he was more often in conflict with his society than in conformity with it. Because the novelist identified with his fictional character rather than with the society in which the character lived, the resultant fiction fulfilled the definition of critical realism. Freed of the patriotic bias implicit in ethography, therefore, the Generation of the 1930s and, with them, older writers, made the advance into modern fiction that writers previous to the Disaster of 1922 could not succeed in making.

The theme of the Asia Minor Disaster itself can be used as a gauge of the maturity of the Greek novel. In the first historical phase, when the theme could be said to have some emotional continuity, the first literary works that are able to convince a reader with their power and authenticity are narratives of a particular man's captivity. Constantly fixed on the individual's experiences, the "narrative" develops as a new and unrecognized art form, a "memoir" unlike the usual Greek form because it is focused on one period of time, on one series of episodes, and on one mood.

Later, the refugee as a type emerges into some importance. As the critics have pointed out, however, he is not as fully represented as he could have been. This is not because the subject is not interesting, or important, but because the critics have tended to measure yesterday's achievements by today's standards. If the Asia Minor Disaster had occurred a generation or two *after* social or modern fiction had been established in Greek letters, then it probably would have been documented more thoroughly. But the critics forget that Greek fiction was in a rudimentary stage in 1922. Besides this, those novels whose interest centers on the Asia Minor theme are highly reflective of the interwar period in which they were written, and are thus at the mercy of external political developments, like the imposition of censorship or the approach of war. By no means are the novelists capable of synthesizing the historical period adequately, for they have no perspective on it. To demand, as some Greek critics seem to do, the grand-scale novel about the Asia Minor Disaster from writers of the Generation of the 1930s is tantamount to demanding a great novel about Napoleon's invasion of Russia not two generations later, when Tolstoy's *War and Peace* was published, but a few years after the burning of Moscow.

The second phase of the Asia Minor theme thus appears after the chronological and esthetic distance has been achieved and after a fairly rich fictional tradition has been established. Writers can consequently detach themselves from their material, supplement it by research, and approach the writing not as people personally overwhelmed by their experiences but as artists — free to take certain liberties with their subject matter, to subordinate it as background for another story, to exploit its unfamiliarity if a strange locale is needed, and to destroy sequential time if their purposes demand this.

The impact of the Asia Minor Disaster has been, as we have seen, two-fold. Greek fiction would not be what it is today if the events of 1922 had not occurred. Without the Disaster, there would, of course, have been no "theme," and the retreat from ethography and the advance into modern fiction would have been more gradual, less decisive than it was. Assuming that Hellenism would have existed still in Anatolia, the older writers either would have had their beliefs in the Megale Idea confirmed — in case of a military victory — or would have maintained their confidence that its realization was imminent, in case of a military defeat of less than Disaster proportions. Men in their middle years, like Varnalis and Kazantzakis, would still have been Marxists, perhaps, but their personal lives would not have been as overturned as they were. The Generation of the 1930s, assuming that they would have emerged as they did, would not have had "the shadow on their soul" that Constantine Dimaras saw, and their need to document the change in national fortunes and to renew Greek fiction would have had less of a mandate from history than it did.

The Asia Minor Disaster of 1922, in short, drove a wedge between the Greeks of the present and the Greeks of the past. Coming one century after the reemergence of the Greek nation, it sealed the modern Greek destiny and stamped the modern Greek personality. Though it meant a permanent impoverishment for the Greek people and definite limits to their future, the Disaster also unified them in one geographical area and allowed them to develop a modern, national culture. The Greek people, their state, and their culture reacted to this body blow and recovered from it with the determination and resilience to be expected of them. In the province of literature, and prose fiction in particular, the events of 1922 have left their mark, in specific novels whose importance to the national tradition cannot be questioned, and in the establishment of a rich and comprehensive genre.

Bibliography

Adamantiadis, Ad. N. "Ta Teleftaia Chronia tis Ellinikis Koinon-ias tis Proussis," *Mikrasiatika Chronika*, Vol. 4, 1948.

Afthoniatis, Petros. *Prosfyges.* Paris; Agon Publishers, 1929.

Alexiou, Elli. *Yia Na Yinei Megalos.* Athens: Dorikos, 1966.

Angelomatis, Christos. *Chronikon Megalis Tragodias – To Epos tis Mikrasias.* Athens: Estia, 1963.

Antoniadou, Sophia. "Nea Revmata stin Neoelliniki Logotechnia apo to 1922 ki' epita," *Nea Estia*, 46, nos. 531-532, Aug. 15-Sept. 1 (1949), pp. 1034-1040; 1125-1130.

Apostolidis, Renos. *Kritiki tou Metapolemou.* Athens, 1962. "Apantisi stous k.k. F. M. Pontani kai M. Vitti: I Neoelliniki Logotechnia kai oi Xenoi Meletites tis." *O Aionas mas,* 5, No. 7, July (1951), pp. 171-178.

Bakolas, Nikos. *O Kipos ton Prinkipon.* Thessaloniki: Gkonis, 1966.

Bien, Peter. *Kazantzakis and the Linguistic Revolution in Greek Literature.* Princeton: Princeton University Press, 1972.

_____. "A Kazantzakis Checklist," *Mantatophoros,* Birmingham No. 5, Nov. 1974, pp 7-53.

Bierstadt, Edward Hale. *The Great Betrayal.* London: Hutchinson and Co., n.d.

Bryer, Anthony. "The Great Idea," *History Today,* 15 (1965), pp. 159-168.

Dafnis, Grigoris. *I Ellas Metaxy Dyo Polemon.* Athens: Ikaros, 1955.

_____. *Ta Ellinika Politika Kommata.* Athens: Galaxias, 1961.

Dawkins, R. M. "The Red Apple," *Archeion tou Thrakikou Laographikou kai Glossikou Thisavrou,* Supplement, Vol. VI. Athens, 1940.

Delta, Penelope. *Allilographia tis P. S. Deltas, 1906-1940,* edited by X. Lefkoparidis. Athens: Estia, n.d.

Dieterich, Karl. *Hellenism in Asia Minor.* Trans. Carroll N. Brown. New York: American Hellenic Society, 1918.

Diktaios, Aris. *Anoichtoi Logarismoi me to Chrono.* Athens: Fexis, 1963.

Dimaras, Alexis. *Neoelliniki Ekpaidefsis (Istorikon Schediasma),* Athens, 1965.

Dimaras, Constantine. *Istoria tis Neoellinikis Logotechnias.* 3rd ed. Athens: Ikaros, 1964. Available in English as *A History of Modern Greek Literature,* translated by Mary Gianos and published by the State University of New York Press, 1972.

_____. " 'Treis Meres sta Monastiria tis Kappadokias' tou Yiorgou Seferi," *Vima,* June 12, 1953, pp. 1-2.

_____. "Megale Idea," *Vima,* January 9 and 16, 1970, pp. 1-2.

Doukas, Alekos. *Stin Pali, Sta Neiata.* Melbourne, Australia: Coronation Press, 1953.

Doukas, Stratis. *Istoria enos Aichmalotou.* 2nd ed. Athens, 1932.

Eddy, Charles B. *Greece and the Greek Refugees.* London: George Allen and Unwin, Ltd., 1931.

Esperas, Chrysos. *To Mythistorima.* Athens: Flamma, 1940.

Floros, Pavlos. *Apoikoi.* Athens: Estias, 1934.

_____. *O Anthropos tis Epochis.* Athens: Pyrsos, 1939.

_____. "To Englima tis Vithleem," in *I Amaranta ki' alla diigimata,* Athens: Pyrsos, 1938.

_____. "To Telos tou Theiou Bembou," in *Nostalgoi.* Athens, 1943. See also *Nea Estia,* 27, No. 321 (1940), pp. 552-555.

_____. "Kanena Ambelaki," "O Kitsinias," "O Soupas kai to Syntagma," and "O Prodotis" in *I Vouvi Orchistra.* Athens, 1966. "O Kitsinias" and "O Soupas kai to Syntagma" also appeared in *Nea Estia.*

_____. "Theomania," *Nea Estia,* 82, No. 962 (1967), pp. 1008-1010.

_____. "I Kideia tou Despoti," *Nea Estia,* 82, No. 970 (1967), pp. 1601-1603.

_____. "To Loutro me ta Karydy Phylla," *Nea Estia,* 83, No. 973 (1968), pp. 87-88.

_____. "Raki," *Nea Estia,* 84, No. 989 (1968), pp. 1224-1228.

_____. "I Mikra Asia stin Elliniki Logotechnia meta to 1923," *Mikrasiatiki Estia,* No. 1, July-September (1946), pp. 74-85.

Fouriotis, Angelos. *Pnevmatiki Poreia, 1900-1950: Thanasis Petsalis, To Ergo tou.* Athens: Mavridis, 1952.

Glinos, Dimitris. *Eklektes Selides, A'.* Athens: Stochastis, 1970.

_____. *Eklektes Selides, B'.* Athens: Stochastis, 1971.

_____. *Ethnos kai Glossa.* Athens: Athena Publishers, 1971.

_____. "Afieroma ston Glino," *Epitheorisi Technis,* 10, Nos. 119-120 (1964).

_____. "Ena Arthro tou Glinou," in K. Varnalis, *Pezos Logos.* Athens: Kedros, 1957.

Grigoris, Gerasimos. "Enas Laikos Chronographos," *Epitheorisi Technis,* 9, No. 93 (1962), p. 302.

Henderson, G. P. *The Revival of Greek Thought, 1620-1830.* Edinburgh and London: Scottish Academic Press, 1971.

Hourmouzios, Aimilios. "I Prosfygiki Logotechnia," *Nea Estia,* 27, No. 314, January 15 (1940), pp. 106-109.

_____. "Diavazontas ena Mythistorima: O Kapetan Michalis tou Nikou Kazantzaki," *Kathimerini,* November 12, 1953.

_____. "I Neoelliniki Logotechnia metaxy Dyo Polemon," *Ilios Enkyklopaidia,* Vol. 7, pp. 1113-1117.

Housepian, Marjorie. *The Smyrna Affair.* New York: Harcourt, Brace, Jovanovich, Inc., 1971.

Iatridi, Julia. *Ta Petrina Liontaria.* Athens: Fexis, 1963.

International Women's Union. (*Syndesmos Gynaikon, Diethnis*). *Aftoviographiai Prosfygon Koritsion, Paidikai Perigraphai ton Diogmon tis Mikrasias.* Athens, 1926.

Kambanis, Aristos. *Istoria tis Neoellinikis Logotechnias.* 5th ed. Supplemented. Athens: Estia, 1948.

Kamberoglou, Byron. *Ston Iskio tis Istorias, ap' tin zoi enos perastikou.* Three volumes. Athens: Kedros, 1961, 1962, 1966.

Kapsis, Yiannis. *Hamenes Patrides: apo tin apeleftherosin sti Katastrophi tis Smyrnis.* Athens, 1962.

Karandonis, Andreas. *Pezographoi kai pezographimata tis Genias tou '30.* Athens: Fexis, 1962.

————. "Chronika: Apologismos," *Nea Grammata,* 2, No. 1, January (1936), pp. 85-86.

Kazantzakis, Nikos. *Tetrakosia Grammata ston Pandeli Prevelaki,* Athens: Helen Kazantzakis, 1965.

————. "Salvatores Dei; Askitiki," *Anagennisi.* 1, Nos. 11-12, July-August (1927), pp. 599-631.

————. *O Christos Xanastavronetai.* Athens, 1948. Available in English as *The Greek Passion,* translated by Jonathan Griffin, and published by Simon and Schuster, 1953.

————. *Epistoles pros tin Galateia,* ed. Aris Diktaios. Athens: Difros, 1958.

————. *The Saviors of God: Spiritual Exercises.* Translated and with an Introduction by Kimon Friar. New York: Simon and Schuster, 1960.

————. *Anaphora ston Greko,* Athens, 1961. Available in English, as *Report to Greco,* translated by Peter Bien and published by Simon and Schuster, 1964.

K. B. *Apo tin Aichmalosia: Kata to Imerologio tou Aichmalotou Aeroporou B. K.* Athens, 1923.

Kontoglou, Fotis. *Istories kai Peristatika.* Athens: S. Nikolopoulos, 1944.

————. *Fimismenoi Andres kai Lismonismenoi.* Athens: Aetos, 1942.

Kordatos, Yianis. *Istoria tis Neoellinikis Logotechnias, apo to 1453 os to 1961.* Prologue by Kostas Varnalis. Two volumes. Athens: Vivlioekdotiki, 1962.

Koumendareas, Menis. *To Armenisma: Tria Chronika*. Athens: Estia, 1966.

Kriaras, Emmanuel. *Psycharis*. Thessaloniki, 1959.

Ladas, Stephen D. *The Exchange of Minorities: Bulgaria, Greece and Turkey*. New York: Macmillan, 1932.

Laourdas, Basil. "I Ailoliki Ghi," *Philologika Chronika*, I, No. 2, March 15 (1944).

_____. "Modern Greek Historical Novels," *Balkan Studies*, 6 (1965), pp. 55-66.

_____. "To Tragoudi tou Daskaloyianni," by Barba-Pantselios, edited by B. Laourdas. Heracleion, Crete: Mourmel, 1947.

Liatsos, Dimitris. *I Mikrasiatiki Katastrophi sti Neoelliniki Logotechnia*. Nikaia, Piraeus: To Elliniko Vivlio, 1962.

Marriot, I. A. *The Eastern Question, A Historical Study in European Diplomacy*, 4th ed. Oxford: The Clarendon Press, 1940.

Maskaleris, Thanasis. *Kostis Palamas*. Twayne World Authors Series 197. New York: Twayne Publishers, Inc. 1972.

Megas, Georges. "La Prise de Constantinople dans la poésie et la tradition populaires Grecques," *L'Hellénism Contemporain, Le Cinq-Centième Anniversarie de la Prise de Constantinople, 1453-1953,* Athens, May 29, 1953.

Melamed, Laura. "Gyrevontas enan Andra." *Athinaika Nea,* June 4, 1936. Published also in French as *J'ai cherche un homme*. Paris, 1936.

Meraklis, Michalis. *I Poiisi mas, O Dichasmos, To Metaichmio.* Kalamata: Nestor Publishers, 1959.

_____. "I Elliniki Pezographia tis Teleftaias Dekaetias," *Nea Poreia, "Ta Deka Chronia: 1955-1965,"* 10, nos. 119-123, January-May (1965).

Milioris, Nikos. *To Kylisma kai alles Istories apo tin zoi ton Vourliotion.* Athens, 1958.

_____. "I Mikrasiatiki Paradosi kai oi Neoteres Genies," Lecture No. 9 in a series sponsored by the Union of Smyrniots. Athens: Enoseos Smyrnaion, 1969.

————. "I Mikrasiatiki Tragodia sti Logotechnia kai sti Techni," *Mikrasiatika Chronika*, 13 (1967).

————. "I Pnevmatiki Prosfora ton Mikrasiaton," *Mikrasiatika Chronika,* 11, (1962).

Miller, William. *The Ottoman Empire and Its Successors, 1801-1927.* 4th ed. Cambridge: The University Press, 1936.

Mitsakis, K. "I Xeni Epidrasi stin Elliniki Logotechnia," *Nea Estia,* 73, Nos. 854-855, (1963), pp. 180-186 and 251-257.

Morgenthau, Henry. *I Was Sent to Athens,* in collaboration with French Strother. New York: Doubleday, Doran and Company, 1929.

Myrivilis, Stratis. *I Zoi en Tafo,* 10th ed. Athens: Estia, 1959.

————. *I Daskala me ta Chrysa Matia,* 10th ed. Athens: Estia, 1956. Available in English as *The School-Mistress with the Golden Eyes,* translated by Phillip Sherrard, London, 1964.

————. *I Panaghia I Gorgona* 2nd ed. Athens: Estia, 1955. Available in English as *The Mermaid Madonna,* translated by Abbott Rick, New York: Thomas Y. Crowell, 1959.

————. *O Vasilis O Arvanitis,* Athens: Pegasos, 1943.

Omiridis, Dimos. "Dyo Anekdota Grammata tou Glinou," *Epitheorisi Technis,* Nos. 122-123, (1965).

Pallis, Alexander A. *Greece's Anatolian Venture – and After.* London: Methuen and Company, 1937.

Panayotopoulos, I. M. *Ta Prosopa kai ta keimena,* II. *Ta Anisycha Chronia.* Athens: Aetos Publishers, 1943.

————. *Hamozoi: Chroniko tou Palaiou Kairou,* 2nd ed. Athens: Ikaros, 1960.

————. *Astrofengia, I Istoria mias Efivias,* 2nd ed. revised. Athens: Astir Publishers, 1971.

————. "Istoria kai Logotechnia," *Eleftheria,* October 7 (1962), pp. 1-8.

Papadimas, Adamantios. *Nea Elliniki Grammatologia.* Athens, 1948.

Papadimitriou, Elli. ed. "Pente Laikes Afigiseis," *Epitheorisi Technis,* 9, No. 93, September (1962).

Paraschos, Kleon. "I Nea Elliniki Pezographia," *To Neon Kratos,* 1, No. 1, September (1937).

Pentzopoulos, Dimitri. *The Balkan Exchange of Minorities and its Impact upon Greece.* Publications of the Social Science Center, Athens, Paris, and The Hague: Mouton and Company, 1962.

Peristeris, George. "O Prosfygas," *Nea Estia,* 59, No. 690, April 1 (1956).

Petsalis-Diomidis, Thanasis. "Ta Trianta Chronia apo tin Katastrophi tou Mikrasiatikou Ellinismou," *Nea Estia,* 61, No. 717 (1957), pp. 694-695. Reprinted from *Kathimerini,* September 5, 1952.

Plaskovitis, Spyros. "I Klimatoverga," in *I Thyella kai to Fanari.* Athens: Estia, 1955.

Politarchis, G. M. "Voutyras," *Megali Enkyklopaidia Neoellinikis Logotechnias,* 4, pp. 327-334. Athens: Haris Patsis, 1969.

Politis, Kosmas. *Stou Hadzifrangou, Ta Sarantachrona mias Hamenis Politeias.* Athens: Karavias, 1963.

Politis, Linos. *Istoria tis Neas Ellinikis Logotechnias, synoptiko diagramma, vivliographia.* 2nd ed. Thessaloniki, 1969.

_____. *A History of Modern Greek Literature,* Oxford: The Clarendon Press, 1973.

Politis, Nicholaos. *Meletai peri tou Viou kai tis Glossis tou Ellinikou Laou: Paradoseis.* Athens, 1904.

_____. *Eklogai apo ta tragoudia tou Ellinikou Laou.* 3rd ed. Athens: P. Leonis, 1932.

Polybius. *Greece Before the Conference,* with a Foreword by T. P. O'Connor. London, 1919.

Pontani, Filippo Maria. "I Synchroni Elliniki Poiisi," *O Aionas mas,* 5, No. 6, June (1951).

Prevelakis, Pandelis. *Chroniko mias Politeias.* Athens: Galaxias, 1965.

_____. *O Poiitis kai to Poiima tis Odysseias.* Athens: Estia, 1958.

Prokopiou, Angelos G. "Kontoglou," *Angloelliniki Epitheorisi*, 3, No. 5, September (1947), pp. 129-138.

Prokopiou, Socrates. *San Psemmata kai san Alitheia, Mikrasiatikon Istorikon Mythistorima me eikones*. Athens, 1928.

Psycharis, Yiannis. "Cabinet de Lecture," in *To Taxidi Mou: Apanta*, 4th ed. Thessaloniki: Makedonikes Ekdoseis, 1962.

Psyroukis, Nikos. *I Mikrasiatiki Katastrophi, 1918-1923*. Athens: Anexartitos Dromos Publishers, 1964.

Raftopoulos, Dimitris. "Mikrasiatiki Anadromi," in *Oi Idees kai ta Erga*. Athens: Difros, 1965.

Rodas, Michalis. *I Ellada stin Mikra Asia*. Athens, 1950.

Runciman, Stephen. *The Great Church in Captivity. A Study of the Patriarchate of Constantinople from the Eve of the Turkish Conquest to the Greek War of Independence*. Cambridge: Cambridge University Press, 1968.

_____. *The Last Byzantine Renaissance* (Wiles Lecture, 1968). Cambridge: Cambridge University Press, 1970.

Sachinis, Apostolos. *Anazitiseis tis Neoellinikis Pezographias stin Mesopolemiki Eikosaetia*. Athens: Ikaros, 1945.

_____. *I Pezographia tis Katochis*. Athens: Ikaros, 1948.

_____. *I Synchroni Pezographia mas*. Athens: Ikaros, 1951.

_____. *To Istoriko Mythistorima*. Athens: Difros, 1957.

_____. *To Neoelliniko Mythistorima, Istoria kai Kritiki*. Athens, 1958.

_____. *Neoi Pezographoi, Eikosi Chronia Neoellinikis Pezographias, 1945-1965*. Athens: Estia, 1965.

_____. *Pezographoi tou Kairou mas*, Athens: Estia, 1967.

Seferiadi, Erse. "Apou," *Nea Estia*, 64, Nos. 747-748 (1958), pp. 1219-1223 and 1293-1297.

Seferis, George. *Treis Meres sta Monastiria tis Kappadokias*. Athens: The French Institute of Athens, 1953.

_____. "The Other World." trans. Ian Scott-Kilvert, *The London Magazine*, 6, No. 5 (1966), pp. 45-64.

Societe des Nations. *L'éstablissement de réfugees en Grèce*. Geneva, 1926.

Sotiriou, Dido. *Oi Nekroi Perimenoun.* Athens: Kedros, 1959.

_____. *Matomena Homata.* Athens: Kedros, 1962.

Souliotis, Athanasios. *Oi Katoikoi tis Mikras Asias.* Athens, 1921.

Spandonidis, Petros. *I Pezographia ton Neon, 1929-1933.* Thessaloniki, 1934.

Spanomanolis, Christos. *Aichmalotoi ton Tourkon.* 2nd ed. Athens: Estia, 1969.

Spanoudi, Sophia. *O Poiitis Omiros Bekes. Biblio A'.* Athens: Eleftheroudakis, 1924.

Spencer, Terence J. B. *Fair Greece, Sad Relic.* London: Weidenfeld and Nicolson, 1954.

Statistical Service of Greece. *Statistical Yearbook of Greece.* Athens: Ministry of Coordination, 1970.

Stavrianos, L. S. "Antecedents to the Balkan Revolution of the 19th Century," *Journal of Modern History,* 29, No. 4 (1957).

_____. *Balkan Federation: A History of the Movement Toward Balkan Unity in Modern Times.* Smith College Studies in History, Northhampton, Mass., 27, Nos. 1-4, October 1941-July 1942.

Stavrou, Tatiana. *Ekeinoi pou Emeinan.* Athens, 1933.

_____. *Oi Protes Rizes.* Athens: Kyklos, 1936.

_____. *To Kalokairi Perase.* Athens: Glaros, 1943.

Sykoutris, Ioannis. *Meletai kai Arthra.* Athens: Ekdoseis tou Aigaiou, 1956.

Theotokas, George. *Elefthero Pnevma.* Athens: Rhallis, 1929.

_____. *Argo,* 3rd ed. Athens: Estia, n.d. Available in English, translated by Ares Tsatsopoulos and E. Margaret Brooke, and published by Methuen, 1951.

_____. *Imerologio tis Argos kai tou Daimoniou.* Athens: Pyrsos, 1939.

_____. *Evripidis Pentozalis ki' alles Istories.* Athens: Pyrsos, 1937.

_____. *Leonis.* Athens: Estia, 1940.

_____. "Gyro sto Thema tou Kommounismou," *Nea Estia,* 44, No. 512 (1948), pp. 1334-1339.

_____. *Pnevmatiki Poreia*. Athens: Fexis, 1961.

Thrylos, Alkis. *Morphes tis Ellinikis Pezographias*. 2 vols. Athens: Difros, 1962, 1963.

Travlandonis, Andonis. *Leyilasia mias Zoïs*. Athens: Galaxias, 1966.

Triandafyllidis, Manolis. *Stathmoi tis Glossikis mas Istorias*. Athens, 1937.

Triandafyllou, Kostas N. *I Mikrasiatiki Katastrophi, Eisagogi eis tin Istoriographikin Theorisin tou Thematos*. Patras, 1962.

Trumpener, Ulrich. "German Military Aid to Turkey in 1914, An Historical Reevaluation," *The Journal of Modern History*, University of Chicago Press, 32, No. 2 (1960), pp. 145-149.

_____. "Turkey's Entry into World War I: An Assessment of Responsibilities," *Journal of Modern History*, 34, No. 4 (1962), pp. 369-380.

_____. "Liman von Sanders and the German-Ottoman Alliance," *Journal of Contemporary History*, London, I, No. 4 (1966), pp. 179-192.

Tsirimokos, Markos. *Istoria tou Ekpaideftikou Omilou*. Athens, 1927.

Vakalopoulos, Apostolos. *I Poreia tou Genous*. Athens: Ekdoseis ton Philon, 1966.

_____. *Ai Prosfygikai Enkatastaseis en ti Periochi Thessalonikis*, with M. Maravelakis. Thessaloniki: Foundation for Macedonian Studies, 1955.

Valetas. George. *Aioliki Vivliographia*. Athens, 1939.

_____. *Anthologia tis Dimotikis Pezographias*. 3 volumes. Athens: Ranos Publishers, 1949.

Varikas, Vasos. "To Chroniko mias Epochis," *Vima*, July 1, 1962.

Varnalis, Kostas. *Pezos Logos*. Contains "I Alithini Apologia tou Sokrati," "To Imerologio tis Pinelopis," and "O Laos ton Monouchon." Athens: Kedros, 1957.

_____. *Ta Penintachrona tou Ergou tou*. Athens: Kedros, 1957.

Veinoglou, Alex. "*I Nekropoli,*" *Nea Estia,* 8, Nos. 92-93 (1930), pp. 1086-1091 and 1140-1145.

Venezis, Ilias. *O Manolis Lekas kai alla Diigimata. Athens, 1928.*

_____. *To Noumero 31,328.* 3rd ed. Athens: Skazikis, 1952.

_____. *Aigaio.* Athens: Estia, 1941.

_____. *Galini.* 7th ed. Athens: Estia, 1957.

_____. *Anemoi.* Athens: Estia, 1944.

_____. *Aioliki Ghi.* 4th ed. Athens: Estia, 1955. Available in English as *Beyond the Aegean,* translated by E. D. Scott-Kilvert, published by the Vanguard Press, 1956.

_____. "I Prosfygia tou 1922 stin Elliniki Logotechnia," *Prosfygikos Kosmos,* January 24, 1943, pp. 1-2.

Vitti, Mario. "I Neoelliniki Pezographia apo ti Genia tou '20 os Simera," *O Aionas mas,* 5, No. 7 (1951), pp. 166-171.

Vlami, Eva. *Ta Oneira tis Angelikas.* Athens: Ekdoseis tou Aigaiou, 1958.

Voutieridis, Ilias. *Istoria tis Neoellinikis Logotechnias.* 2nd ed., with a supplement by Dimitris Yiaghos. Athens, 1966.

Voyatzidis, J. C. "La Grande Idée," *L'Hellénism Contemporain, Le Cinq-Centième Anniversaire de la Prise de Constantinople,* 1453-1953, Athènes, May 29, 1953, pp. 279-287.

_____. "I Archi kai i Exelexis tis Megalis Ideas," *Imerologion Tis Megalis Ellados* (1923).

_____. "*O Pankosmios Polemos kai I Ellas,*" *Imerologion Tis Megalis Ellados* (1925).

Vrettakos, Nikiphoros. *Nikos Kazantzakis: I Agonia tou kai to Ergo tou,* Athens: P. Sypsas-Chr. Siamantas Publishers, 1960.

Ward, Mark H. *The Deportations in Asia Minor, 1920-1922.* London: Published by the Anglo-Hellenic League and the British Armenia Committee, 1922.

Xenopoulos, Grigoris. *I Smyrnia,* serialized in *Ethnos,* beginning March 30 (1920).

_____. *Prosfyges, Athinaikon Mythistorima* serialized in *Neos Kosmos,* beginning June 1934.

_____. "O Logos tou K^{ou} Gr. Xenopoulou eis tin Dexiosi tou eis tin Akadimia," *Nea Estia*, 2, No. 124 (1932), pp. 176-185.

Yiaghos, Dimitris. "I Ethniki Symfora kai I Logotechnia mas," *Morphes kai Themata Logotechnias*, Athens, 1964.

Yialourakis, Manolis. "Myrivilis," *Megali Enkyklopaidia Tis Neoellinikis Logotechnias*, Vol. 10. Athens: Haris Patsis. n.d.

Zakythinos, Dionysios. "Apo tis Ptoseos tou Mikrasiatikou Ellinismou eis tin 28^{in} Oktovriou, 1940," Panygeric Conference of 27th October, 1966, *Records of the Academy of Athens*, 41 (1966).

Zoumboulidis, Kostas. *Niovi, Smyrnaiiko Aisthimatiko Mythistorima*. Athens: Zikakis, 1926.

Index